GEONOMICS INSTITUTE FOR INTERNATIONAL ECONOMIC
ADVANCEMENT SERIES
Michael P. Claudon, Series Editor

Debt Disaster? Banks, Governments, and Multilaterals Confront the Crisis
edited by John F. Weeks

*The Canada-U.S. Free Trade Agreement: Implications, Opportunities,
and Challenges*
edited by Daniel E. Nolle

Perestroika and East-West Economic Relations: Prospects for the 1990's
edited by Michael Kraus and Ronald D. Liebowitz

Perestroika and East-West Economic Relations

Prospects for the 1990's

Edited by Michael Kraus
and Ronald D. Liebowitz

NEW YORK UNIVERSITY PRESS
New York and London

Library of Congress Cataloging-in-Publication Data

Perestroika and East-West economic relations : prospects for the 1990's /
edited by Michael Kraus and Ronald D. Liebowitz.
    p.   cm. — (Geonomics Institute for International Economic
Advancement series)
  Based on a conference held at Middlebury College in September 1988,
and cosponsored by the Geonomics Institute for International Economic
Advancement and ISKAN.
  ISBN 0-8147-4604-7
  1. Soviet Union—International economic relations—Congresses.
2. Perestroika—Congresses. 3. East-West trade (1945-)— Congresses.
I. Kraus, Michael. II. Liebowitz, Ronald D. III. Geonomics Institute
for International Economic Advancement. IV. Institut Soedinennykh
Shtatov Ameriki i Kanady (Akademiia nauk SSSR). V. Series.
HF1557.P46 1990
337.470171'3—dc20   90-5446
                                                                          CIP

New York University Press books are printed on acid-free paper,
and their binding materials are chosen for strength and durability.

CONTENTS

ACKNOWLEDGMENTS

Many have contributed to the success of this East-West venture. In the first place, this volume has benefited from the conference participation of a large and diverse group of specialists on East-West relations. It included Ib Alken, Russian Research Center, Harvard University; Oleg Alyakrinski, Institute for the Study of the USA and Canada (ISKAN); Peter Bakewell, Department of External Affairs, Government of Canada; Bela Balassa, World Bank; Alexander Belov, ISKAN; Raymond Benson, American Collegiate Consortium, Middlebury College; John Bonin, Department of Economics, Wesleyan University; Jozef M. van Brabant, United Nations; Josef C. Brada, Department of Economics, Arizona State University; Michael P. Claudon, President, Geonomics Institute, and Department of Economics, Middlebury College; James Douglas, Secretary of State, Vermont; Alexander Dvoretsky, ISKAN; Robert English, Department of Politics, Princeton University; H. Stephen Gardner, Department of Economics, Baylor University; Sergei Geivandov, ISKAN; Ed A. Hewett, Brookings Institution; Franklyn Holzman, Department of Economics, Tufts University; Robert A. Jones, Chairman of the Board, Geonomics Institute; Craig Karp, U.S. Department of State; Valeriy Khrutskiy, Soviet Mission to the UN; Robert Krattli, WJS Inc.; Michael Kraus, Department of Political Science, Middlebury College; Alexei Kvasov, ISKAN; Russell Leng, Department of Political Science, Middlebury College; Ronald D. Liebowitz, Department of Geography, Middlebury College; Ed Lord, Mytre Holdings, Ltd.; David Macey, Department of History, Middlebury College; Igor Malashenko, ISKAN; Michael Marrese, Department of Economics, Northwestern University; Peter Murrell, Department of Economics, University of Maryland; Vladimir Popov, ISKAN; Peter Reddaway, Department of Political Science, George Washington University; Olin Robison, President, Middlebury College; David Rosenberg, Department of Political Science, Middlebury College; Leonard J. Santow, Griggs and Santow; Catherine Sokil, Department of Economics, Middlebury College; Allison Stanger, Center for Science and International Affairs, Harvard University; William C. Taubman, Department of Political Science, Amherst College; Alexander Volkov, ISKAN; and John Walsh, Chaplain, Middlebury College.

The staff of the Geonomics Institute, especially Colleen Duncan, Elizabeth Leeds, and Nancy Ward, ably assisted in organizing the conference program. Elizabeth Leeds and Terry Plum provided editorial assistance; Shirley Benson translated Soviet contributions; and Colleen Duncan shepherded the preparations of the volume for publication from the September 1988 conference through several stages of revisions, to this updated final version. Their contribution is greatly appreciated.

                                                        The Editors

FOREWORD

The dramatic evolution of the Soviet economic and political systems over the past five years calls for a reexamination of the prospects for East-West economic and political relations. Soviet academicians and government officials today debate how to reform an economic system that has failed to provide basic goods and services and has proven unable to develop and assimilate advanced technology.

From the start of his program, Mikhail Gorbachev recognized a link between political and economic reform. While some argue that a free-market system will provide the incentive for greater productivity and will help integrate the Soviet economy into the world economy, others see the changes as a threat to the security the centralized system provides and ensures most citizens.

The week-long conference, Implications of Soviet Reforms for East-West Relations, which took place in September 1988, was co-sponsored by the Geonomics Institute for International Economic Advancement and ISKAN.[1] Middlebury College professors Michael Kraus and Ronald D. Liebowitz organized the conference, which explored the economics and politics of East-West economic cooperation under diverse reform scenarios. The different viewpoints and backgrounds represented by the conferees and their papers make this a particularly rich and often provocative volume.

What distinguished this conference from others—and comes through clearly in this volume—is the spirit of glasnost. Not only did the new openness make an unusually large (and young) Soviet presence possible, it also enriched the tone and substance of the discussions. Although a significant East-West divergence of per-

---

1. ISKAN is the Moscow-based Institute for the Study of the USA and Canada of the Soviet Academy of Sciences. Under a unique joint venture agreement, our two institutes are working together to break down barriers to greater Soviet-American commerce.

spectives on some issues is clearly evident in the volume, there is also a notable convergence of views on many key questions. The outcome, as the reader will note, is a timely contribution to the debate about greater East-West economic cooperation and expanded business opportunities in the 1990s.

This volume contributes exceptionally well to Geonomics' mission to bring together business leaders, government policymakers, and academicians. Geonomics seeks to promote initiatives that facilitate international business, and it sponsors and disseminates policy-oriented research and seminars. To that end, the conference was followed in July 1989 by a workshop that resulted in the world's first multilateral proposal for making the Soviet ruble convertible. And in October 1989, Geonomics released a plan for the first Soviet-American venture capital firm to be capitalized in both rubles and U.S. dollars.

Geonomics is privately funded, nonpartisan, and not for profit. We welcome ideas and opinions for better achieving our goals.

Michael P. Claudon
President and Managing Director
Geonomics Institute

INTRODUCTION

The emerging Gorbachev era represents a rebirth of reformist politics in the Soviet Union on an unprecedented scale. The developments sweeping the Soviet Union and East Europe at the end of the 1980s were fully anticipated by neither East nor West. They are best understood as a product of the long-term changes within the Soviet and East European societies on the one hand, and as consequences (both intended and unintended) of Mikhail Gorbachev's policies, designed at least in part to address those changes, on the other. At the heart of Gorbachev's strategy of political, economic, and social reform, or what the Soviets call perestroika, is the attempted transformation of the relationship between the state and society. Economic reforms have been an essential component of that strategy. In fact, falling growth rates, a large budget deficit, lagging technology, and declining standards of living provided an original impetus for the reforms that began with Gorbachev's accession to power in March 1985.

Since then, Soviet policymakers, academicians, and financial specialists have proposed, debated, and, at least to some extent, enacted a series of measures designed to resuscitate the ailing Soviet economy and revitalize the economic mechanism so as to avert the prospect of a systemic decline of socialism. These steps have, among other things, aimed at a decentralization of decision-making and a partial privatization of the command economy, thereby seeking to reduce the controls of central planners and the bureaucratic powers of the state.

Despite these changes, Soviet economic performance five years into the Gorbachev era has not improved. Although reasons for this failure are complex (and they are analyzed or alluded to in the following chapters), they certainly include the inadequacies of some and the inconsistencies of other reform policies. However, at least in hindsight, it is also clear that a reform process as ambitious as perestroika was bound to be accompanied by disruptions. In other words, while the old economic system no longer works well, the new economic mechanism is not yet in place. Particularly alarming to the Soviet leadership has been the deterioration in the consumer sector since 1987, which spurred on the large-scale working class protest in the summer and fall of 1989—a walkout by nearly half-a-million Donbas, Kuzbas, and Vorkuta miners that has paralyzed the mining industry, causing close to $5 billion in losses.

Most Soviet and western economists would agree that the ultimate prospects of perestroika will depend on the long-term modernization of the economy and the short-term improvement in the living standards of the Soviet people. Thus, in the early 1990s, Moscow faces the challenge of finding methods to restructure its economic mechanism on the one hand, and to enhance the consumer sector on the other. It is a dilemma whose resolution can benefit from—if, in fact, it does not require—increased trade and economic interaction with the West. Hence, a major Soviet objective is to obtain substantive agreements on economic cooperation in the form of greater trade, government and bank credits, and joint ventures from the West. This goal, in turn, raises the fundamental question of what role western economies can or will play in the Soviet reform effort.

Soviet reform policies and objectives, especially in the foreign economic sector, the questions they raise, their East-West implications, and the prospects for a major breakthrough in East-West economic relations form the focus of this volume. In Chapters 1 and 2, Peter Reddaway, Igor Malashenko, and Academician Georgi Arbatov provide contrasting perspectives on the political context of reform that influences the Soviet economic agenda. While the first two specialists debate the extent to which differences of outlook within the party leadership reflect contending reform programs that may affect the reform process, Arbatov's contribution examines some of the roots of economic difficulties that lie outside the economic system.

Chapters 3, 4, 5, and 6 focus on Soviet economic perestroika, primarily on its relationship to the international economic sphere. H. Stephen Gardner begins with a general overview of the role of foreign economic ties in the Soviet economy, discussing the legacy of protectionism and autarky. His chapter highlights the key foreign trade and financial reforms to date and analyzes the massive structural changes necessary for substantive and qualitative improvements in Soviet economic performance. Many of these same themes—though from a Soviet perspective—are taken up in Chapter 4 by Vladimir Popov, who examines the limited role the foreign sector has historically played in the Soviet economy. Against the backdrop of a critical assessment of the reform measures adopted through 1989, Popov advocates radical reform, including early (if partial) ruble convertibility. He maintains that partial reform measures, or "stop and go" policies characteristic of other reforming planned economies, would only lead to spiraling inflation, further international indebtedness, and a wasted opportunity for systemic change. In Chapter 5, Bela Balassa and Michael P. Claudon argue that major institutional changes must accompany price reform, the introduction of product quality-enhancing measures, and export expansion if the Soviet foreign sector is to develop a major role in world trade. The decentralization of decisionmaking, they conclude, is a necessary condition for these changes to become reality. In Chapter 6, Peter Murrell evaluates how the reform of socialist economies and an increase in East-West trade might affect the market economies. Like Popov, Murrell believes that only through radical reform measures— more radical than those instituted by Kadar's Hungary, for example—can the planned economies change enough to affect the market economies and to have a tangible impact on global trade. For Murrell, internal reorganization of economic institutions to create a noninterventionistic milieu analogous to that of the multi-national corporation is the key to effective reform of the socialist economies' foreign sector, and is far more important than simply expanding international economic cooperation.

Chapters 7, 8, 9, and 10 deal with two themes: (1) the impact of perestroika on the Council for Mutual Economic Assistance (CMEA), and (2) the implications of the earlier reformist attempts for the current wave of changes. The enthusiasm for both economic and political reforms varies greatly among CMEA states, so a look at changes in CMEA operating procedures provides a barometer of relative strength of the pro- and anti-reform attitudes. Jozef M. van

Brabant reviews the history of CMEA policies in Chapter 7, outlining some of the proposed mechanisms for greater integration, including closer economic ties with the European Economic Community and further integration in the world economy. He maintains that greater integration will depend on a successful perestroika in all CMEA states. In Chapter 8, Michael Marrese focuses on Hungary's efforts to reform its foreign economic mechanism in light of the Soviet Union's restructuring program. A central question of Marrese's chapter is whether a reforming CMEA economy is better served by increasing its trade with western capitalist countries—despite obvious barriers—or by further expanding ties with the CMEA instead. His conclusion, namely that Hungary's economy will do better by turning to the West, is partly disputed in the Soviet commentary by Alexei Kvasov that follows in Chapter 9. Kvasov questions Marrese's conclusions on the grounds that socialist states need not choose one direction at the expense of the other, for trade could substantially increase with both CMEA states and the West. Josef C. Brada concludes the CMEA discussion in Chapter 10, with a summary of the achievements of the CMEA along with a proposal for intra-CMEA currency convertibility. As the first step in moving toward convertibility against western currencies, Brada advocates a partial marketization of the planned economies so funds generated through the sale of so-called "fixed-priced" goods could finance the purchase of "free-price" marketized goods. Such an approach would minimize major problems in CMEA trade, such as bilateralism and commodity inconvertibility.

The final portion of the book views East-West relations in a broader framework. In Chapter 11, Alexander Volkov analyzes the prospects for East-West economic relations in the context of global economic trends. His conclusions are based on three projections: (1) West European integration in the 1990s will not significantly change the overall structure of the world economy; (2) despite the *relative* decline of its foreign sector, the United States will retain a leading role in forging greater East-West economic cooperation; and (3) Japan's position in world financial institutions will necessarily change as old markets for Japanese exports become saturated and, as a consequence, loaned capital will begin to be replaced by Japanese direct investments in many markets.

Finally, he argues that the question of Soviet integration into the world economy is, above all, a political question. On a related note, Catherine Sokil in Chapter 12 scrutinizes the issues arising out of new Soviet interest in membership to the GATT, IMF, and World Bank. Sokil argues that, although the regulations for membership in such institutions ought to be upheld and not amended to ease Soviet entry, Moscow's participation in the international economic system should be welcomed. Past Soviet attitudes toward participation in international economic organizations are critiqued by Igor Malashenko in Chapter 13. He criticizes the old way in which Soviet leaders pursued autarkic economic policies as a perceived means toward promoting national economic security. Today, Malashenko argues, economic interdependence is a path to security and is the only way for the Soviet Union to take advantage of technological developments that, due to self-imposed economic isolation, have for decades been inaccessible. In Chapter 14, the point of departure for Georgi Arbatov's analysis of Soviet-American economic relations in a global context is the primacy of political over economic factors as the driving force of those relations. He advocates a new approach based on a series of concrete measures that would bring about a "movement from estrangement to rapprochement." Arbatov views the bilateral relationship as a stepping stone toward a new East-West strategy aimed at resolving intransigent North-South issues and major global concerns, including debt, food, energy, and the environment. The volume concludes with Ed A. Hewett's assessment in Chapter 15 of the Soviet reform program to date and of the prospects for East-West economic relations in the 1990s. His contribution takes the form of six propositions about East-West relations for the future. Although Hewett's propositions center on economic issues, they—like Arbatov's arguments—have political implications.

Collectively, the essays in this volume examine the impact of the rapidly changing political and economic climate in the Soviet Union and East Europe on East-West economic relations. While it appears that many political obstacles to greater East-West economic interaction are quickly disappearing—witness the East European Revolution of 1989—the enormous structural and social changes needed for a successful transformation of the centrally planned economies will most likely ensure a long and difficult process. Yet a major step along the path was taken at the Malta Summit in December 1989, when President Bush and General Secretary Gorbachev broached for the first time the issue of Soviet participation in western-dominated international economic organizations and the global economy. This volume, we hope, reflects some of the new thinking, East and West, that is essential for establishing a framework for a post-Cold War international order.

Michael Kraus and Ronald D. Liebowitz
December 1989
Middlebury, Vermont

CHAPTER 1 ⸻

Soviet Political Reform: Diversity or Division?[1]

PETER REDDAWAY *and* IGOR MALASHENKO

Reddaway:

I think you have seen the development in the last two years of two broad political programs in the Soviet Union, programs that can be called, for the sake of convenience, "Gorbachevism" and "Ligachevism." They have become better defined as time has gone by, and they are very, very different from each other. Gorbachevism is a program of democratic socialism, and Ligachevism is a more authoritarian sort of socialism. Gorbachev stands for what can be called a radical perestroika, Ligachev stands for a moderate perestroika. To put it in terms of the forces that these individual leaders are appealing to and from whom they derive their political support, Gorbachev pulls support from the center-left forces in Soviet politics, and Ligachev looks for support from the center-right forces.

A number of Soviet commentators take the view that this distinction does not really matter very much, and that it is good that there are different programs represented by different leaders within the Politburo. This view argues that it is not a problem to Gorbachev that Ligachev has a different program, because Ligachev reassures the conservative elements in the *nomenklatura* that their point of view is well represented at the top, and that they have some influence in matters. Ligachev helps to stabilize the regime

⸻

1. This chapter is based on an exchange that took place during the conference roundtable.

in a period of transition. I think this position has an element of truth about it, but it is probably misleading. Ultimately, the elements are here for an unstable leadership situation.

Let me, in case anybody is uncertain or disagrees with my view that there are two different programs emerging, try to define what I mean. With regard to political reform, the Gorbachevites are very strong on the electoral principle, and widening or deepening it, both in the way it works in the party, the way it works in the soviets, and the way it works in the people's workplaces. The Ligachevites are less enthusiastic about widening or deepening the electoral principle, fearing that the traditional basis on which the *nomenklatura* mechanism has worked is being seriously undermined. The Gorbachevites are very keen to transfer power from the traditional party apparatus, both at the local level and at the top, to a number of other bodies, including the soviets, the socialist market, and even a free market. Power has been transferred from the party, and from the ministries as well. The ministries do not arouse much concern from the Ligachevites, because they too dislike the ministries to a large extent. However, taking away power from the party does very much bother the Ligachevites. Ligachev sees himself as a guardian of the interests of the party apparatus.

Another conflict with regard to political reform is over the extent of the glasnost policy. How far should it go? The lines became extremely clear at the 1988 Party Conference, where the Gorbachev view of radical glasnost was very severely challenged by the Ligachevites, who felt that it had already gone quite far enough. Gorbachev was compelled to retreat somewhat on that issue at the conference.

There is also the question of political order throughout the country. The Gorbachevites take the view that it is important for people to be able to express their views on economic, political, and social issues in the form of demonstrations, which should not have to be licensed in advance nor necessarily under official control. The workers should be allowed to protest vigorously at abuses in their workplaces, or even call a strike occasionally, and the government should not panic or become alarmed. Strikes are a reasonable and normal occurrence. The Ligachev group, by contrast, thinks that such a situation is incipient political anarchy, has already gone too far, and certainly should not be allowed to go further. In his Gorky speech, Ligachev made some very strong remarks on this score, recapitulating the old argument that states, "Why should workers strike against their own enterprises? They own them. Why should they sabotage them through strikes?"

The nationality issue focuses other differences in viewpoint between the Gorbachevites and the Ligachevites. We see remarkable developments in the Baltic Republics, which are an experiment for the country as a whole and for the minority republics. Far-reaching liberalization is being allowed and even encouraged to see whether or not it is workable. The reasons for going as far as they have appear to be economic. Estonia, possibly Latvia, and possibly Lithuania are being turned into economic free zones, which, according to some reports, is the ultimate purpose, or one of the purposes, of this policy. There is a chance that the policy of economic decentralization will really be pushed, because, needless to say, Estonians and the others would embrace it. They want to have much stronger control over their local economy, and that impetus will assist the general process of economic decentralization throughout the country. To support the local leaderships in these republics, the authorities have gone further. They have allowed the national independent flag of Estonia to become a legitimate flag again, and they have made other concessions to the sovereignty of those republics.

It is clear from an interview that Yuri Afanasev gave to an Italian journalist, that he, at any rate, is absolutely for a comprehensive, liberal approach to the nationalities issue, to allow the national republics to control their own affairs. He feels that it is a logical path of radical perestroika, and that the Soviet Union must go the whole way. Gorbachev has not said anything so radical, but it is the sort of advice that he is hearing from his radical advisers.

The Ligachevites are very much more skeptical. They fear that it is planting the seeds of the breakup of the Soviet Union. They remember what happened in 1917, and they are afraid it might happen again. Gorbachevites say, in effect, that we do not think it is going to lead to a breakup, and we should take the risk.

The whole Armenian-Azerbaijan issue is another on which, I think, there are differences. The Ligachevites say they would have taken a tougher line at a much earlier stage. Gorbachev disagreed, trying to treat the issue delicately. I think there is a significant clash on this issue.

On the economic reform, Ligachev spelled out in his Gorky speech his deep suspicion of the whole principle of the market. He just does not like the notion of a market, even a socialist market. To have this sort of opposition voicing the views of the status quo, representing the conservative elements in the apparatus of the party, is clearly a problem for the Gorbachevites.

We see another clash developing in foreign policy, and it will be fascinating to see how far it goes. Again in the Gorky speech, Ligachev acted as a spokesman for the elements within the regime who are anxious at what they see as a strong trend to move away from the traditional attitude to foreign policy, based on the class approach and class principles, toward an increasing appeal to all human interests in foreign policy, all human concerns, ecology, and preserving peace. Ligachev warned, in very direct language, that this trend in Soviet policy was confusing and disorienting to the Soviet people and the Soviet Union's allies. It will be very important to see whether the course Ligachev has taken up will have an effect on the conduct of Soviet foreign policy.

If this line is pushed, the leaderships in East Europe (I think Ligachev was particularly hinting about East Europe) are going to be very uncertain as to what Soviet intentions are. What are they going to do? Are they going to allow East Europe to move along its own path, even if it means a threat to communist rule or to the purpose of the rulers there? Again, the Afanasev interview is extremely interesting. He said, in effect, that the Soviets must tell the East European states they can do what they want. They are sovereign republics with their own legitimacy. If trends move in the direction of capitalism in East Europe, that is not good for the Kremlin, but the Soviets would have to live with it.

How do these differences in political programs transfer into political conflict? The main elements here could be summed up under three headings: the Yeltsin case in November 1987, the Andreyeva episode in March and April of 1988, and the Party Conference at the end of June 1988.

Gorbachev has moved from what I regard as a position of leading perestroika from the left to a much more center-left, or even in some respects centralist, position to preserve his political power. The Yeltsin affair was the first big push in that direction, because after that incident it was clearly dangerous to lead perestroika from the left. Gorbachev was forced to denounce and to lead the criticism of Yeltsin. The effects on the elements of the party apparatus that had been taking a radical perestroika line were profound. They had been urged by Gorbachev, for the previous year at least, to be radical, to be urgent, to be bold in their application of perestroika. Yeltsin was a model radical who embraced these principles. Once he found himself out on a limb, Gorbachev was there with Ligachev chopping it off. Inevitably, radicals subsequently felt that it would be wiser to wait and see how things worked out at the top, and not to be too radical or too bold. We find Gorbachev increasingly critical of such cautious thinking in officials, but it became more prevalent after the Yeltsin affair.

The Andreyeva case is very important, and it has not yet been fully understood in the West. It is difficult to interpret, but the Andreyeva letter clearly appeared with Ligachev's endorsement, and probably at his initiative, or at the initiative of elements around him.[2] It was a clear challenge, an anti-perestroika manifesto, though dressed up in the disguise as being in favor of a conservative sort of perestroika. Ligachev and his allies did their best to provoke this article. They even reprinted it in many newspapers and had a television discussion in Leningrad supporting it. To paraphrase what Demidov wrote in the *Zhurnalist* (1988, No. 5), "For 23 days, we did nothing. We, the liberals, the Gorbachevites, did nothing. We were terrified. We waited. We thought the whole thing was going to move in a new direction. And, by contrast, the conservatives knew what was happening, and they were acting. They were pushing at the limelight for all they could, but we were too terrified to do anything."

The paralysis of the liberals indicates how delicate the political balance is at the top. The liberals felt that maybe the events were not going their way, and they stood transfixed and immobile until eventually the *Pravda* article entitled "Principles of Restructuring: The Revolutionary Nature of Thinking and Acting," gave them some reassurance.[3]

2. *Sovetskaya Rossiya,* March 13, 1988.
3. *Pravda,* April 5, 1988.

It is absolutely clear there is severe political conflict all the time. It was especially apparent at the 1988 All-Union Conference of the Communist Party of the Soviet Union at the end of June, when some of this conflict was actually portrayed on television screens. The Gorbachevites suffered two major setbacks during the conference. Before the conference began, the Gorbachevites had made it clear that they wanted to use the conference to produce a heavy turnover in the Central Committee. They mentioned 25, 30, and even 50 percent. However, when the delegates were elected to the Party Conference, it turned out they were the wrong delegates—they would not produce new Gorbachevite members of the Central Committee, but rather the reverse. Therefore, it was decided simply not to have any turnover in the Central Committee, because it would be counterproductive to the Gorbachevite point of view.

The second setback was the very strong reaction against glasnost by many of the delegates. Some of the delegates in favor of the current level of glasnost were shouted down.

On the positive side, from the Gorbachev point of view, most of the resolutions that came out of the conference were radical and corresponded to what Gorbachev wanted in politics and economics. The big question, however, is implementation. A series of impressive, radical resolutions in the Central Committee, or even more impressive laws translating the Party Conference resolutions into legal form, may never be implemented. Obviously, if there is a Central Committee that has not been reconstructed in its membership, the more conservative, centralized elements are going to be in a powerful position to sabotage the implementation of radical Gorbachevite resolutions.

One of the fascinating questions in Soviet politics at the moment is whether Gorbachev's shift from the left wing to a more center-left position to preserve stability within the regime is a tactical move to accommodate the more conservative currents of the last year, or whether it is a permanent move on his part. If it is more permanent, then we can expect the problems of perestroika to continue, and the radical resolutions will have trouble being implemented. On the other hand, if it is a tactical move by Gorbachev, we can expect him to be looking for new angles from which to attack the status quo in an effort to knock the conservatives and the center-right groups off balance, and finding new ways of pressing forward in much the same way Khrushchev did some thirty years ago.

Malashenko:

Frankly, I have a number of disagreements with Mr. Reddaway. I disagree with his analysis of the current political situation in the Soviet Union. Perestroika is a process of major political and economic change, not a personal contest. The crucial question from my point of view is the question that is very rarely asked in this country or in the Soviet Union. It is a crucial question about the Russian and Soviet political culture: To what extent does this political culture permit democratic reform and democratic achievement?

If we are talking about political divisions, I would present the situation in different terms. I would say it is democratization versus liberalization. I do not think that there are now very strong or really formidable political forces in the Soviet Union that are trying to block the process of reform completely. The period of stagnation has made reform absolutely inevitable. But what kinds of reforms are we actually talking about? The crucial distinction between democratization and liberalization is a qualitative difference, because liberalization is a process that can be encouraged from the top. Four years ago, we initiated a process of liberalization, not democratization, of the society.

When I am asked the question about the irreversibility of perestroika, I think exactly in these terms. Perestroika is irreversible to the extent that there is real democracy in the society, not liberalization. Liberalization is always reversible. There can be enormous liberalization today and no liberalization tomorrow. You cannot do this with a real democracy. The forces for democratization actually started later than the slogans of perestroika or glasnost. But now that they have started, it is increasingly difficult to reverse the process of perestroika.

Irreversibility, democratization, and liberalization all have to do with the distribution of power. It has been said that the party should give up power, or something to this effect. I would ask the question: Give up power to whom, or to what? It is not fair to say that the party should give up the power it does not actually have.

The party apparatus has the power, but that is quite a different story. We should democratize the party itself, and then we will see how much democratization it can provide for the society. I think it will be significant. By the way, I am encouraged by the American model, because it is absolutely impossible for the average Russian to understand the difference between the Republican and Democratic parties, and yet you still have a democracy!

The major problem now is not the fact that we have a difference at the top, even in the Politburo or Central Committee. The problem is that Ligachev is missing from the Politburo. If we look at Soviet history, we see that the most productive periods were when there were actual political divisions within political organizations. When there was a united front, little good happened. Look at, for example, the Brezhnev stagnation. I am actually sad that Yeltsin is gone, despite the fact that I dislike him. You have presented the Yeltsin case in a very sympathetic way. If we are talking on personal terms, I am also very sympathetic about it. I have no doubt that he is a very sincere person. But if I look at his ideas and his programs, I am absolutely horrified by them. It is the ideology of the big jump. We have had many big jumps in our history, and we know the net result of the big jump, even if we talk only in economical terms. You can jump, but you know that you will hit the bottom.

Still, Yeltsin's presence was very fortunate, because there was a productive balance in the Politburo. Then he made an absolutely unbelievable and stupid political move. I could not believe my ears and eyes when I heard and saw this. There should be consensus within the Politburo, of course, but not homogeneity. It is a prescription for stagnation and some absolutely unreasonable reforms. For the sake of diversity, I hope that some other person like Yeltsin will be incorporated into the Politburo.

The same is true for the diversity of opinions in foreign policy. There was complete agreement about our foreign policy for many years, and it did not quite function because there was no apprehension of the alternatives. For example, when foreign policy leaders were making the decision on Afghanistan, there was a very limited number of people involved. As far as we understand now, there was not a single voice raised in opposition.

As Mr. Reddaway has pointed out, the problem of implementation is crucial. There is no way to implement the reforms only working through the party apparatus. It is a prescription for a complete disaster. In several years there will just be some mock reforms. If we have the active participation on the part of the general public, many resolutions can be implemented and many mistakes corrected. It is my hope that the development of our political culture will reach that crucial point, but it is not a stable process, and it will take some time. Sooner or later, there will be a shift in the paradigm, a qualitative and not just a quantitative change. That is the reason why I am personally optimistic, despite the enormous political difficulties we are facing during this process.

Reddaway:

I was very interested in much of Mr. Malashenko's comments. I think we are being presented with a somewhat novel theory of politics, one that states that for leaderships to be divided against themselves is good. Despite this brave face, the situation is not so convenient and has many disadvantages. One of the leaders Mr. Gorbachev and other East Europeans have looked to with admiration has been Mrs. Thatcher of England. Mrs. Thatcher has gone to great trouble at an early stage in her administration to assemble a united cabinet. She has rid herself of various people who criticized her and had reservations about particular policies. In my opinion, she has been successful because she managed to achieve a reasonably united cabinet. The same was true of President Reagan. He was criticized for having too much disagreement within his cabinet, but I do not think it was anywhere nearly as fundamental as the disagreement in the Soviet leadership. I am thus rather skeptical about this line of argument.

The proposal that the periods during which there was division in leadership were the most fruitful in Soviet history also bears some examination. At the beginning of the Brezhnev period, there was weak economic reform during those four or five years, but it did not really lead anywhere. There was also the invasion of Czechoslovakia in those years. Obviously, in a period like that there are some initiatives, but I do not think we can call them tremendously fruitful, and they can lead to rather bad situations, like the invasion of Czechoslovakia.

Malashenko:

I do not mean an institution divided against itself, but a system of checks and balances. We are talking about politics, and the margins are extremely important. I was talking about a diversity of opinion. We cannot absolutely compare these different systems. You are talking about a very liberated, western system. Mrs. Thatcher was fortunate enough to have very little opposition, but still there was some opposition. This is not the case in the Soviet Union. Perhaps it will be in the future, but it is a political fiction right now. The system could work this way, and I hope it will in the future.

Reddaway Postscript (July 1989):

Since the above exchange took place, two especially notable developments have occurred. First, Gorbachev has made determined, if not wholly successful, efforts to increase his personal authority in the leadership, to diminish Ligachev's, and thus to increase the Politburo's cohesiveness. Second, he has made equally determined efforts to transfer much power and authority from the party apparatus to the two-part legislature of the Congress of People's Deputies and the Supreme Soviet. These developments strongly suggest that Gorbachev, with all his tactical skill, is a committed radical. However, his increased authority is now threatened by the deepening crises in the economy and in nationalities conflicts, and by the rise of worker discontent, which is taking the form of large-scale strikes. All this gives the conservatives hope that they may soon be able to force a change of course. My analysis of Kremlin politics over the last year—"The Threat to Gorbachev"—appears in *The New York Review of Books*, August 17, 1989, pp. 19-24.

CHAPTER 2

Perestroika: An Agenda for Change

GEORGI ARBATOV

The future of Soviet-American economic cooperation and coordination of efforts undertaken by the two countries to solve global problems of the modern civilization will depend to a large extent on the future of perestroika in the Soviet Union. One can argue that perestroika, its success or failure, is becoming one of the major developments in the international economic system.

Wide-ranging discussions of economic problems in the Soviet Union have taken place at the highest levels, including the 27th Congress of the Communist Party of the Soviet Union (CPSU), the 19th Party Conference, and the Plenary Meetings of the CPSU Central Committee. Similarly, intense debates of economic issues are aired in the press. In no other topic have Soviet readers shown a more lively interest. Gradually, the discussions have broadened beyond the limits of pure economic problems, which is quite natural. As I see it, many of our economic difficulties, as well as the means of overcoming them, are not confined exclusively to the economy. They are to be found in politics, in legislation, in ideology, and even in psychology.

Economists, as well as representatives of other social sciences, are now under heavy criticism. They deserve that criticism, though one should not forget that the development of these sciences has been deformed and supressed for many years. But I do not think that even if our best economists could now offer the most precise, well-founded, and concrete recommendations on every economic problem, our managers today would be able to implement them.   It is well known that our managers are not even able to implement many party decisions that are mandatory.

To be sure, there are some fundamental reasons for this situation. At a certain stage of the historical development of our country, under truly extraordinary conditions and for the sake of speedy industrialization and the strengthening of our defense, an appropriate model of the economy—an administrative-command economy—was created. By means of continuous and strong political and ideological pressure, corresponding organizational structures, methods of management, and the system of economic norms have emerged.

The question of alternative paths of development is now being studied by historians. From the viewpoint of contemporary practice, a different question is most important: Can the projected radical economic reform, which has already become an approved party directive, "grow" out of the command economy created at an earlier stage of development?

Judging by the evidence available thus far, the answer is no. The difficulties accompanying the process of implementing economic reforms (such as independence of the enterprises, cost accounting, self-financing, self-repayment, and others), as well as the implementation of new forms of economic activity (such as the lease, contract production, cooperatives, and joint ventures), are not accidental by any means. These difficulties are not just the result of ineptitude or ill will of some officials. In fact, because the new economic measures are alien to the administrative-command economy, they are adopted by that system only with immense effort. Without ongoing assistance "from above," they would be quickly and mercilessly rejected by the old economic system.

If this is so, then several conclusions follow. First, we need to strengthen the already existing act of political will, to back up party decisions concerning the reform with an adequate political or administrative action. This is essential to ensure the success of the reform. In other words, it is impossible either to crush or to re-make the old economic superstructure without administrative and political pressure. For a certain period of time, some leading departments of the Council of Ministers and the Planning Committee must become a kind of "liquidation commission," whose task it would be to clean up a construction site for the new economic system. These bodies should use their power to remove all obstacles—obsolete organizational structures and management methods, as well as the entire system of economic norms of the bureaucratic-command practice—that lie in the path of the reform.

Second, it is necessary to bring to a logical end the work on developing the strategy (and perhaps the tactics) of the practical implementation of the economic reform, of a transition from the old economy to the new one. Major steps in this direction have been made recently, especially at the 19th Party Conference and at the July 1988 Plenary Meeting of the CPSU Central Committee. These steps include a more precise definition of our priority tasks, such as the improvement of the food supply, increasing the production of consumer goods, and the development of services.

Other crucial aspects of the economic strategy in the transitional period were also discussed at the Party Conference. One aspect concerns the tension between striving to fulfill the current five-year plan, which was adopted earlier, and the policy line aimed at implementing the economic reform. It is certainly difficult to remove this tension, especially when our everyday needs dictate that we choose between these conflicting goals.

An eminent American economist, who has followed the development of Soviet economy for a long time, said to me in a private conversation: "You try to make a major overhaul of your house while living in it normally. If I were you, I would try to move somewhere else for a while." Considering that we have no place to move to, I would propose a different simile, drawing upon assistance in child delivery. When a fatal outcome seems inevitable, it is an established rule to save the mother first, because she can give birth to other children. Similarly, we should realize that the reform takes precedence over the fulfillment of our current plan, as we already see that the incipient "child" is suffering from many genetic diseases inherited from the administrative-command practice: volume-oriented indicators, disproportions, and inadequate structural goals, to name a few. It is not the real needs of society toward which the plan is oriented. The goals of the plan are set according to the interests of various departments, or simply to "show-off" a nice figure in the report. Should we overstrain ourselves in an effort to save such a "child"? Is it worth such a sacrifice as perestroika?

On the other hand, the plan should not be undermined. It should be thoroughly, thoughtfully, but resolutely corrected. Such a maneuver under the given circumstances is unavoidable. We should view the remaining two years of the current five-year plan from the standpoint of the implementation of the reform, considering it a kind of transitional period enabling us to throw the burden of the past off our shoulders and at the same time freeing us to set priority tasks before the next five-year plan begins.

Another important issue of the economic strategy came up at the Party Conference: how to ensure the transition from the unlimited power of planning agencies to the independence of enterprises. This question is linked not only to the problem of streamlining the system of state orders for the input of enterprises, but to the problem of eliminating redundancies of management and the reduction of the staff. Again, here is a difficult choice we have to make. It seems not only more human but also more rational to bear additional costs through more generous allowances and pensions instead of artificially holding back the scrapping of useless bureaucratic organizations.

Another question concerning economic strategy has to do with a whole host of problems, including enormous losses of vegetables, fruits, and other agricultural products, the import of grain, which has become chronic, the system of city-to-village labor assistance, the fantastic scale of unfinished construction, and others. These problems are easily solved in the rest of the world, and it is high time for us to solve them as well. This does not mean adding some new decrees and programs to the large number that already exist. First of all, we need to take an intolerant attitude toward the present state of affairs. Secondly, the administrative and material responsibility of the culprits must be recognized.

The third conclusion is that the time factor has become much more critical. Most of our people probably understand very well that the solution to the problems that have been accumulating over the years and the implementation of the all-around economic reform can be achieved only over a long period. But at the same time, the feelings of anxiety and dissatisfaction with economic conditions are growing. This dissatisfaction (which was also noted at the recent Party Conference) has its reasons—four years are enough to show more significant results than what we have accomplished. Time becomes a decisive factor. We must not let people grow disappointed, disillusioned, or skeptical. After all, the whole idea of perestroika is rooted in stimulating the creative activities of people, in getting them involved in changing and innovating society.

OVERCOMING OBSTACLES TO PERESTROIKA

Competition

Four other issues must be addressed, the first of which is competition. We are used to quoting Lenin's remark about monopoly leading to degradation as one referring only to capitalism. But we did not realize for a long time that probably in no other country in the world is there such monopolization as there is in the Soviet Union. And we could have already seen for ourselves that a socialist monopoly is a source of no less degradation than a capitalist one. Here is an important source of negative phenomena in such spheres as prices, quality level, and the state of scientific and technological progress. And as a corollary and a consequence of this unlimited monopoly, we see a complete contempt for the interests of consumers. In my view, it would not be an exaggeration to say that without a thoroughly conceived and consistently implemented antimonopolistic policy, the restructuring of the economy will fail.

Of what should such a policy consist? First, we should outlaw the monopolistic practices of every kind and institute strong sanctions against violating these laws. Second, we need to introduce new forms of the organization of production, which would legislatively rule out or limit monopoly even while industrial ministries still exist. Such steps should be taken in the entire sphere of services and the production of consumer goods, which are a major part of the total goods production. Similar "antitrust" measures should be used against such monopolies as Aeroflot and Intourist. Finally, we should create conditions for our producers to make them compete with foreign firms, including capitalist ones. It will be possible if we introduce a realistic exchange rate for a convertibility of the ruble. Then the buyer will have a choice:

either to buy a domestic product or a foreign one, but at a higher (sometimes much higher) price for better quality. This concerns both the means of production and consumer goods.

Corruption

The second problem is the existence of vast deformed spheres of economic activities, which degenerated into something parasitic, harmful to society, and contradictory in their spiritual and moral values. They include domestic trade, catering, and a major part of the service sector. Everyone seems to know about the situation in these spheres, and some problems are addressed by our press. For example, recently we have read that, according to the head of the Moscow branch of the Agency Against Theft of Socialist Property, fifty-seven out of fifty-eight salesmen cheat buyers. But the press gave neither honest assessment of the state of affairs nor practical conclusions. Thus, the corruption can negate any achievements in industry or agriculture. Clearly, we cannot raise the level and quality of Soviet living standards without a profound perestroika and a real revolution in these spheres. Unfortunately, corruption is a reality that considerably affects the social and moral climate in our society. It is difficult to say how to restructure these spheres, and an open, serious discussion of the problem has yet to appear in the press.

Decline in Living Standards

The third problem is the Soviet living standard, a situation that is uppermost in everybody's mind, if only because of the discussion of prices in the press. It seems that a number of our economists look in fear at the monster they helped create—in bureaucratic offices, a proposed reform of the pricing system was quickly converted into a proposal for higher prices on top of the price rise that occurred spontaneously. In the discussion of the pricing reform, the very assumption that perestroika should call for new sacrifices seems wrong, which is not to say that the pricing system does not need a radical reform (though its outlines do not emerge quite clearly from the current debate). But price changes should not be to the detriment of living standards; rather, they should be compatible with their overall improvement. One can hardly reach modern frontiers in the national economy without raising living standards.

Where will the resources come from to march ahead and, at the same time, remove the bottlenecks formed over the past few years? Clearly, we do need major sources of inputs right now. The principal of these—and our economists say it loud and clear—is the abandonment (either complete, once and for all, or temporary and partial) of many costly and inefficient economic programs and construction projects, including the giants—the "projects of the century," such as the Baykal-Amur Mainline and the reversal of rivers from North to South and from East to West. Clearly, the ill-conceived development program for nonblack soil areas, while badly needed, calls for rethinking. The activity of the Ministry of Irrigation, with its staff of two million and a 10-billion ruble annual budget, is seen as a striking example of squandering resources. The proposal to reorient its activities to, say, road construction, probably merits consideration. More broadly, an open and public "stock-taking" of all long, drawn-out construction projects is well overdue.

A related but separate source of new resources is the abandonment of redundancies in defense through an active use of political opportunities for safeguarding security. This is not simple, but the new political thinking opens up such a door. In addition to a stringent but reasonable policy of austerity in all areas, it will probably provide us with "primary accumulation" necessary for perestroika.

In this connection, the idea of a more active use of new opportunities in foreign trade put forward by a number of our economists merits attention, especially because the resources saved as a result of giving up nonessential programs and construction projects will not be converted immediately into useful commodities and services. Therefore, the use of foreign trade potential, including credits, will provide the necessary breathing space. But much can be done even without credits by drastically reducing the imports of equipment.

Coercion

The fourth problem concerns the reliance of the administrative-command economy on coercion—the use of administrative and judicial reprisals—as its necessary tool. Judicial reprisals assumed a variety of forms, from the trials of dissenters (beginning with the Chayanov-Kondratiev trial), to the monstrous excesses of the dispossession of the *kulaks*, and to the different forms of confiscation and restriction against private holdings. The practice of persecution and victimization of resourceful and enterprising managers, whose work undermined the bureaucratic restrictions and whose successes challenged the administrative-command system, was widely used until recently, though it has not been completely eradicated even now. Charges brought against plant managers such as Chebanov in Cherkassy or Chebanenko in Gorky, managers of prospectors' teams and cooperatives, and collective-farm chairmen, such as Khudenko and Snimshikov and the Starodubtsev brothers from the Tula region, put them and others under investigation for many months, shattering their nerves and ruining their health in the process. In fact, there is hardly a single collective-farm chairman of national renown who has escaped such a fate. A new practice developed in law enforcement, which was facilitated by the character of the existing laws and regulations, that enabled some unscrupulous people to frame any manager.

Owing to the enormous economic and social harm of this practice, I propose that a commission be established under the Central Committee to reexamine such cases and to rehabilitate those unjustly convicted of economic offenses. This is necessary to ward off the threat of victimization still facing resourceful and innovative managers. This problem should also find its solution in the legal reform now being prepared.

CONCLUSION

The most important ingredient for the success of radical economic reform and perestroika is the full confidence of the millions of people in the party's political course, not only in terms of dedication to socialism and patriotism, which we already have. There is today already a belief in perestroika, a confidence in the correctness of the path of social renovation chosen by the party. It is a great achievement of recent years, but it should also be supplemented by more prosaic and concrete steps. The working people must be confident that if they buy a cow today, become farmers under a family contract, organize a cooperative, or begin to exercise their right as owners of an enterprise, the legalities of their actions will not be abolished tomorrow or the day after. Many people do not have such confidence yet.

Innovations should be encouraged, and not only morally. A reason for mistrust is the existing gap between words and deeds, the fact that a "fly in the ointment" is added to many innovations, be it an unreasonably large state order, an excessive tax, or a catch in the instructions completely leveling off the essence of a new law or resolution. In addition, the continuing interference of numerous bodies in the affairs of enterprises, collective farms, cooperatives, and "self-employed" citizens must be stopped. This can come about only by the use of authority—not in the spirit of the years that are best forgotten, of course, but sensibly, by means of reinforcing economic measures with political guarantees.

CHAPTER 3

The Implications of Greater East-West Economic Cooperation for the Soviet Economy

H. Stephen Gardner

Several years ago, Ed A. Hewett (1983, 304) offered a scenario for Soviet foreign trade reform that seemed, at the time, rather optimistic: "[If] in 1990 they are beginning to talk about a Hungarian-type reform, and if by the year 2000 they are beginning to introduce such a reform, that will be a more rapid and fundamental change than they have undergone in the last twenty years . . .". Viewed from that perspective, the pace of change in recent years has surpassed all expectations. The Soviets are beginning to introduce a preliminary set of Hungarian-style reforms a decade ahead of schedule.

At the same time, the rhetoric of perestroika—the promise of democratization, radical reform, acceleration, openness, and internationalization—has raised hopes and expectations to a new level that will be difficult to fulfill. Every effort to change the system is challenged by the national legacy of authoritarianism, which predates Stalinism, and by the devilish ability of the command system to reproduce itself in new shapes, forms, and surroundings. Extensive reform of the foreign trade system has been initiated, and much more has been proposed, but the early results are both hopeful and disappointing. What will be the role of international trade and investment in perestroika? What are the prospects for a major breakthrough in East-West economic

relations?   How will improved trade relations affect the performance of the Soviet economy?   These are difficult questions, addressed during unpredictable times.

This paper begins with a general review of the role of foreign
economic relations in the Soviet economy.   First, it considers the
continuing legacy of protectionism and autarky and then surveys
several possible motivations for Soviet involvement in trade
relations: comparative advantage, technology transfer, competitive
pressure, and political influence.   The second part of the paper
reviews the foreign trade and financial reforms that have been
introduced or proposed, and assesses their implications for East-
West trade and Soviet economic performance.

THE ROLE OF FOREIGN TRADE IN THE SOVIET ECONOMY

Dating back to the early days of the empire, Russian politicians
and theorists have had fickle attitudes toward foreign economic
relations.   In recent years, the legacies of Tsarist protectionism and
Stalinist isolationism have given way slowly to a broader understanding, based on comparative advantage, technology transfer,
political interdependence, and, finally, the motivating force of
foreign competition.

Protectionism and Autarky

The roots of protectionism are planted deep in Russian history and
culture.   "Despite the most shameful underpayment of the work-
people," Karl Marx (1867, 526) noted, "Russian manufacture
manages to vegetate only by the prohibition of foreign competition."   After the Revolution, under the threat of "capitalist
encirclement," the state monopoly of foreign trade made it possible
to progress from mere protectionism to autarky.   During the late
1930s, Soviet trade fell well below 1 percent of national income,

"surely a record of sorts," according to Wiles (1969, 437). Abolition of the monopoly, Stalin warned, "would mean an inundation of the U.S.S.R. with goods from capitalist countries, a decrease in industry because of its relative weakness, [and] an increase of unemployment . . .".[1]

Under the autarkic system, imports were restricted to three basic categories: (1) important products that could not be produced at home under any circumstances; (2) goods that could be produced at home, but were needed to fill temporary gaps in the annual plans; and (3) capital goods that were needed to extend autarky to new sectors of the economy. As a Soviet scholar noted in 1938: "Imports into the U.S.S.R. are planned so as to aid in freeing the nation from the need to import."[2] Exports were delivered from sectors that were able to produce beyond domestic requirements, with little consideration of comparative advantage.

According to current Soviet thinking, autarky was the "correct" policy during the 1930s, when it was "dictated by the necessity to ensure the full technical and economic invulnerability of the young Soviet economy." It has become an anachronism, however, now that the state is a superpower, surrounded by allies, and "the demands of the times call for active participation in the world-wide process of scientific-technical progress" (Rybakov 1988, 69).

Anachronism or not, the legacy of protectionism and autarky still exerts a strong influence on Soviet trade policy. Opponents of broader economic cooperation are able to point to the disappointing results from imports of machinery and equipment (more on this below), the danger of dependency on western supplies of food, and the ruinous burden of debt on the economies of East Europe. According to Shastitko, "You talk with any of our economic managers today who has nothing to do with foreign ties, and he will tell you that dependence on foreign trade is bad."[3] Yuri Konstantinov (1987, 13), in a book that proclaims the importance of the

1. Quoted in Smith (1973, 10-11).
2. D. Mishustin quoted in Holzman (1974, 382).
3. Interviewed by Cherepanov (1987, 8).

international division of labor, says that import policy should be based on "the strictest economy, on parsimonious use of foreign exchange, and on refusal to buy goods that we can do without."

On the export side of the equation, although the need to rationalize production along lines of comparative advantage was officially recognized in the Soviet Union at least twenty years ago, the "residual principle of planning" has proved durable. "In the plan for 1988, no absolute priority has been given to exports," according to Ivan Ivanov (1988, 6), the Deputy Chairman of the State Foreign Economic Commission. About 60 percent of petroleum exports, he says, were scheduled for delivery in the second and third quarters, when international demand was soft, but domestic requirements were satisfied. Likewise, the State Planning Commission (GOS-PLAN) descended on a machine tool factory in Kuybyshev that had 444 pieces of equipment committed for delivery to western clients, and claimed all but 150 of the machines for domestic use.[4]

In his comprehensive review of the events and discussions that led to Gorbachev's program of "radical reform," Ed A. Hewett (1988, 299) found that foreign trade received "virtually no attention in the debate, even from the radicals . . .". This is not too surprising when we consider the limited role that trade has traditionally played in the Soviet economy, but it is remarkable when we recall that improvement in trade performance was the chief motivation for reforms in East Europe. Not until the summer of 1986, when the falling price of oil caused Soviet hard-currency export earnings to decline for the third consecutive year, was a significant program of perestroika devised for the foreign sector.

This is not to suggest, of course, that autarky is still the dominant theme in Soviet international economic relations. Some would say, in fact, that Soviet trade participation rates are already on par with those in market economies (Treml 1980; Ofer 1987). This is a difficult comparison to make because Soviet domestic prices, most of which are strictly controlled, are very different from those on the world market.

4. *Wall Street Journal,* March 9, 1988, p. 21.

As the data in Table 3-1 indicate, participation ratios estimated from trade and output levels in dollar prices are quite different from those in domestic ruble prices. This is a classical index number problem that cannot be resolved simply.[5] At any rate, all of the series in Table 3-1 indicate an upward trend in Soviet trade participation ratios since 1950, although that trend was interrupted after 1980 by the decline in world oil prices and the political fallout from events in Afghanistan and Poland. The highest ratios are those for imports in current domestic prices, reflecting not only the index number effect (the tendency to import products that have relatively high domestic prices), but also an apparent increase in the domestic prices of imported goods relative to other domestic prices.[6]

Despite its increase, Soviet trade participation still seems to lag behind the levels achieved by market economies. In Table 3-2, Soviet export shares in GNP are compared with those for four other large countries and regions.[7] According to these estimates, Soviet participation is lower than that for any of the other areas, including Latin America, which has a much larger population and a lower level of industrial development.[8]

Soviet trade dependency is much higher, of course, in a number of industries and product groups. More than one-fifth of the state's output of crude oil, automobile, and woodworking equipment is

5. For a discussion of this problem, with reference to Soviet trade dependency ratios, see Bergson (1980); Treml (1982); and Desai (1989).

6. The relatively rapid rate of inflation for domestic prices of imported goods may have been caused by their growing interdependence with external prices. See Treml (1980, 191-96).

7. Trade within the European Community and Latin America is excluded from the export totals, allowing us to treat these regions as if they were united countries, trading with the outside world. Trade and production are measured in current dollars for all countries.

8. This general conclusion is confirmed by Vyacheslav Dashichev, a Soviet historian (interviewed in Cherepanov [1987, 7]). He says that "today foreign trade accounts for only about 8 percent of Soviet national income, while it is close to 15 percent for the U.S." These figures evidently relate to the sum of exports and imports, and it is not clear whether "national income" is the Soviet or the western concept.

exported, and nearly half of the equipment used by the textile, chemical, and food processing industries is imported (Table 3-3). In the mid-1980s, the Soviets used western equipment to produce about 30 percent of their ethylene and propylene, nearly half of their benzine, two-thirds of their nitrogenous fertilizers, and 90 percent of their xylene, polyethylene, and synthetic fibers equivalent to Orlon and Dacron (Braithwaite 1987; Sagers and Shabad 1987).

The dependency ratios reported in Tables 3-1, 3-2, and 3-3 are based on trade with all countries. For our present purposes, we should recall that the largest share of Soviet trade is conducted with other socialist countries. Trade with nonsocialist countries accounted for about one-third of Soviet commerce in 1987, measured either in current or 1970 prices (Table 3-4). The nonsocialist shares of exports and imports have declined since 1980, measured in current prices. The export share has increased, however, if it is measured in constant prices, because a larger physical volume of exports was required to compensate for the decline in oil prices.

Comparative Advantage

Until 1953, Soviet economic science was kept in a tight ideological noose; all discussion of comparative advantage and other "bourgeois conceptions" was silenced because "the law of value cannot function under our system as the regulator of production" (Stalin 1952, 20). Within a year of Stalin's death, Borisenko and Shastitko attempted to assess the economic rationality of Soviet trade along lines of comparative cost, but their results were never published. An interdepartmental group of economists began work on an official methodology for measurement of foreign trade efficiency in 1962, and after protracted debate, a "provisional" document was published in 1968 (Gardner 1983).

Ever since the publication of the 1968 methodology, Soviet trade specialists have complained that the branch ministries take little

Table 3-1. Alternative Valuations of the Share of Foreign Trade
in Soviet Gross National Product, 1950-1987

(Percentages)

	Current Dollar Prices		1976 Dollar Prices		Current Ruble Prices		1970 Ruble Prices	
	Exp.	Imp.	Exp.	Imp.	Exp.	Imp.	Exp.	Imp.
1950	1.3	1.1	na	na	na	na	na	na
1955	1.7	1.5	na	na	2.4	na	na	na
1960	1.8	1.8	na	na	2.9	6.6	na	na
1965	1.9	1.9	na	na	3.3	6.3	na	na
1970	1.9	1.8	2.7	2.2	4.8	6.5	4.8	6.5
1976	3.0	3.0	3.0	3.0	5.8	11.5	4.8	9.0
1980	4.4	3.9	3.4	3.7	5.3	14.5	5.2	10.2
1985	3.5	3.3	3.3	4.5	na	na	5.0	12.5
1987	3.8	3.5	3.4	4.0	na	na	5.4	10.8
1988	3.5	3.4	na	na	na	na	na	na

Sources: See Appendix A.

Table 3-2. Export Shares of Gross National Production in
Selected Countries and Regions, 1960-1986[a]

(Percentages, Based on Current Dollar Valuations)

	U.S.S.R.	U.S.	Japan	EC	Latin America
1960	1.8	3.8	4.8	4.3	4.5
1970	1.9	4.2	6.1	5.6	3.5
1975	3.0	6.7	10.2	9.1	5.0
1980	4.4	8.2	12.9	11.4	5.8
1986	3.7	5.3	12.6	8.6	4.3
1985 Population (Millions)	277	239	121	322	410

a. Trade within the EC and Latin America is excluded (see explanation in the text).
Sources: See Appendix B.

account of foreign trade efficiency in their investment decisions. They also point to several trends in the foreign trade structure that are "not progressive."

Take, for example, the small share of machinery and equipment (M&E) in Soviet exports. According to a 1977 Soviet study, M&E earned more foreign exchange per ruble of domestic cost than any other aggregate product group (Kirillov 1977). The Ninth Five-Year Plan called for an increase in the M&E share of total exports from 22 percent in 1970 to 29 percent in 1975. Numerical targets have not been published for the subsequent plans, but they routinely include a goal "to improve the structure of trade with foreign countries, primarily by increasing sales of machinery, equipment, and other highly-processed goods."[9]

A number of actions have been taken since the 1960s to promote manufactured exports (more on this below), but the 29-percent goal that was set in 1970 has not been met to this day. In 1987, M&E accounted for about 16 percent of total exports in current prices or 25 percent in 1970 prices.[10] In trade with nonsocialist countries, the M&E share of exports has never exceeded 20 percent, even in 1970 prices (Table 3-5). Thus, the primary motivation of the foreign trade reforms that will be described below is to reduce Soviet dependency on fuel exports and to conform more closely to the pattern of comparative advantage by increasing exports of manufactured goods.

Along with their displeasure over the small share of M&E and the large share of energy in total exports, Soviet economists and officials are also unhappy with their heavy dependence on agricultural imports. According to Treml (1986), about 22 percent of domestic food consumption, measured in calories, was provided by imports in 1981. The share of food in total imports from nonsocialist countries was significantly larger in the first half of

---

9. This was the language of the "Basic Directions" for the Twelfth Plan (1986-1990), but similar statements have been inserted in all of the other plans since the 1960s.
10. The estimate in 1970 prices is explained in Gardner (1988a).

Table 3-3. Shares of Foreign Trade in Soviet Production and
Domestic Utilization of Selected Products, 1960-1986
(Percentages)

	1960	1970	1980	1987
Export Shares Of Production:				
Cameras	4.3	30.4	28.8	37.5
Potash Fertilizer	-	32.0	34.1	29.3
Woodworking Equipment	3.2	13.6	34.5	40.2
Cotton Fiber	25.3	24.3	30.1	31.7
Watches	15.5	26.7	33.6	21.3
Automobiles	22.0	24.5	24.9	25.5
Crude Oil	12.1	18.9	19.7	21.9
Natural Gas	0.5	1.7	12.5	11.6
Import Shares of Utilization:				
Textile Ind. Equipment	13.6	23.3	48.8	57.7
Chemical Equipment	36.7	40.3	68.1	46.6
Food Ind. Equipment	23.3	27.6	48.8	48.0
Tea	26.7	25.1	29.9	33.0
Raw Sugar	20.4	25.4	31.4	25.5
Steel Pipe	9.4	9.9	14.9	20.6
Grain	0.2	1.2	13.7	13.7

Source: Narkhoz (1987, 605 and 607).

Table 3-4. Share of Nonsocialist Countries in Soviet Foreign Trade, 1946-1987
(Percentages)

	Soviet Exports		Soviet Imports	
	Current Valuta Prices	1970 Valuta Prices	Current Valuta Prices	1970 Valuta Prices
1946	42	na	48	na
1950	16	18	22	20
1960	35	27	29	25
1970	35	35	35	35
1975	39	34	48	43
1980	46	34	47	42
1985	39	37	39	39
1987	35	39	31	35
1988	35	na	31	na

Sources: Vneshtorg (annual); Gardner (1988a).

the 1980s than in the 1970s, measured either in current or constant prices (Table 3-6). This pattern of trade is not justified, according to Abel Aganbegyan (1988), "in the country in which 80 percent of the 'black earth' soil in the world is concentrated—the best soil, with enormous richness, fertility and the most varied of conditions; a country which used to *export* agricultural produce." Soviet food imports, in other words, are not based on the country's resource endowment, but on "an unsatisfactory system of agricultural management." Purchases of grain, meat, and dairy produce should cease in the 1990s, he says.

In contrast to the Soviet view, Vanous (1984) has argued that comparative advantage considerations should encourage the Soviet Union to *increase* their grain imports. According to his calculations for 1980, 1 ruble of marginal cost in the oil industry could yield a product that, if exported, could buy enough grain to save over 6 rubles of marginal cost in grain production. If gas rather than oil exports were increased, the savings would be nearly 16 rubles per ruble of production cost. These results are challenged in recent work by Liefert (1987), who includes a depletion charge in his estimates of the marginal cost of oil and gas production. With that adjustment, his intermediate estimates indicate that exchanges of oil for grain were advantageous for the Soviet Union only in 1974 and 1978-1982, when the world price of oil was exceptionally high. However, exchanges of natural gas for grain were still very advantageous in all years.

The Vanous and Liefert estimates are based, of course, on historical patterns of production cost. Aganbegyan hopes, on the other hand, that improvements in agricultural management will drastically reduce the cost of food production, allowing the Soviet Union to regain its resource-based status as a grain exporter. Agricultural reforms are moving ahead, but a goal of self-sufficiency in the 1990s will be difficult to meet. Thus, the U.S.-U.S.S.R. Long-Term Grain Agreement was renewed in November 1988, and Soviet purchases of U.S. grain were running at a record pace in mid-1989.[11]

11. For details, see U.S. Department of Agriculture (1989, 39-56).

At any rate, comparative cost considerations have become an important element in the debate over the Soviet trade structure. Despite Stalin's distrust of the "law of value," it is likely to play a much more important role as price controls are relaxed, and more enterprises are allowed to make their own trade decisions on a basis of "self-financing."

Technology Transfer

Frequently, Soviet officials affirm the importance of the *international division of labor*, but they speak even more often about the need to keep pace with the *worldwide scientific-technical revolution*. The backward state of Soviet production technology has been documented extensively in the West and acknowledged openly in the Soviet Union. According to the CIA and DIA (1988a, 17), the Soviets cannot begin series production of computers and flexible manufacturing systems at current American technological levels for at least seven or eight years. Western academic studies have reached similar conclusions, and they have uncovered longer technological lags in some sectors (Brada 1985). Furthermore, according to the CIA, the technology gap has been growing, not shrinking, in recent years (*Allocation* . . . 1988, 86). This may be true, in part, because Soviet machinery and equipment is used long after it is obsolete; it is kept in service about twice as long as equipment in the major market economies.[12]

After years of denial, these problems are now openly discussed by Soviet economists and leaders. Aganbegyan (1988, 183) affirms that "we have so far lagged far behind" in technology. He cites a 1985 study that found 71 percent of the equipment in the civil engineering industry was obsolete and should be replaced as soon

---

12. See Cohn (1987, 17). According to Chawluk (1987), excessive service lives may reduce Soviet labor productivity by anywhere between 1 and 16 percent, depending on the specification of the aggregate production function. Excessive capital repair expenses may reduce national income by another 3 percent.

Table 3-5. Commodity Structure of Soviet Exports to
Nonsocialist Countries, 1970-1987
(Percentages of Total Trade)

	1970	1975	1980	1985	1987
Machinery & Equipment					
Current Prices	17	11	8	9	11
1970 Prices	17	17	15	18	16
Fuel & Electricity					
Current Prices	15	40	55	57	44
1970 Prices	15	19	19	20	16
Nonfood Raw Materials					
Current Prices	24	19	13	11	14
1970 Prices	24	23	20	18	18
Food & Food Raw Materials					
Current Prices	9	4	1	1	2
1970 Prices	9	3	2	2	3
Manf. Consumer Goods					
Current Prices	2	3	2	2	3
1970 Prices	2	4	4	4	5
Other					
Current Prices	33	23	20	20	26
1970 Prices	33	34	40	39	42

Source: Gardner (1988a).

Table 3-6. Commodity Structure of Soviet Imports from
Nonsocialist Countries, 1970-1987
(Percentages of Total Trade)

	1970	1975	1980	1985	1987
Machinery & Equipment					
Current Prices	27	29	23	21	27
1970 Prices	27	34	28	22	27
Fuel & Electricity					
Current Prices	2	5	4	11	9
1970 Prices	2	2	1	4	4
Nonfood Raw Materials					
Current Prices	37	31	31	29	33
1970 Prices	37	32	32	34	38
Food & Food Raw Materials					
Current Prices	21	25	31	26	16
1970 Prices	21	19	26	25	19
Manf. Consumer Goods					
Current Prices	8	6	6	8	7
1970 Prices	8	7	8	11	8
Other					
Current Prices	6	4	5	5	8
1970 Prices	6	6	5	4	3

Source: Gardner (1988a).

as possible. Thus, the 1986-1990 Plan calls for an ambitious increase in the rates of investment and capital retirement. Investment is scheduled to double in the machine-building sector; it grew only 24 percent in the previous five years.[13]

Western assessments of the Soviet modernization campaign generally have found that major investment goals cannot be met without substantial importation of equipment from the West.[14] Technology trade is also encouraged by the current relaxation of East-West political relations and the recent adoption of joint-venture legislation in the Soviet Union. At the same time, several obstacles stand in the way. The drop in world oil prices has seriously reduced the import capacity of the Soviet Union. While western export controls are softening, they remain in place. Moreover, Soviet officials are divided in their attitudes toward dependence on western technology.

Many Soviet officials are unimpressed with the results obtained from previous machinery imports. After a sustained chemicalization campaign, based on technology purchases that began during the Khrushchev years, the U.S.S.R. is still a large net importer of chemical products. Rapid expansion of East-West trade during the 1970s was accompanied by a rapid deceleration of economic growth.

According to Soviet and western research, several factors have reduced the impact of imported technology. First, despite their growth in the mid-1970s, the scale of machinery imports has been relatively small. M&E imports from the West accounted for these estimated proportions of Soviet investment in M&E during 1971-1986:[15]

---

13. We should note that Soviet economists are not unanimous in their support for a major investment drive. Chernikov, for example, argues that excessive investment will interfere with the assimilation of new technology, which will *slow* the rate of capital stock retirement (see Leggett 1982, 146). Selyunin (1988) argues that a continuation of economic growth based on forced saving and excessive investment will yield no improvement in the consumers' standard of living.

14. Braithwaite (1987); Leggett (1987); Sagers and Shabad (1987); and Hewett, Roberts, and Vanous (1987).

15. Author's estimates, based on trade in 1972 domestic prices estimated in Gardner (1988a) and investment data in 1969 rubles found in *Narkhoz* (various years).

1971-1975	6.0 percent
1976-1980	7.5 percent
1981-1985	5.9 percent
1986	5.1 percent

Second, according to the classification scheme developed by Martens (1984), "high technology" goods accounted for only 18 percent of Soviet manufactured imports from the West in 1970, and only 12 percent in 1981. The sophistication of Soviet imports is limited not only by western export controls, but by domestic requirements. Machinery is often imported that could be produced domestically if suppliers were able to overcome construction and supply bottlenecks.

Third, the impact of machinery imports has been blunted by the inefficient systems of central planning and state trading. After a domestic enterprise asks its branch ministry for an imported machine, it routinely takes two or three years to have the item included in the import plan, and then it takes the foreign trade organization (FTO) another year or two to complete the purchase (Guk 1987). Furthermore, in the past, the FTOs communicated poorly with domestic final users. Thus, according to data compiled by the Moscow Chamber of Commerce and Industry, about 9 percent of the M&E imported in the central districts of the RSFSR did not meet the needs of domestic enterprises (Zhukov 1986). This problem has been addressed by recent trade reforms, which allow some ministries and large enterprises to conduct their own purchases, and require the FTOs to work more closely with final users.

Fourth, after the equipment has been imported, construction problems may delay its installation for additional months or years. According to surveys of western exporters, it takes the Soviets from two to six times longer to complete an installation than it would take in the West.[16] In the interim, imported equipment is often left outside in shipping containers, gathering rust and obsolescence. At the beginning of 1988, more than 12 billion rubles

16. See Hanson and Hill (1979); Rothlingshofer and Vogel (1979); and Goldman (1987).

worth of equipment (domestic and imported) was waiting for installation in the energy, metallurgy, chemical, timber, machine-building, and agro-industrial sectors (Berger and Pashkov 1988).

Fifth, after the equipment is installed, its productivity is reduced by a host of operational problems, including raw material shortages, overstaffing, poor training and incentives, and limited access to spare parts. Thus, according to western exporters, the productivity of equipment installed in the Soviet Union is about one-third lower than in the West.

Finally, and perhaps most importantly, there has been little evidence of a "learning curve" in the sectors that have relied heavily on foreign technology. In the chemicals industry, each new line of production—ammonia, plastic, and synthetic fibers—has required new purchases of turnkey plants from the West (Braithwaite 1987). Unlike the Japanese, who have been able to build their export base by improving foreign products and technologies, the Soviets have suffered from poor coordination of their international trade and domestic research programs (Brada 1985). This problem has been acknowledged by Soviet specialists (Bogomolov 1983), and it has apparently influenced the plans for perestroika of research and development.

The net impact of imported equipment on the Soviet economy is difficult to assess. In the 1970s, some western econometric studies concluded that technology imports contributed significantly to Soviet economic growth; a more recent analysis found that "no superiority can be claimed for western capital employed in the Soviet Union over indigenous Soviet equipment" (Brada and Hoffman 1985).

According to a Soviet study of compensation-based projects in the chemicals industry, the performance of imported equipment has fallen short of original expectations, but it has still delivered labor productivity and profitability levels that are from 50 to 100 percent better than the industry average (Borin 1988). Unfortunately, the relatively strong performance of the imported chemical plants, which have preferential access to raw materials, may have been secured at the expense of poor performance elsewhere in the economy (Goldstein 1984).

At any rate, assimilation of western technology is a most important goal of Soviet economic policy, and recent reforms, *if* implemented properly, should improve their performance in that area. Joint ventures should contribute to the scale of technology imports, and they should strengthen communication and cooperation with western suppliers. Decentralization of the foreign trade system should speed the acquisition of western equipment and ensure that it meets domestic needs. The moratorium on new construction should speed the installation of equipment in existing plants. Shortages of raw materials should be alleviated by the development of the wholesale trade network. Under new systems of management and material incentives, enterprises should be willing and able to reduce overstaffing.

Competitive Pressure

The benefits of comparative advantage and technology transfer have been recognized officially in the U.S.S.R. for many years, but a new theme has appeared in recent pronouncements. Slowly but surely, Soviet economists and officials are acknowledging that foreign competitors should be allowed to exert pressure on domestic enterprises to improve the efficiency and quality of their operations.

In contrast to Stalin's "two camp" thesis, the "new political thinking" of Ivan Ivanov (1988, 4), Deputy Chairman of the State Foreign Economic Commission, says that the Soviet Union is now part of "one single world economy," and any improvement in Soviet performance "is now inconceivable without comparison and contrast with the world market." Likewise, Rybakov (1988, 66) argues that traditional protectionism is largely responsible for the poor performance of the economy: "The internal hothouse conditions of the economy, the monopolization of the internal market, gave rise to technological and economic stagnation . . . and reduced the efficiency and growth of international cooperation."

Monopoly power is a natural legacy of the Stalinist economic system. Understandably, economic planners prefer to communicate with a small number of very large producers. If the basic elements of perestroika—enterprise autonomy, profit incentives, and price flexibility—are implemented successfully, foreign competition will be needed to prevent their abuse. "What is especially important," according to Gorbachev (1987a), is "strengthening the influence of the foreign market on the work of our industries and enterprises, on the quality of their production, and on their scientific and technical progress." One will look in vain through speeches of previous general secretaries to find similar language.

At present, foreign competition on the Soviet market is extremely limited. As we have seen, the traditions of protectionism and autarky are very strong, and they are still evident in the statements of national leaders. According to western exporters, their Soviet customers are permitted to buy imported equipment only after the Soviet ministry that produces similar equipment certifies that it cannot fill the order.[17] On the other hand, joint ventures operating in the Soviet Union have been given permission to trade on the domestic market at "contractual prices," which are explained by the advertising agency *Vneshtorgreklama* (1987):

> 'Contractual' means negotiable, and these prices may differ from the official domestic wholesale and retail prices, enabling joint ventures to compete with domestic producers. This competition has been introduced intentionally with the aim to increase the efficiency and quality of production.

Before the economy opens to foreign competition in a significant way, Aganbegyan (1987) says that "we must first reform prices so as to enhance the ability of our products to compete," and then move toward ruble convertibility. Under current conditions, he implies, a heavy dose of competition would cause massive adjust-

17. *Business Eastern Europe*, February 15, 1988, p. 50.

ment and payments problems. Here, of course, we have a classic "chicken and egg" problem: foreign competition is needed to encourage greater domestic efficiency, and greater domestic efficiency is needed for the economy to withstand foreign competition. The problem has not been solved, but it is a subject of open discussion.

Financial Balance

For many years, the Ministry of Finance has valued foreign trade as a source of revenue for the state budget. Thus, one of the most important tools used in foreign trade planning is the so-called "index of budgetary efficiency," which measures the budgetary impact of 1 ruble of trade in a particular commodity (Gardner 1983, 48-54). Data on the earnings from foreign trade in domestic prices are seldom published, but western estimates place them at about 20 percent of total budget revenues in 1988 (CIA 1988, 18).

The financial impact of foreign trade has grown much more important in recent years, as growing budget deficits have been financed by monetary emission, resulting in a huge "overhang" of rubles and growing shortages of goods. To mitigate these problems, and to quell the rising tide of labor unrest, several Soviet economists have proposed a shift in import priorities toward consumer goods. According to Nikolai Shmelev, for every dollar spent on imported consumer goods, the "overhang" can be reduced by about 8-10 rubles. Thus, Gorbachev has approved about 10 billion rubles (about $15 billion) of new spending on consumer goods, which is about a 30-percent increase over the original plan for 1989.[18]

International Relations

Any assessment of the role of East-West economic relations is incomplete if it disregards their role in foreign policy. As

18. For more on this, see *Business Eastern Europe,* July 31, 1989, pp. 241-42.

Khrushchev told a group of U.S. senators in 1955: "We value trade least for economic reasons and most for political reasons as a means for promoting better relations between our countries."[19] The western business community, in the eyes of the Soviet leadership, can be a sinister force of imperialism, or it can serve as an important lobbying group for improvement of East-West relations.   Playing on the latter theme, Gorbachev said this to a 1988 meeting of the U.S.-U.S.S.R. Trade and Economic Council:

> Among those present are people who are well known not only for their achievements in the field of business, but also for their public, and I would say, political activity.   They have put their energy, business capabilities, and communication skills at the service of mutual understanding, and have assisted in the practical resolution of a number of issues of international significance.[20]

In the end, the most important political repercussions of expanded East-West trade may be felt within the Soviet Union. Expansion of trade will require broader and deeper economic reforms, and economic freedom cannot proceed without a corresponding development of political freedom.

REFORM OF THE FOREIGN TRADE SYSTEM[21]

We have seen that Soviet officials are dissatisfied with the foreign trade performance of the Stalinist system.   On the export side, the country is overly dependent on sales of fuel and raw materials. Domestic enterprises have little incentive to produce manufactured goods for export, and they have little knowledge of the foreign market.   On the import side, each transaction must pass through a maze of bureaucratic procedures and paperwork, with little consideration for the needs of the final user.   In the end, the

19. *New York Times*, September 18, 1955, p. 48.
20. *Pravda*, April 14, 1988, p. 1.
21. Some of the material in this section is drawn from Gardner (1988b).

wrong products are often purchased, and imported equipment may be obsolete before it is purchased and installed. To deal with these and other problems, the Gorbachev leadership has reduced and reorganized the foreign trade bureaucracy, has made major progress toward decentralization of foreign trade management, and has revamped the system of export incentives. In addition, new ground is being broken through the formation of joint ventures, through new forms of participation in international capital markets, and through efforts to affiliate with GATT and other international organizations.

Reorganization of the Central Apparatus

The prelude to foreign trade reform began in October 1985, seven months after Gorbachev came to power, when Foreign Trade Minister Nikolai Patolichev was replaced by Boris Aristov. Patolichev had held the position since 1958, and he had successfully defeated previous efforts to decentralize the foreign trade system. In 1976, for example, the Politburo approved a major trade reform, but the most significant sections of the decree were never even published. Aristov, who came from the Foreign Affairs Ministry, mounted little resistance to the subsequent demise of the Ministry of Foreign Trade.

In August 1986, the Central Committee and the Council of Ministers approved a major reform of foreign trade management. Most importantly, the decree gave a number of agencies and enterprises the right to engage in trade on their own account, and it established a new State Foreign Economic Commission (SFEC) to regulate and coordinate the work of the ministries and agencies involved in foreign trade, export production, international finance, tourism, and transport (*Foreign Trade* 1987). The SFEC is responsible for preparation of reform proposals, and it has the authority, within its jurisdiction, to issue directives. The first chairman of the SFEC was Vladimir M. Kamentsev, a deputy prime minister and a former minister of the fishing industry. In July 1989, deputies to the new Supreme Soviet accused Kamentsev of nepotism, incompetence, and bureaucratism, and he was the first of several ministers to be denied confirmation. As of this writing, the SFEC post remains unfilled.

The internal management of the Foreign Trade Ministry was reorganized in February 1987. In particular, the number of sectoral "main administrations" was cut in half, reducing the staff of the central apparatus by about 30 percent.[22] In January 1988, the Foreign Trade Ministry was merged with the State Committee for Foreign Economic Relations (SCFER, the foreign aid agency) to form a unified Ministry for Foreign Economic Relations. The new ministry was placed under the leadership of Konstantin Katushev, the former chairman of the SCFER. Consolidation of the two agencies made it possible to release 5,000 staff members, most of whom have found jobs in organizations that are now allowed to trade on their own account.[23] Thus, significant progress has already been made toward the reduction and rationalization of the foreign trade bureaucracy.

Decentralization of Foreign Trade Management

Outside of the central foreign trade bureaucracy, the August 1986 reform authorized twenty-one national agencies (fourteen industrial ministries, five state committees, and two others) and sixty-eight large enterprises and research institutes to handle their own foreign transactions, beginning in January 1987. During 1987 and 1988, trading rights were extended to about 100 other ministries, industrial associations, enterprises, and union-republic councils of ministers. Since April 1989, *all* Soviet enterprises, associations, and cooperatives with competitive goods or

22. According to I. Ganin of the State Foreign Economic Commission, in *Ekonomicheskaya gazeta*, No. 49, November 1987, p. 21.
23. *Wall Street Journal*, June 24, 1988, p. 8.

services have been allowed to handle their own foreign trade operations, and by June 1989, some 2,000 Soviet enterprises had fulfilled their registration requirements with the Ministry of Foreign Economic Relations.[24]

The new autonomy of Soviet enterprises is restricted in two important ways. First, because of the inconvertibility of the ruble, enterprises are expected to operate on a basis of "foreign exchange self-recoupment." In most cases, this means that they must sell exports to finance their own imports (more on this below).

Secondly, under licensing procedures established in March 1989, the individual enterprises, associations, and cooperatives are subject to a strict system of trade regulation. While the traditional FTOs are able to obtain a "general purpose" (*general'nyy*) license, allowing them to operate without interference for up to one year, the new trading organizations must apply for a "single-purpose" (*razovyy*) license for each individual export or import trans-action.[25] For several product groups, the authority to issue licenses has been assigned to the industrial ministries. Because these ministries must fulfill their own export plans, they are under-standably reluctant to approve licenses for enterprises and coopera-tives outside their orbit. Thus, some enterprises have found it more difficult than ever to export their products.[26]

Of course, like businesses in other countries, the majority of Soviet enterprises are too small to support internal foreign trade divisions. Under the new regulations, these producers are able to hire the services of specialized FTOs on a commission basis. On the export side, the old system of order-requisitions, which gave

24. The extension in trading rights in April 1989 was allowed by a Council of Ministers decree in December 1988, published in *Foreign Trade* magazine (Moscow), No. 2, 1989, pp. 44-49. The number of registered enterprises was reported in Prime Minister Ryzhkov's speech to the Congress of People's Deputies on June 7, 1989.

25. This differentiated licensing system was established by the Council of Ministers and the State Foreign Economic Commission. The regulations may be found in *Foreign Trade* (Moscow), No. 4, supplement, 1989, pp. 1-4; and *Ekono-micheskaya gazeta*, No. 13, 1989, p. 23.

26. *Business Eastern Europe*, July 3, 1989, pp. 209-10.

the FTOs dictatorial control over production enterprises, has been replaced by a contractual system. On the import side, the FTOs are required to work much more closely with Soviet purchasers than in the past. A western firm negotiating with Tekhnopromimport was surprised to learn that the FTO could not make even minor changes in a contract without consulting the purchaser. According to the western client, "Two years ago they would not even have *told* the end user. Now they need his permission."[27]

For western companies that trade on the Soviet market, the new system of enterprise autonomy presents a mixture of advantages and disadvantages. On the plus side, it is now possible to trade directly with suppliers and purchasers of products, without the bureaucratic interference of the Ministry of Foreign Trade. Lines of communication are shorter, and contracts can be negotiated more quickly. On the minus side, American firms that were able to handle their business through one large FTO must now identify and serve a larger number of Soviet entities. The autonomous Soviet enterprises are more selective in their purchases, and they face a shortage of qualified foreign trade personnel.

Joint Ventures

Joint venture laws have been operating in East European countries such as Yugoslavia, Romania, and Hungary since the early 1970s, and in China since 1979. The Soviets were slow to accept foreign investment, preferring instead to buy turnkey plants with long-term foreign credit. This arrangement added to Soviet indebtedness, and it failed to improve the country's foreign trade performance. Western suppliers of turnkey plants had little incentive or authority to ensure their success. Many of the facilities never reached rated capacities, and their products remained non-competitive on world markets.

27. *Business Eastern Europe,* February 15, 1988, p. 50. For more on this, see Kuvshinov (1987).

In January 1987, a Council of Ministers resolution opened the door, for the first time since the 1920s, to Soviet joint ventures (JVs) with western partners.[28] The resolution was amended in October 1987 and again in December 1988 to expedite formation of the ventures and to make them more attractive to foreign investors; and the terms are still negotiable.

Initially, the law set a 49-percent limit on foreign ownership of the ventures, but now any distribution of shares can be negotiated by the partners. Likewise, the original law stipulated that the board chairman and the general director had to be Soviet citizens; now it is possible for foreigners to hold either of these jobs. Joint ventures have special authority under Soviet labor law to hire and fire employees and to establish new systems of work evaluation and payment. Recently, the Soviet government promised that customs duties on equipment imported by the ventures would be reduced "to a minimum" or canceled altogether.

In response to these incentives, new JVs have been forming at an accelerating rate. During the first two years of the JV legislation, the following numbers of registrations were reported by the Ministry of Finance:

Quarter	Registrations this Quarter	Cumulative Registrations
1987/II	5	5
1987/III	3	8
1987/IV	15	23
1988/I	13	36
1988/II	27	63
1988/III	42	105
1988/IV	86	191
1989/I	174	365

28. For the texts of the most important regulations, see *Foreign Trade* (Moscow), No. 2, supplement, 1987, pp. 16-19; *Ekonomicheskaya gazeta*, No. 4, 1987, pp. 18-19; and *Foreign Trade* (Moscow), No. 2, 1989, pp. 48-49.

Thus, the number of registrations has roughly doubled during each quarter since the beginning of 1988. Indeed, by the end of 1988, the Soviet Union had established more ventures with western countries than any of the other CMEA member countries.[29] By the end of January 1989, thirty-three ventures were registered with West Germany, thirty-two with Finland, twenty-seven with Austria, twenty-one with Italy, fifteen with the United States, and twelve with France.

Most of the registered ventures are relatively small. In mid-January 1989, the average JV had an initial capitalization of 4.3 million rubles (about $6.7 million). The largest projects were a 48-million ruble machine-building complex with West Germany and a 41-million ruble aluminum plant with France.[30]

Hundreds of other ventures are under negotiation, and some very large projects are presently on the drawing board. For example, a letter of intent has been signed between the Soviet Ministry of the Oil Industry and an international group led by Occidental Petroleum to build a $6-8 billion petrochemicals complex at the Tenghiz oil field near the Caspian Sea. Negotiations are also proceeding between the Soviet Ministry of Oil Refining and Petrochemicals, Combustion Engineering (U.S.), and McDermott International (U.S.) to build two large petrochemicals complexes in western Siberia at a cost of more than $20 billion, with financial backing from Japan.

Despite these early results, several aspects of the JV campaign have been disappointing to Soviets and westerners alike. On the western side, the most serious problem is caused by the inconvertibility of the ruble. Profits earned by a joint venture from sales within the Soviet Union cannot be repatriated by the western partner without difficulty. Western partners also have trouble obtaining the raw materials they need through the Soviet

29. For a breakdown of joint ventures by CMEA countries and western partners, see Moscow Narodnyy Bank Limited, *Press Bulletin,* June 21, 1989, p. 16.

30. For additional details on the registered ventures, see *PlanEcon Report,* March 24, 1989, pp. 1-65.

planning and supply system, and they are dissatisfied with the 30-percent profit tax, the 20-percent tax on repatriation of hard-currency profits, and the annual deduction from profits to form an enterprise reserve fund.

Soviet trade officials are disappointed with the industrial structure of the ventures. More than half of them are involved in consulting, light industry, food, tourism, construction, building materials, and publishing. The JVs are promoting closer cooperation between Soviet and western enterprises, but they may not provide the technological boost that the Soviets need. The big petrochemicals projects are controversial because they will require huge investments in infrastructure and housing, which will certainly conflict with other national priorities, and they pose a serious threat to the environment.

Foreign Trade and Price Reform

Decentralization of the Soviet economy will be meaningless or even harmful if producers are not confronted with an appropriate system of prices and incentives. Over a period of several years, perestroika is supposed to introduce a system of "real prices" and "self-financing," turning part of the economy over to a limited and regulated market system. Reforms of this kind are particularly controversial in the foreign trade sector, where they may expose the population to international business cycles and inflation.

Under the Stalinist system, enterprises that produce exports and purchase imports are required to trade with the FTOs at controlled, cost-based, prices. Thus, the producers are unresponsive to relative prices on the international market. A minor reform of this system began in 1959, when supplements were added to the wholesale prices of machinery and equipment produced for export. The price supplements were designed to compensate producers for the special qualitative standards and packaging required in export production. Still, the adjusted prices were linked to production costs rather than foreign market conditions. The supplements were raised in subsequent years, but industrial managers continued to complain about unprofitable export production.

On the import side, alterations of the price system began in 1960. The State Price Committee found it difficult to set cost-based prices on imported items that did not have close domestic analogues, so they introduced a set of coefficients to convert the "foreign trade ruble" prices of imported machinery and equipment into domestic prices. The coefficients were differentiated by product groups to maintain consistency between import prices and the cost-based prices of domestic substitutes. Thus, Soviet enterprises still were not exposed to relative prices prevailing on the world market, and the coefficients applied only to imports of machinery and equipment.[31]

In 1987, GOSPLAN and the Ministry of Finance introduced a new set of conversion coefficients to set domestic prices for imports and exports of all products.[32] In effect, the new coefficients operate like a set of multiple exchange rates. Thus, export producers are now able to benefit directly from an increase in the international price of their product, whether it is caused by a specific qualitative improvement or by general market forces.

Unfortunately, there are too many of these coefficients; about 3,000 were introduced in 1987, differentiated by commodity groups and countries, and ranging in value from 0.3 to 6.0 (Zakharov 1987). When applied to foreign prices, they yield domestic prices that are nearly identical to the old cost-based valuations. Thus, the system "reproduces the old administrative-financial mechanism in the guise of new terminology," says Burov (1988), and still insulates the domestic economy from relative prices on the world market. Burov goes on to suggest that the Ministry of Finance

31. For more on this, see Gardner (1983, 54-59); and Treml and Kostinsky (1982, 19-22).

32. Interestingly, the State Price Committee, which published the earlier sets of conversion coefficients, was not mentioned as a participant in this reform (Burov 1988).

lobbied for this inefficient system because it provides stability and revenue for the State budget.[33]

At any rate, an October 1987 resolution of the Central Committee and Council of Ministers instructed the State Price Committee to narrow the differences between international and domestic prices, and to move toward the future use of a single unadjusted exchange rate to set the domestic prices of imports and exports. Another decree in December 1988 affirmed the need to "gradually abandon" the system of differentiated coefficients and introduce a unified exchange rate.[34] According to Komin (1988, 113), world prices are playing an important role in the preparation of a price reform. In particular, he says that domestic prices of coal, oil, and natural gas need to be doubled to end the "illusion" that exports of these products are highly profitable for the country.

Foreign Exchange Retention

Under the Stalinist system, export producers are paid with domestic currency, and all foreign exchange earnings are captured by the central planners. This arrangement allows the government to maintain firm control over the volume and composition of imports, but it provides little incentive for export production. Furthermore, with the allocation of foreign exchange under central control, decisions are made slowly and inefficiently, opportunities are lost, and corruption is common.

Beginning in 1964, export producers were allowed to retain a small percentage of their foreign exchange earnings in special accounts at the Foreign Trade Bank. The accounts could be used to

33. On the other hand, a spokesman for the Ministry of Finance claims that the coefficients have allowed exporting enterprises to increase their incomes by about 80 million rubles per year above the levels they would have earned with the old wholesale prices. See *Ekonomicheskaya gazeta*, No. 29, 1989, p. 18.

34. *Ekonomicheskaya gazeta*, No. 41, 1987, pp. 18-19; and *Foreign Trade*, No. 2, 1986, p. 46.

purchase imported machinery, raw materials, or licenses that would contribute to export production (Gardner 1983, 78-79). Still, these foreign exchange allotments provided little incentive to export producers because: (1) they were too small, initially only 3-5 percent of export proceeds; (2) they could not be used to buy consumer goods; (3) they could be deducted from the conventional import allocation of the enterprise; and (4) they were often diverted to other uses by the branch ministries and the Foreign Trade Bank.

The foreign trade reform that began in January 1987 significantly strengthened the rights and responsibilities of industrial enterprises in foreign exchange management. The retention quotas have been raised to 25 percent for timber exports, 35-45 percent for machine-building, and 70-90 percent for computers and high-technology products. Export producers received about $700 million in hard currency in 1987, $1.4 billion in 1988, and $2 billion in 1989.[35]

Just as importantly, the foreign exchange accounts of export producers are now supposed to be inviolable and easy to use. The August 1986 decree said that the branch ministries could "centralize" up to 10 percent of the foreign exchange received by their subordinate enterprises, but promised that the remainder would not be subject to confiscation by higher bodies. The supplementary decree of October 1987 and December 1988 removed some of the red tape involved in spending the funds, declaring that the enterprises may decide how to spend their money without approval, and that their purchases should be given the highest priority by FTOs.

Industrial managers have been given more freedom and authority to engage in foreign trade, but they also shoulder a heavier burden of responsibility. The August 1986 decree warned that heads of enterprises and ministries are now "personally responsible for the rational and efficient use of their currency

35. Ivan Ivanov (1987, 203); *Pravda*, October 20, 1987, pp. 3-4; and *Business Eastern Europe*, April 10, 1989, pp. 113-14.

funds." During May-September 1986, *Ekonomicheskaya gazeta* published a series of articles and letters under the banner, "Imported Equipment is Under Strict Control!" By all accounts, Soviet managers are now paying closer attention to the quality and quantity of their purchases. According to one western machinery supplier, he received more claims from Soviet customers in 1987 than in all of his previous experience.[36]

The eventual aim of the reform program is to establish a regime of "foreign exchange self-recoupment" (*valyutnaya samookupayemost'*). According to the plan, domestic enterprises will be required to earn or borrow (with repayment expected) the foreign exchange needed to modernize and retool their plant, to buy equipment and materials for research, and to pay compensation for their failure to meet contractual commitments. Centralized currency funds will be used for new construction, for large purchases of raw materials, and, presumably, for importation of consumer goods.

All of this represents an improvement over the old system, although several problems still remain. First, in many industries, the foreign exchange allotments are still very small. In the huge fuel and raw materials sectors, for example, they are only 2-5 percent. Second, foreign exchange allotments give workers and managers only an indirect incentive to engage in export production, because they cannot, in general, be used to buy consumer goods.[37] Exporting allows the enterprise to buy machinery and equipment, which *may* contribute to the productivity of the enterprise, and that *may* enhance the income and job security of its workers. When the government expanded the foreign exchange retention system, it simultaneously suspended the special salary bonuses that had been paid since 1964 for fulfillment of export plans (Maltsev 1988).

36. *Business Eastern Europe*, November 30, 1987, p. 381.

37. There are now two important exceptions to this rule: (1) since 1987, it has been possible to use balances of transferable rubles to import medical, cultural, and recreational equipment for the collective use of enterprise employees, and (2) since April 1989, it has been possible to use 10 percent of hard-currency balances to import consumer goods.

A third problem with the retention system, coupled with the inconvertibility of the ruble, is that it may encourage an inefficient pattern of imports. Enterprises that are able to sell exports do not always have the greatest need to buy imports. To make things worse, foreign exchange often is awarded only to enterprises that produce final products for export, with little consideration for the contributions of suppliers and subcontractors (Zverev 1988). Thus, the structure of imports is likely to violate the laws of comparative cost, and it is likely to encourage development of a dual industrial structure—a modern sector, integrated with the world economy, and a backward, autarkic sector.

A fourth problem, according to Soviet exporters, is that bilateral balancing in CMEA trade makes it difficult for them to spend their "soft" transferable ruble accounts. Purchases from other CMEA countries must be ordered far in advance and included in annual trade agreements (Zverev 1987). To mitigate this problem, the October 1987 decree ordered the state planning and supply agencies to organize a system of wholesale trade in products imported from other CMEA countries, beginning in 1989, with payment in transferable rubles.

International Payments and Finance

In the long run, Soviet officials hope that foreign trade reform will boost exports of manufactured goods, agricultural reform will reduce grain and meat imports, and foreign partners in joint ventures will finance more equipment imports. In the meanwhile, it will be impossible to improve living standards and modernize industry without debt-financed imports of machinery, equipment, and consumer goods. This is particularly true at the present time, when oil prices are low and foreign technology is advancing rapidly.

Unfortunately, it is difficult to assess recent developments in the debt and payments situation of the Soviet Union because glasnost has not removed the veil of secrecy from Soviet balance-of-payments statistics. A number of western scholars and statistical agencies have attempted to fill this void, but their estimates are very crude. The CIA estimates of the hard-currency balance of payments, for example, include an "errors and omissions" residual that is almost always larger than either the current- or capital-account balance. Thus, their results for 1988 show a $1.4 billion current-account surplus, but a much larger ($3.1 billion) debit entry for errors and omissions (CIA and DIA 1989).

At any rate, CIA estimates indicate that Soviet net hard-currency indebtedness remained at about $10 billion from 1980 until early 1985. After Gorbachev entered office, the debt ballooned to $27 billion by the end of 1988, leaving the Soviet Union with annual debt-service equal to about 25 percent of its export earnings. According to Abel Aganbegyan, one of Gorbachev's principal economic advisers, "We are already in the danger zone in terms of indebtedness." He believes that borrowing should stop until the country is better able to meet its own consumer demand, but he adds, "I'm a minority with my colleagues in that opinion."[38] Nikolai Shmelev, for one, has argued that the Soviet Union could borrow another $30-50 billion to rebuild its export industries without amassing an excessive debt burden.[39]

With their expanded reliance on international credit markets, the Soviets are experimenting with new forms of financing. In particular, as western banks have been forced to curtail their conventional international lending, the Soviets have turned to greater securitization of their debt (Brainard 1987). They have allowed western suppliers to sell their promissory notes in the forfaiting market, for example, for several years. By the end of 1986, about one-quarter of the world's forfaiting claims were held against the Soviet Union.[40] In January 1988, the Bank for Foreign Economic Affairs sold a SFr100 million ($78 million) offering of

38. *Euromoney*, December 1988, p. 9.
39. *Financial Times*, February 4, 1988, p. 2.
40. Moscow Narodnyy Bank Limited, *Press Bulletin*, December 16, 1987, p. 23.

bonds in Switzerland, the Soviet Union's first public offering on western capital markets since the Revolution.

In keeping with their new role in international trade, the domestic enterprises also have obtained access to international credit markets. The August 1986 decree authorized the Bank for Foreign Economic Affairs to grant loans to industry for development of export production, with repayment periods up to four years. The decree of October 1987 extended the repayment period to eight years on investment loans and allowed financing of up to two years for operating costs. In general, the Bank for Foreign Economic Affairs charges its domestic customers an interest rate 0.25 percent above its cost of funds on the world market (Y. Ivanov 1987). In keeping with the new decentralization of the banking system, some of the other new specialized banks hope to break the monopoly of the Bank for Foreign Economic Affairs and win the right to handle international transactions (Levikov 1988).

The October 1987 decree also declared that enterprises may pool their foreign exchange resources and lend them to other enterprises, ministries, banks, or even foreigners, with permission from superiors. This arrangement was necessitated by the foreign exchange retention system, which scatters a small amount of foreign currency among many enterprises. The new credit facility should allow enterprises to assemble funds for larger purchases, and it may reduce their dependence on countertrade.

Convertibility of the Ruble

As we have seen, nearly all of the Soviet foreign trade reforms are disabled by a common illness—the inconvertibility of the ruble. Without convertibility, domestic prices cannot be tied directly to foreign prices, the home market cannot be opened to foreign competition, western partners in joint ventures will be unwilling to accumulate ruble balances, and Soviet exporters will not be able to sell their foreign exchange to enterprises that need imports. Thus, the June 1987 CPSU Plenum called for a step-by-step progression toward convertibility of the ruble, first in CMEA trade and then on the world market.

According to Ivan Ivanov of the State Foreign Economic Commission, his personal expectation is that full convertibility could be achieved in the second half of the 1990s. Before that can happen, however, he identifies four preconditions that must be met: (1) a reasonable balance must be established between the money supply and the supply of goods in the Soviet Union; (2) a major price reform must be enacted, which will make it possible to determine the purchasing power of the ruble; (3) an effective system of wholesale trade must be established; and (4) a competitive base of industrial exports must be developed.[41]

These are ambitious goals, and many western observers do not believe they can be accomplished without the adoption of a true market economy and a massive increase in the general price level. In the meanwhile, several partial measures are being taken to ease the pain of inconvertibility. We have already noted, for example, the plan to establish a system of wholesale trade in products imported from other CMEA countries, beginning in 1989, with payment in transferable rubles. A working group at the State Bank is also exploring the possibility of setting up a specialized company to coordinate countertrade operations (Mozhaiskov 1988). Another proposal calls on the International Bank for Economic Cooperation (the CMEA clearing bank) to establish special accounts in transferable rubles that would be convertible into hard currency. Thus, the CMEA countries would be able to use their hard currency on a fractional reserve basis to expand their mutual hard-currency trade (Rybalko 1988).

Western participants in joint ventures have also devised several methods to cope with the currency problem. Many of the JVs earn hard currency from exports abroad or from sales to westerners in the Soviet Union, allowing repatriation of their ruble profits to purchase "hard goods," such as oil, that can be sold readily for hard

41. *Financial Times*, February 4, 1988, p. 2; and *Interflo*, May 1988, p. 33.

currency. Ventures that are aimed at import substitution can be allowed to repatriate hard-currency *savings*.

The repatriation problem may also be alleviated by cooperation among western firms. For example, the American Trade Consortium (ATC), which includes RJR-Nabisco, Chevron, Archer-Daniels-Midland, Johnson & Johnson, and Eastman Kodak, signed a general trade agreement with the Soviets in March 1989. The ATC is designed to act as a clearinghouse for negotiation of JV contracts and for pooling of hard-currency savings. Chevron will earn hard currency by exporting Soviet oil products, and other members of the consortium will use these earnings for their import and repatriation needs.

Another step toward partial convertibility was taken in April 1989, when a new system of foreign exchange auctions came into being. Reportedly, the auctions will be held once every four months, and any enterprise or joint venture partner with foreign exchange will be allowed to participate. As producers are allowed to retain more of their export earnings, this system could allow a gradual transition to full convertibility on current account.

CONCLUSION

What are the prospects, we asked earlier, for a major breakthrough in East-West economic relations? How will Soviet perestroika contribute to this process? What sort of perestroika will be required in the West? Again, much has already been accomplished, but expectations are high, and much remains to be done.

Against the background of previous failures in Soviet reform and East-West relations, we can hope that several important lessons have been learned. First, it seems that the Soviet leaders have finally accepted the fact that modernization cannot proceed within the confines of the Stalinist economic system. Central planning must be dismantled, and central control must be limited to the "commanding heights" of the economy. The pace of reform, they have learned, can no longer be governed by the Russian proverb "The slower you travel, the farther you will go." Instead, in the words of Axel Lebahn (1988) of Deutsche Bank, they know that the necessary pace "has long ceased being determined by the standards of individual nations, it is measured by the global standards of international competition."

Most importantly, the slow pace of perestroika has convinced many Soviet leaders that bureaucratic and dictatorial traditions in Soviet society cannot be overcome without a major change in the political system. The delegates to the new Supreme Soviet have made remarkable progress, but they are sailing in uncharted waters.

Despite their sense of urgency, the Soviets have also learned that systemic reform cannot be accomplished overnight. They realize that major adjustments in trade relations, industrial structure, financial balance, managerial methods, and income distribution must be introduced in a sequence that is economically rational and politically defensible. A major price reform, for example, must precede a significant enhancement of enterprise autonomy, but price reform cannot be introduced in a political vacuum. Thus, a system of compensation must somehow be devised that will not begin a new round of financial disequilibrium.

In the West, hopefully we have learned that a major improvement in relations with the East will require concessions, adjustments, and perestroika on all sides. In the foreseeable future, companies involved in East-West trade will continue to cope with limited information, countertrade, and political, institutional, and legal reform, disturbed by episodes of international conflict. From the Siberian pipeline and Toshiba-Kongsberg affairs, we should learn that expansion of East-West cooperation will require a balanced reassessment of western export controls. The reaction of U.S. ammonia producers to Soviet competition reminded us that East-West trade must also battle the forces of western protectionism.

In the end, for East-West economic cooperation to reach its full potential, confidence must be rebuilt on both sides. Before they make a major commitment to Soviet joint ventures, western corporations must be convinced that their investments are safe, that profits can be transferred to their stockholders, and that perestroika is indeed "irreversible." Before they increase their dependence on western imports and indebtedness, the Soviets must know that they can export on western markets to service their debt, and that trade will not be used capriciously as an instrument of foreign policy. To build confidence on both sides, pessimism must be replaced with hopeful realism, suspicion with understanding, and empty rhetoric with hard work and open communication.

APPENDIX A: SOURCES AND METHODS FOR TABLE 3-1

Export and Import Data: For *current dollars*, trade totals from *Vneshtorg* (annual) were converted to dollars at the official exchange rates. For *1976 dollars*, the dollar data for 1976 were extrapolated to the other years using physical volume indices, disaggregated by commodity and country groups, described in Gardner (1988a). Estimates in *current domestic rubles* are from Treml (1982) and from Treml and Kostinsky (1982), with the exception of export data for 1976 and 1980, which are estimated from national income shares reported in Shagalov (1983, 11) and Konstantinov (1987, 7). For estimates in *1970 domestic rubles*, the current price data for 1970 were extrapolated to other years with indices in 1972 rubles, described in Gardner (1988a).

Gross National Product Data: CIA estimates in *1970 domestic rubles* for 1960-1980 are taken from Pitzer (1982), and they are moved forward to other years using volume indices from CIA and DIA (1988b). Data in *current domestic rubles* for 1960, 1970, 1976, and 1980 are from CIA (1983). GNP in 1955 is taken to be 26 percent larger than national income produced (Soviet concept), based on the ratio for 1960, and GNP in 1965 is taken to be 30 percent larger than national income produced, based on an average of ratios for 1960 and 1970. Estimates in *1976 dollars* are derived by applying growth indices in Pitzer (1982) and CIA and DIA (1988b) to the dollar estimates for 1976 in Edwards, Hughes, and Noren (1979). These estimates, in turn, were adjusted into *current dollars* with the U.S. GNP deflator.

APPENDIX B: SOURCES AND METHODS FOR TABLE 3-2

Export Data: For the Soviet Union, see Appendix A. For all other countries, data are taken from the United Nations *Monthly Bulletin of Statistics* (June issues). Direction-of-trade data from that source were used to exclude trade within the EC and Latin America.

GNP Data: For the Soviet Union, see Appendix A. For the United States, Japan, and the EC, estimates in 1986 dollars are taken from CIA (1987), and they are adjusted to current dollars with the U.S. GNP deflator. For Latin America, data for 1960-1977 are derived from Kravis, Heston, and Summers (1982, 343), and they are moved forward to other years with real GNP indices for the region in IMF (1987, Table A1) and the U.S. GNP deflator.

REFERENCES

Aganbegyan, Abel. 1987. "Basic Directions of *Perestroika*." *Soviet Economy* 3, 4: 277-83, October-December.

———. 1988. "The Economics of *Perestroika*." *International Affairs* (London) 64, 2: 177-85, Spring.

Allocation of Resources in the Soviet Union and China—1986. 1988. Hearings before the U.S. Congress, Joint Economic Committee, Subcommittee on National Security Economics. Washington, DC: Government Printing Office.

Berger, M., and A. Pashkov. 1988. "The Uralmash Incident." Translated from *Izvestiya*: 3, March 3. *Current Digest of the Soviet Press* 40, 12: 28-29, April 20.

Bergson, Abram. 1980. "Comment." In *The Impact of International Economic Disturbances on the Soviet Union and Eastern Europe*. Eds. Egon Neuberger and Laura D'Andrea Tyson. New York: Pergamon Press, pp. 207-11.

Bogomolov, O. 1983. "Nauchno-tekhnicheskiy progress v SSSR i ego vneshnepoliticheskie aspekty" (Scientific and Technical Progress in the USSR and Its Foreign Policy Aspects). *Planovoye khozyaystvo*: 110-16, April.

Borin, Vadim. 1988. "USSR Compensation-Based Cooperation with Developed Capitalist Countries." *Foreign Trade* (Moscow): 30-34, February.

Brada, Josef C. 1985. "Soviet-Western Trade and Technology Transfer: An Economic Overview." In *Trade, Technology, and Soviet-American Relations*. Ed. Bruce Parrott. Bloomington: Indiana University Press, pp. 3-34.

Brada, Josef C., and Dennis L. Hoffman. 1985. "The Productivity Differential between Soviet and Western Capital and the Benefits of Technology Imports to the Soviet Economy." *Quarterly Review of Economics and Business* 25, 1: 6-18, Spring.

Brainard, Lawrence J. 1987. "Soviet International Financial Policy: Traditional Formulas or New Innovations?" In *Gorbachev's Economic Plans*, Vol. 1, pp. 100-15.

Braithwaite, Jeanine D.   1987.   "The Soviet Chemical Industry: Chemicalization, Capital, and Compensation." In *Gorbachev's Economic Plans*, Vol. 1, pp. 342-58.

Burov, A.   1988.   "Podkhody k valyutnomu samofinansirovaniyu" (Approaches to Foreign Exchange Self-Financing). *Ekonomicheskaya gazeta*, No. 20: 16, May.

CIA.   1983.   *Soviet Gross National Product in Current Prices, 1960-80*. SOV 83-10037, March.

———.   1987.   *Handbook of Economic Statistics, 1987*.   CPAS 87-10001, September.

———.   1988.   "USSR: Sharply Higher Budget Deficits Threaten *Perestroika*." SOV 88-10043U, September.

CIA and DIA.   1988a.   "Gorbachev's Modernization Program: A Status Report." In *Allocation of Resources . . .* (1988).

———.   1988b.   "Gorbachev's Economic Program: Problems Emerge." A report presented to the U.S. Congress, Joint Economic Committee, Subcommittee on National Security Economics, mimeo, April.

———.   1989.   "The Soviet Economy in 1988: Gorbachev Changes Course." A report presented to the U.S. Congress, Joint Economic Committee, Subcommittee on National Security Economics, mimeo, April.

Chawluk, Antoni.   1987.   "Is Soviet Capital Too Old?" *Economica* 54, 215: 335-54, August.

Cherepanov, A.   1987.   "What is Slowing Us Down? Foreign Economic Ties, Reality and Prospects." Translated from *Izvestiya*, October 10, p. 6. *Current Digest of the Soviet Press* 39, 41: 7-8, November 11.

Cohn, Stanley H.   1987.   "Soviet Intensive Development Strategy in Perspective." In *Gorbachev's Economic Plans*, Vol. 1, pp. 10-26.

Desai, Padma.   Forthcoming.   "How Should the Role of Foreign Trade in the Soviet Economy be Measured?" *Journal of International Economics*.

Edwards, Imogene, Margaret Hughes, and James Noren. 1979. "U.S. and USSR: Comparisons of GNP." In *Soviet Economy in a Time of Change*, Vol. 1, pp. 369-401.

Gardner, H. Stephen. 1983. *Soviet Foreign Trade: The Decision Process*. Boston: Kluwer-Nijhoff.

———. 1988a. "The Commodity and Factor Composition of Soviet Foreign Trade with the West and the East." A paper presented at the annual meeting of the Eastern Economic Association, Boston, March.

———. 1988b. "Restructuring the Soviet Foreign Trade System." *The Columbia Journal of World Business*.

Goldstein, Elizabeth Ann. 1984. "The Impact of Technology Transfer on Production and Productivity in the USSR: The Case of the Ferrous Metals Industry." In Smith, ed. (1984), pp. 63-94.

Gorbachev, Mikhail S. 1987a. "O zadachakh partii po korennoy perestroyke upravleniya ekonomikoy" (Tasks of the Party Related to the Radical Restructuring of the Management of the Economy). *Ekonomicheskaya gazeta*, No. 27: 2-9, July.

———. 1987b. *Perestroika: New Thinking for Our Country and the World*. New York: Harper & Row.

Gorbachev's Economic Plans. 1987. U.S. Congress, Joint Economic Committee. Washington, DC: Government Printing Office.

Guk, S. 1987. "Mercury in the Labyrinth: The Difficult Paths of Foreign Trade." Translated from *Izvestiya*: 2, May 25. *Current Digest of the Soviet Press* 39, 21: 18-19, June 24.

Hanson, Philip, and Malcolm R. Hill. 1979. "Soviet Assimilation of Western Technology: A Survey of U.K. Exporters' Experience." In *Soviet Economy in a Time of Change*, Vol. 2, pp. 582-604.

Hewett, Ed A. 1983. "Foreign Economic Relations." In *The Soviet Economy Toward the Year 2000*. Eds. Abram Bergson and Herbert S. Levine. London: George Allen & Unwin, pp. 269-310.

———. 1988. *Reforming the Soviet Economy: Equality versus Efficiency*. Washington, DC: The Brookings Institution.

Hewett, Ed A., Bryan Roberts, and Jan Vanous. 1987. "On the Feasibility of Key Targets in the Soviet Twelfth Five Year Plan (1986-1990)." In *Gorbachev's Economic Plans*, Vol. 1, pp. 27-53.

Hoch, R. 1986. "Open Economy and Domestic Consumption." *Acta Oeconomica* 37, 3-4: 189-203.

Holzman, Franklyn. 1974. *Foreign Trade Under Central Planning*. Cambridge, MA: Harvard University Press.

IMF. 1987. *World Economic Outlook*. Washington, DC, April.

Ivanov, Ivan. 1987. "Restructuring the Mechanism of Foreign Economic Relations in the USSR." *Soviet Economy* 3, 3: 192-218, July-September.

———. 1988. "The State Monopoly of Foreign Trade: Today's Forms and Problems." *Foreign Trade* (Moscow): 4-11, April.

Ivanov, Yuri. 1987. "Vneshtorgbank of the USSR and Restructuring of the Mechanism of Foreign Economic Activities." *Foreign Trade* (Moscow): 4-11, November.

Kirillov, A. 1977. "Sovetskoye eksport mashin i oborudovaniya" (Soviet Exports of Machinery and Equipment). *Planovoye khozyaystvo*: 80-86, May.

Komin, A. 1988. "Perestroyka tsenovogo khozyaystva" (Restructuring the Price Economy). *Voprosy ekonomiki*: 107-14, March.

Konstantinov, Yu. A. 1987. *Novyy valyutno-finansovyy mekhanizm (The New Foreign Exchange Financing Mechanism)*. Moscow: Finansy i statistika.

Kravis, Irving B., Alan Heston, and Robert Summers. 1982. *World Product and Income*. Baltimore: The Johns Hopkins University Press.

Kuvshinov, Vladislav. 1987. "On Self-Supporting Relations Between Foreign Trade and Industrial Organizations." *Foreign Trade* (Moscow): 33-36, September.

Lebahn, Axel. 1988. "Political and Economic Effects of Perestroika on the Soviet Union and its Relations to Eastern Europe and the West." *Aussen Politik* 39, 2: 107-24.

Leggett, Robert. 1982. "Soviet Investment in the 11th Five-Year Plan." In *Soviet Economy in the 1980s*, Part 1, pp. 129-46.

———. 1987. "Soviet Investment Policy: The Key to Gorbachev's Program for Revitalizing the Soviet Economy." In *Gorbachev's Economic Plans*, Vol. 1, pp. 236-56.

Liefert, William Mark. 1987. "The Soviet Gain from Trade with the West in Fuel, Grain, and Machinery." Unpublished manuscript.

Levikov, Aleksandr. 1988. "Bankiry v 'LG'" (Bankers in the *Literary Gazette*). *Literaturnaya gazeta*, No. 21: 11, May 25.

Lukianov, F. 1988. "Joint Enterprises—1988." Translated from *Izvestiya*: 5, May 5. *Current Digest of the Soviet Press* 40, 18: 10-11, June 1.

Maltsev, Andrei. 1988. "Middle Urals' Export Base." *Foreign Trade* (Moscow): 1-22, May.

Martens, John A. 1984. "Quantification of Western Exports of High-Technology Products to the USSR and Eastern Europe." In Smith, ed. (1984), pp. 33-62.

Marx, Karl. 1954 [1867]. *Capital: A Critique of Political Economy*, Vol. 1. Moscow: Progress Publishers.

Mozhaiskov, O. 1988. "*Ekonomicheskoy gazete* otvechayut" (Reply to the *Economic Gazette*). *Ekonomicheskaya gazeta*, No. 12: 21, March.

Narkhoz. Annual. Gosudarstvennyy komitet SSSR po statistike. *Narodnoye khozyaystvo SSSR v ＿＿ g: statisticheskiy ezhegodnik* (*The National Economy of the Soviet Union in ＿＿ : Statistical Yearbook*). Moscow: Finansy i statistika.

"O dopolnitel'nykh merakh po sovershenstvovaniyu vneshneekonomicheskoy deyatel'nosti v novykh usloviyakh khozyaystvovaniya" (On Additional Measures to Improve Foreign Economic Activities Under New Economic Conditions). 1987. *Ekonomicheskaya gazeta*, No. 41: 18-19, October.

Ofer, Gur. 1987. "Soviet Economic Growth: 1928-1985." *Journal of Economic Literature* 25, 4: 1767-1833, December.

"On Measures to Improve the Management of Foreign Economic Relations." 1987. *Foreign Trade* (Moscow): 2-5, sup., May.

Pitzer, John. 1982. "Gross National Product of the USSR, 1950-80." In *USSR: Measures of Economic Growth and Development, 1950-80.* U.S. Congress, Joint Economic Committee. Washington, DC: Government Printing Office.

Rothlingshofer, Karl, and Heinrich Vogel. 1979. *Soviet Absorption of Western Technology: Report on the Experience of West German Exporters.* Munich: IFO.

Rybakov, O. 1988. "Eshcho raz o novom podkhode k razvitiyu ekonomicheskogo sotrudnichestva SSSR s sotsialisticheskimi stranami" (Once Again on the New Approach to Development of Economic Cooperation of the USSR with Socialist Countries). *Planovoye khozyaystvo:* 65-75, April.

Rybalko, G. 1988. "Konvertabel'nost' rublya v povestke dnya" (Convertibility of the Ruble is On the Agenda). *Ekonomicheskaya gazeta,* No. 9: 20, February.

Sagers, Matthew J., and Theodore Shabad. 1987. "The Soviet Petrochemical Industry." In *Gorbachev's Economic Plans,* Vol. 1, pp. 321-41.

Selyunin, Vasilii. 1988. "Growth Rates on the Scales of Consumption." Translation of *Sotsialisticheskaya industriya:* 2, January 5, 1988. *Current Digest of the Soviet Press* 40, 4: 8-10, February 24.

Shagalov, G. L. 1983. *Effektivnost' ekonomicheskogo sotrudnichestva stran SEV (The Efficiency of Economic Cooperation of CMEA Countries).* Moscow: Ekonomika.

———. 1988. "Novyy mekhanizm vneshneekonomicheskikh svyazey i mezhdunarodnogo sotrudnichestva" (The New Mechanism of Foreign Economic Relations and International Cooperation). *Voprosy ekonomiki:* 138-48, May.

Smith, Glen Alden. 1973. *Soviet Foreign Trade: Organization, Operation, and Policy, 1918-1971.* New York: Praeger.

Smith, Gordon B., ed. 1984. *The Politics of East-West Trade.* Boulder: Westview Press.

Soviet Economy in a Time of Change. 1979. U.S. Congress, Joint Economic Committee. Washington, DC: Government Printing Office.

Soviet Economy in the 1980s: Problems and Prospects. 1982. U.S. Congress, Joint Economic Committee. Washington, DC: Government Printing Office.

Stalin, Joseph. 1952. *Economic Problems of Socialism in the USSR.* New York: International Publishers.

Treml, Vladimir G. 1980. "Foreign Trade and the Soviet Economy: Changing Parameters and Interrelations." In *The Impact of International Economic Disturbances on the Soviet Union and Eastern Europe.* Eds. Egon Neuberger and Laura D'Andrea Tyson. New York: Pergamon Press, pp. 184-207.

———. 1982. "Measuring the Role of Foreign Trade in the Soviet Economy." *Centrally Planned Economies Current Analysis,* Wharton Forecasting Associates, August 6.

———. 1986. "Soviet Foreign Trade in Foodstuffs." *Soviet Economy* 2, 1: 19-50, January-March.

Treml, Vladimir G., and Barry Kostinsky. 1982. *Domestic Value of Soviet Foreign Trade: Exports and Imports in the 1972 Input-Output Table.* U.S. Department of Commerce, Bureau of the Census, October.

United Nations. Annual. *Monthly Bulletin of Statistics,* June issues.

Vanous, Jan. 1984. "Comparative Advantage in Soviet Grain and Energy Trade." In Smith, ed. (1984), pp. 95-108.

Vneshtorg. Annual. Ministerstvo vneshney torgovli SSSR. *Vneshnyaya torgovlya SSSR v _____ g.: Statisticheskiy sbornik (Foreign Trade of the USSR in _____: Statistical Yearbook).* Moscow: Finansy i statistika.

Vneshtorgreklama. 1987. "New Thinking for Foreign Trade." *Business Week,* December 14, pp. 137-42.

Wiles, P. J. D. 1969. *Communist International Economics.* New York: Praeger.

Zakharov, S. 1987. "Po valyutnym koeffitsiyentam" (On Foreign Exchange Coefficients). *Ekonomicheskaya gazeta,* No. 29: 21, July.

Zhukov, V. 1986. "Importnoye oborudovaniye–pod strogii kontrol!" (Imported Equipment Under Strict Control!) *Ekonomicheskaya gazeta*, No. 21: 21, May.

Zverev, A. 1987. "Valyutnyye fondy i otchisleniya" (Foreign Exchange Funds and Allotments). *Ekonomicheskaya gazeta*, No. 31: 21, July.

——. 1988. "Predpriyatiye na mirovom rynke" (Enterprises on the World Market). *Ekonomicheskaya gazeta*, No. 23: 23, June.

Perestroika and the Foreign Economic Ties of the Soviet Union

VLADIMIR POPOV

The large-scale reforms now unfolding in the Soviet economy are designed to bring about, among other things, a radical change in the mechanism and structure of our economic ties with foreign countries. In the future, this should enable the Soviet Union to improve the competitiveness of its manufactured goods on world markets and to make maximum use of the benefits of the international division of labor; in short, it should allow the Soviet Union to become a full-fledged member of the international economic community.

In this paper, the structure of Soviet foreign economic ties is examined in a historical perspective, and some desirable directions of reforms in this area are outlined. First, the paper deals with some data on the growth of Soviet foreign trade during the past sixty years. Second, the current state of external economic ties of the Soviet Union is analyzed. Third, recent changes in Soviet foreign economic policy are evaluated. Fourth, some proposals for changes in the mechanism of external economic contacts are suggested. And fifth, possible implications of western economic policy toward the Soviet Union are examined. Finally, the paper concludes with a discussion of the role of foreign economic relations in the development of Soviet domestic economic reforms.

I. LOOKING BACKWARD

The involvement of the Soviet economy in international trade has fluctuated considerably over time (see Table 4-1).[1] The curtailment of the New Economic Policy (NEP) of the 1920s and the implementation of a command economy at the beginning of the 1930s caused a sharp drop in the volume of foreign trade (which had reached its highest level in 1930) and the isolation of the Soviet economy from the world market. At the end of the 1930s, the share of foreign trade turnover in the national income dropped to less than 2 percent, and the share of exports to less than 1 percent. To some extent, the reduction in trade with foreign countries in the 1930s was due to international factors. A persistent phenomenon of the 1920s and 1930s was a weakening of international trade ties: the physical volume of world trade, which had dropped during World War I, regained its 1913 level only in the mid-1920s, but it soon began to fall again as a result of the Depression and the universal spread of protectionist barriers. The export quota—the ratio of trade exports to GNP—of the United States, for example, fell from 13 percent in 1919 to 4-5 percent in the 1930s; of England from 24 percent in 1913 to 15 percent toward the end of the 1930s; of France from 19 percent to 12 percent; and of Germany from 24 percent to 7 percent for that same period (Yudanov 1983).

But in addition to international factors, there were also internal reasons responsible for the decline in Soviet trade. The administrative economy did not facilitate the growth of an export potential and, on the contrary, suppressed it. The principal export item at that time was grain, but its production fell after collectivization, and by the end of the 1930s, per capita grain production was far below the 1913 level. There was a catastrophic shortage of grain for domestic consumption and export. Because

1. Table 4-1 provides data on the share of foreign-trade turnover (exports plus imports) in the Soviet Union's national income. Because data on national income in current prices were not published until the end of the 1950s, until that time the value of foreign trade was compared with retail trade turnover—the sole aggregate index in current prices for the period of the 1920s to the 1950s. Retail trade turnover averages a little more than half the national income, so the size of foreign trade is thus approximately two times less in relation to national income.

Table 4-1. Soviet Foreign Trade Turnover

	Foreign Trade Turnover in 1983 Prices			Foreign Trade Turnover in Current Prices[a]	
Year	Billions of Rubles	% of Nat'l Income	Year	% of Retail Trade Turnover	% of Nat'l Income
1918-23	2	20.0	1924	9.8	
1924-28	7	20.0	1928	11.4	
1929-32	12	30.0	1932	3.2	
1933-37	6	6.0	1937	2.4	
1938-6/30/41	3	2.6	1940	1.6	
7/1/1941-45	4	3.3	1945	10.1	
1946-50	20	9.5	1950	8.1	
1951-55	45	10.8	1955	11.6	
1956-60	85	12.1	1960	12.9	6.9
1961-65	140	14.8	1965	13.9	7.6
1966-70	200	14.7	1970	14.2	7.6
1971-75	365	20.0	1975	24.1	14.0
1976-80	500	22.1	1980	34.8	20.4
1981-85	625	23.6	1985	43.8	24.6
1986-90	725	22.9	1986	39.4	22.3
(Plan)			1987	37.8	21.5

a. Conversion of hard currency into rubles is at the following rates: 1924 - 0.199 rubles to 1 dollar; 1928 - 0.194; 1932 - 0.199; 1937, 1940, 1945 - 0.530; 1950, 1955, 1960, 1965, 1970 - 0.900; further - according to the rate set by Gosbank.

Source: Narodnoye khozyaystvo SSR for various years; Mirovaya ekonomika i mezhdun-arodniye otnosheniya, 1987, No. 2, p. 147.

grain had been the main exportable commodity, the extremely low level of exports—less than 1 percent of the national income—is not surprising.

Foreign trade increased somewhat during World War II, when the Soviet Union received large deliveries of war material, food products, and other goods from countries in the Atlantic Alliance, both on credit and for gold. Moreover, immediately after the war, deliveries of equipment from Germany in the form of reparations increased sharply: in 1945, imports exceeded exports by a factor of 14. On the whole, foreign trade grew rather sluggishly in the postwar years, despite the formation of new socialist states and the Council for Mutual Economic Assistance (CMEA). The growth of foreign trade turnover just barely outstripped the growth of national income. As late as 1970, foreign trade turnover comprised less than 8 percent of Soviet national income, or approximately 4 percent of GNP.

By contrast, Soviet foreign trade grew rapidly in the 1970s: détente and the boom in world trade helped to draw the Soviet economy into international trade flows. Most importantly, prices for oil and gas, which were the main Soviet products that were competitive on the world market and whose export could be increased quickly, rose substantially. By the mid-1980s, the share of foreign trade turnover rose to 25 percent of the national income (see Table 4-1), or to 12-15 percent of GNP, which was comparable to the same indicators in other industrialized countries. The Soviet share of world trade rose from 4 percent in 1970 to 5 percent in the mid-1980s (*Economic Report. . .* 1986). But for a country that accounted for approximately one-fifth of the entire world's industrial production, it was still a rather low figure. Besides, Soviet involvement in the world division of labor proceeded during the past fifteen to twenty years on the basis of intensifying and reinforcing an archaic, outmoded, and essentially "colonial" trade structure. Exports grew by increasing the exportation of energy sources—oil and gas—while imports of consumer goods and food products, primarily grain, increased.

As Table 4-2 shows, food products, raw materials, and fuel and energy have always dominated the structure of our exports. Formerly, grain was the main export, then raw materials, but fuel became the chief export product in the 1970s and 1980s. The share of machinery and equipment, which accounts for almost one-third of world trade at the present time, has fallen in Soviet trade during the last quarter century and now amounts to only 15 percent of the total. The share of raw materials and fuel in imports, on the other hand, dropped during the postwar period, while the share of food products and other consumer goods simultaneously increased and now accounts for almost one-third of all imports. The share of machinery and equipment also increased, but for a country that has at its disposal virtually all the necessary natural resources and

Table 4-2. Structure of Soviet Exports and Imports (%)

Trade Group	Exports					Imports				
	1913	1940	1960	1985	1987	1913	1940	1960	1985	1987
Raw Material and Semi-Manufactured Goods	24.2	31.6	35.1	15.7	16.7	36.4	40.2	30.0	16.3	16.1
Fuel and Electric Power	3.5	13.2	16.2	52.7	46.5	7.1	6.5	4.2	5.3	3.9
Foodstuffs and Raw Materials for their Production	54.7	27.7	13.1	1.5	1.6	21.2	14.9	13.1	21.1	16.1
Industrial Consumer Goods	4.7	7.8	2.9	2.0	2.6	10.3	1.4	16.9	12.6	13.0
Machinery, Equipment, and Means of Transportation	0.3	2.0	20.7	13.9	15.5	16.6	32.4	31.1	37.1	41.4
Other Goods	12.6	17.7	12.0	14.2	17.1	8.4	4.6	4.7	7.6	9.5
Total Goods	100.0	100.0	100.0	100.0	100.0	100.0	100.0	100.0	100.0	100.0

Source. Narodnoye khozyaystvo SSR for various years.

enormous agricultural areas, it is still unusually low, accounting for only 40 percent of the total.

Thus, Soviet foreign trade to a considerable degree consumes irreplaceable natural riches to support a certain level of consumption, which can be seen as the erosion of our future, a "life of borrowing." One should also keep in mind that the growth in export revenues in the 1970s and early 1980s was due not so much to an increased volume of exports as to the more than tenfold rise in world prices for oil and gas. While the value of trade turnover in 1970-1985 increased almost seven times, its physical volume little more than doubled. In other words, we were simply drawn into the maelstrom of global developments and reaped primarily not the fruits of our own labors, but those of a favorable market for energy products.

For a time, the unexpected "golden rain" of petrodollars concealed the structural deficiencies of our foreign trade, creating an appearance of well-being. Symptoms of illness grew less noticeable, but the disease progressed nonetheless. The collapse of world oil prices in 1986 exposed the shaky foundations and made obvious what, in general, had already been clear to specialists: the trade exchange with foreign countries, despite its rapid expansion from 1970 to 1985, had not become a factor for the Soviet Union's long-term economic growth because it remained oriented on current economic needs and continued to be used to "patch the holes" in an unbalanced economy. Despite the quantitative growth—both absolute and relative—in foreign trade turnover in the 1970s and early 1980s, the Soviet economy continued to be cut off from the world economy, because it was not in effect drawn into those profound qualitative advances that determined the development of international economic ties.

II. THE SOVIET UNION IN THE WORLD ECONOMY

Since the stormy 1970s, the world economy is entering into a new order characterized by global interdependence. A new international division of labor is unfolding: the share of raw materials and semi-manufactured products in world trade is steadily declining, and technological progress is neutralizing comparative advantages associated with natural conditions and geographical location.   Traditional branches of industry (the production of footwear, textiles, ready-made clothing, steel, ships, automobiles, and simple electronic goods) are "relocated" to countries with cheap labor costs—to newly industrializing countries (NICs)— where they become the basis for their exports. The United States is increasingly basing its export potential on high-tech industries— the electronic and aerospace industries, chemistry, instruments and related products, and the export of services. West Europe and Japan continue to export some traditional goods (steel and auto- mobiles, for example), but they are also likely to liberate them- selves in the future from the traditional branches of industry by "relocating" them in NICs and shifting more to high-tech goods.

A leading segment of the world goods market is the trade in machinery and equipment, where exchange is no longer between branches of industry but within a particular branch. Deliveries are made within a framework of production cooperation: specialized firms, which manufacture units and components for one finished product, form stable technological ties.   Trade in services is growing rapidly in such nontraditional spheres as banking, hotel management and insurance, foreign construction, engineering, leasing, consulting, advertising, trade intermediary operations, and the transmission and processing of information.   The total value of international turnover from trade in private commercial services alone (excluding transfers of income on foreign invest- ments and international governmental operations) now amounts to about one-fifth of all world trade in goods and services.[2]

International firms—transnational corporations that, according to minimal estimates, already account for more than one-quarter of the production and more than half of the trade in the nonsocialist world—have moved to the forefront of the world's economy. Purely national firms, exporting from one country alone, are gradually being squeezed into the background, especially in branches of high technology, by international firms that have factories in various countries and carry out operations on a global scale.

International crediting is undergoing rapid growth.   The supranational Eurodollar market, formerly the chief sphere of

2. *Mirovaya ekonomika i mezhdunarodniye otnosheniya*, No. 12, 1986, p. 28.

international credit, is now growing together with national financial markets, thanks to the elimination of earlier restrictions, and it is becoming essentially a unified international market of interest capital. Currency transactions for many tens of billions of dollars are concluded every day, and less than 5 percent of them are connected with the movement of goods, that is, with international trade.[3] Credit in the most varied forms has become a normal and necessary condition for any operation in the world economy.

In combination, these developments signify a gradual disappearance of the economic boundaries between countries, a merging of national economies into some kind of unified economic organism developing according to common laws. The synchronization of the business cycle in western countries apparent during the past two decades is very revealing in this respect—any kind of significant divergence in trends of development of the business activity in leading western countries is scarcely possible in today's interconnected world. A state's national economic policy appears to be effective today only if it is agreed upon on an international scale and coordinated with the national strategy of other countries.

The formation of a new system of international economic interdependence is not proceeding altogether smoothly. As is the norm in a market economy, the present large-scale advances in the world's economy are accompanied by structural crises, disproportions, and sharp conflicts. Periodic outbreaks of protectionism and "trade wars," violent fluctuations in currency exchange rates and interest rates, and poor coordination of national economic policies are all factors that seriously complicate international economic contacts.

Nevertheless, these structural shifts in the world economy are occurring, and the global interdependence of national economies is steadily growing. Protectionist moods are strong in all countries, but the main tendency is nevertheless toward a lowering of trade barriers, at least within the GATT framework. Repeated fluctuations in currency exchange rates and lack of coordination of economic strategies create obstacles for international trade and capital movement, but transnational production still grows,

3. *Financial Times*, March 16, 1984.

financial markets become more and more integrated, and the interpenetration of national economies intensifies. Some countries benefit more from the growth of interdependence, others less; the greatest success is enjoyed most visibly by high-tech international firms, which operate on a global scale and make extensive use of international credit.

Only one major power—the Soviet Union—has so far remained outside these developing worldwide economic processes. The purely quantitative growth of our foreign trade in recent years can in no way be considered genuine participation in international economic relations. The exchange of oil and gas for grain and consumer goods, basically a barter in kind that makes up the core of our international economic contacts, is an outdated form of international trade. Less than 2 percent of Soviet foreign trade with the West consists of machinery and equipment, and only 0.23 percent of trade is comprised of high-technology goods, while the corresponding indicator for developing countries is 13 percent.[4] On the other hand, we receive 80 percent of our income in convertible foreign currency from exports of raw materials, primarily oil and gas.

The situation is not much better in trade with socialist countries: less than 20 percent of our exports to CMEA countries consist of machinery and equipment; deliveries of products within the framework of production cooperation in CMEA account for in all between 5-10 percent of the total volume of trade in machine-technical production and only a few percent of total trade turnover, as compared with 40 percent in the European Economic Community. Moreover, Soviet exports of machinery and equipment to European CMEA members are four times less than such imports from those countries; the share of machinery and equipment in Soviet exports varies from 10 percent (to Czechoslovakia) to 21 percent (to Bulgaria), while the share of these goods in imports from CMEA countries varies from 40 percent (from Romania) to 69 percent (from the GDR); the Soviet foreign trade deficit in this category in 1985 totaled about 15 billion rubles (from 0.5 billion rubles with Romania to 4.3 billion rubles with the GDR).[5]

4. *Izvestiya*, October 9, 1987.
5. *Voprosy eknomiki*, No. 5, 1987, p. 140.

What prevents us from exporting more machinery and equipment? What are the root causes for the obsolete structure of our foreign trade? The main cause, of course, is the low quality of our manufactured goods. As was noted at one of the Supreme Soviet sessions, only 29 percent of serially produced machine-building products (including 14 percent in machine-tool production and 17 percent in instrument construction) meet world standards.[6] Only 20 percent of the automobiles produced in the Soviet Union correspond to world standards of quality; the rest are not competitive on the world market because of their technical performance and would be sold 30-50 percent cheaper than similar models from foreign companies.

The 1988 Plan called for world standards to be met for 2.6 percent of the tractor motors, 19.5 percent of the gas turbine units, 25.3 percent of the trucks, and so forth—a total of 55 percent of the major types of machinery and equipment, as compared with 23 percent in 1985. The goal is for 90 percent of the most important types of machinery and equipment to comply with world standards by 1990 and 100 percent by 1993. It is, however, very doubtful that these goals are attainable: according to the most optimistic estimates, only 17-18 percent of the output of our manufacturing industry will be competitive on the world market, and only 7-8 percent by the most pessimistic estimates.[7] As far as new scientific-technical plans and newly created models of products are concerned, less than 10 percent of their total meet world standards, and consequently even their rapid introduction will not improve the situation in the near future.

Clearly, without a fundamental and decisive improvement in product quality, we cannot count on breaking into the world market for sophisticated technological goods, where competition is especially sharp. But there is another side of the coin. We cannot expect to first raise the quality level of our manufactured products and subsequently put them on the world market; one cannot learn to swim without getting one's feet wet. Both processes must develop simultaneously and in a parallel fashion, supporting, nourishing, and supplementing each other. Entry into the world market is

6. *Ekonomicheskaya gazeta,* No. 32, 1986, p. 20.
7. *Novyy mir,* No. 6, 1987, p. 154.

necessary for quality to improve, and an improvement in quality is
necessary for entry into the foreign market. Meanwhile, our
producers did not have entry into the world market until very
recently, and in fact they had a poor idea of the world standards
that they were constantly urged to meet.

Soviet industry faces limited if any foreign competition on the
Soviet internal market. Until very recently, imports as well as
exports were strictly centralized: neither the immediate suppliers
of goods to the world market nor the immediate consumers of
imported goods saw any convertible currency—they carried on all
operations only in Soviet rubles through intermediaries, those
specialized foreign trade organizations dealing on the world
market and subordinate to the Ministry of Foreign Trade
(Vneshtorg).

Some industrial ministries and enterprises today have the right
to enter the foreign market independently and may keep a part of
the currency they earn. Still, competition with foreign producers
is not succeeding. Only those few enterprises and ministries that
make export deliveries and have the right to keep part of their
foreign currency earnings may import the goods they need; they
are indeed free to choose where to buy—whether on the domestic
market or abroad—though within certain limits. But the overwhelming majority of other enterprises, which do not export their
products or do not export them through Vneshtorg, that is, without
direct access to the foreign market, have no such choice—they may
buy something on the world market only if those "above" agree to
appropriate the funds.

The convertibility of the ruble and the decentralization of
imports—the effective exposure of the closed economy—are necessary to achieve comparability with world standards of efficiency
and quality. The ruble, however, has long ceased to be convertible.
In the 1920s, during NEP, the ruble was freely exchanged for
foreign currency on a currency exchange at the rate of 19.4 kopecks
to the dollar (the same rate as the Tsarist ruble—1.94 rubles "old
money" for 1 dollar). At the end of the 1920s, free currency
exchange was stopped, and the rate set by Gosbank since that time
is hardly used in making real computations. Change in this rate
has reflected (though with delays and only imperfectly) the actual
depreciation of the Soviet currency as a result of inflation; at times,

the rate of inflation in the Soviet Union exceeded the rate of price increases in the principal western countries by several times. Devaluation of the ruble occurred: in 1937, 1 dollar cost 53 kopecks; in 1950, it cost 40 kopecks; in 1961, it cost 90 kopecks; and during the 1980s, it cost 60-80 kopecks.[8]

The exchange rate set in 1950 (4 rubles in "old money" or 40 kopecks of "new money" to 1 dollar) reflected nothing but Stalin's personal opinion. According to W. Belkin, a member of a group of experts established on Stalin's personal instructions to calculate the real purchasing power parity between the ruble and dollar, the experts were aware that Stalin wanted the ruble to have a high value. Therefore, they chose to compare goods whose relative prices were especially favorable to us, comparing American gabardine overcoats to Soviet re-dyed military surplus greatcoats, for example. Plus, they added 15-percent premiums, supposedly to reflect better quality, the "excellence" of our goods. But even such a tendentious approach resulted in a ratio of 14 rubles (in "old money") to 1 dollar. In the end, Stalin's blue pencil decided the matter; after looking at the calculations, he scowled, crossed out the number 14, and wrote "4 rubles." However, Stalin's figure was of absolutely no economic significance, because the established official ruble rate was not used practically in any operations.

The situation has not changed much since that time. Today, the so-called differentiated exchange rate coefficients, already exceeding 10,000 in number, are used in carrying out foreign trade operations, and not the ruble rate established by Gosbank. In essence, at present, every branch of industry and practically every type of product has its own exchange rate. When exporting, say, lumber products, foreign trade associations change the hard currency received into rubles at one exchange rate, but when importing equipment, they receive hard currency for rubles at a completely different rate. There is no free convertibility of the ruble as yet, and the vast majority of Soviet producers are therefore cut off from global scientific-technical progress and do not know how their costs compare to those in other countries.

Moreover, one country, no matter how large it is, cannot always be the leader, and all competent departments taken together are

8. *Narodnoye khozyaystvo SSSR*, various years.

not physically capable of computing on paper what the hard-currency coefficient should be designated in order to receive a well-founded price in rubles for a particular imported machine. Therefore, even with a growth in the scale of foreign trade, the absence of currency convertibility turns into economic autarky.

Further, our full participation in world economic processes is hindered by numerous prohibitions on all types of international nontrading operations. We are referring here to the exchange of services, foreign investment and the establishment of firms abroad, international financing, and many other types of activity that are still not "traditional" for us.

In carrying out the construction of many manufacturing and nonmanufacturing projects abroad—mainly in socialist and developing countries (there have been more than 3,000 such projects completed in the postwar period)—the Soviet Union until recently did not have its own firms abroad. According to western estimates, by the end of 1983 there were 116 companies in western countries, formed with the participation of Soviet organizations and possessing a general capital fund of about $400 million. Only eleven such companies carried out operations in the sphere of material production, while the rest were concentrated in the spheres of trade (marketing and post-sales services, for example), credit and finances (four banks with total assets of about $10 billion, and others), and the provision of transport and other services. An additional twenty-seven Soviet companies operated in the developing countries. Meanwhile, the value of foreign direct investments by leading western countries now amounts to tens and hundreds of billions of dollars.

Our participation on the international market of interest capital has also been insignificant. Of the $79 billion in pure debt owed by CMEA countries to the West at the beginning of 1987, the Soviet Union's debt was $16 billion in all.[9] We are a creditor rather than a debtor with respect to socialist and developing countries, but because claims are mainly expressed in rubles and obligations in freely convertible currencies, they are not mutually cancellable.

Furthermore, the quantitative scale of neither our foreign construction projects nor our debts and credits is of great signifi-

9. *Argumenty i fakty,* Nos. 41-42, 1987.

cance here. Much more important is the fact that these foreign economic ties, like foreign trade, are extraordinarily centralized, so that in essence these are contacts with foreign contractors by the Soviet government, not by Soviet producers.

Until recently, construction work abroad has been carried out by the State Committee on Foreign Economic Ties, which has merged with the Ministry of Foreign Trade. Everything in this area was decided in the most centralized fashion—where to build, what to build, and what resources to employ. Small wonder that this method resulted in prestigious, pompous projects: large projects were carried out more for show than for practical purposes, regardless of the real economic needs of our partners.

Many "superprojects" built with Soviet participation are now only half-utilized, because they are clearly not suited to the existing economic structure and do not meet actual economic needs. For example, the large auto repair plant in Santiago-de-Cuba built with our help in Cuba, which has a capacity of 4,000 trucks a year, is only utilized to 27 percent of capacity. To operate at full capacity, virtually all trucks in need of repair would have to be brought there from all over the country—but there are fifteen similar plants on the island.

Soviet enterprises could probably come to better agreements with foreign partners in a private way and could provide the assistance needed on a commercial basis (with full or partial state financing). But our enterprises do not have such rights for now, just as they do not have the right to use completed projects (plants) while retaining joint ownership.

The establishment of credit contacts abroad is no less strongly centralized. The government (Gosbank and the Foreign Economic Bank) again appears as the sole lender and creditor; enterprises and organizations are deprived of the right independently to borrow money abroad, to extend credit to foreign firms, and generally to invest their hard-currency profits in any type of foreign financial assets.

Such are the most general features of the structure of the Soviet Union's foreign economic ties. Clearly, the structure in its present form does not serve the national interests of the country because it isolates the Soviet economy from the world economy and does not permit the realization of potential benefits from the international economic integration now developing on all levels.

III. A NEW FOREIGN ECONOMIC STRATEGY

A reform of foreign economic ties is an essential component of the economic restructuring now underway. These changes must make the Soviet economy more open, create a modern export potential, give Soviet producers entry into foreign markets, and attract foreign firms to participate in projects carried out in the Soviet Union. In the future, the Soviet Union must become an active participant in global economic processes and a full-fledged member of the world economic community to take full advantage of the benefits of the international division of labor and the internationalization of economic life.

Since 1987, twenty-two ministries and departments and seventy-seven associations, enterprises, and organizations have received the right to carry out export-import operations directly on the foreign market. These organizations accounted for 20 percent of the Soviet Union's foreign trade turnover, including two-thirds of the export of machinery and equipment, and 12 percent of exports and 18 percent of imports.[10] The number of such ministries and enterprises has increased since then; by the autumn of 1988, most of the ministries and departments and all-union republics, and more than 100 enterprises, interbranch scientific-technical complexes, and other organizations had received the right of direct access to the foreign market. In 1987, their share of total exports was 12 percent and their share of total imports was 28 percent; corresponding figures for the first three quarters of 1988 were 22 percent and 32 percent. It is planned that in 1989 the foreign exchange funds of the enterprises will increase up to 2 billion rubles.

The administration of foreign economic ties has also been restructured. A State Foreign Economic Commission and a Ministry of Foreign Economic Ties have been created; control over contacts abroad, which was formerly dispersed, has now been concentrated in these bodies.

At the beginning of 1987, the creation of joint enterprises and associations with the participation of foreign firms was authorized by edict of the Supreme Soviet Presidium and by decrees of the Soviet Council of Ministers. The capital of these companies is

10. *Kommunist,* No. 15, 1987, p. 26; *Pravda,* January 1, 1988.

formed from shares held by Soviet and foreign firms; in the case of joint companies with partners from capitalist and developing states, the Soviet share must be no less than 51 percent. No plan is set for these companies; they are supplied on a priority basis, and their profits are distributed among the participants in accordance with their shares. After the first two years, joint companies begin to pay taxes—30 percent of the profits remaining after investments and deductions for reserve funds, plus another 20 percent when the profit due to the foreign partner is transferred abroad.

The question of establishing a "preferential economic regime" in a number of regions (Far East, Leningrad, Novgorod) is being discussed (to give producers the right of direct access to foreign markets and independent use of hard-currency earnings). Plans call for creating special "joint business enterprise zones" in the Far East, which would have a privileged system of customs assessment, licensing of foreign economic transactions, and taxation.

By the middle of 1988, agreement was reached on using the national currencies of three CMEA member countries (the Soviet ruble, Czechoslovak koruna, and Bulgarian lev) in joint accounting. So far, this right is enjoyed only by participants in agreements on direct ties, joint enterprises, and international associations.

Rapprochement with some international economic organizations has begun. The Soviet Union has stated its desire to obtain the status of observer in the GATT, with a view to gaining full membership. In the summer of 1987, the Soviet Union became a member of the General Fund for Raw Material Commodities, which was formed within the framework of UNCTAD and is an international bank for financing programs to stabilize prices of raw material goods and projects for expanding the production and consumption of raw materials. More than 100 countries participate in the International Monetary Fund, including most western states. The United States, which signed this agreement in 1980, subsequently refused to ratify it.

In December 1988, a new and important step was taken. When the Soviet Council of Ministers decided to grant as of April 1, 1989, to all enterprises and associations whose products can compete on the foreign market the right to carry on export and import operations directly (on the basis of hard-currency self-financing).

Also, unwarranted limitations on the activity of joint enterprises (in particular, the requirement that at least 51 percent of the capital belong to the Soviets) have been removed, and plans call for the gradual elimination of differentiated hard-currency coefficients for enterprises to exchange their foreign currency funds for rubles in accordance with agreed prices set by foreign exchange auctions, and for the transition to a new exchange rate in international transactions beginning January 1, 1991. Implementation of these measures will effectively signify the introduction of market principles in allocating that part of foreign exchange currency earned by exports (the part that accrues to an enterprise's foreign exchange funds, about 30 to 50 percent of all export earnings). If, in addition, the state assumes the obligation to exchange the foreign currency it withdraws from enterprises into rubles at a realistic rate, we will obtain a limited, but nonetheless real, convertibility of the ruble for current operations, which will mark a principled change in the entire mechanism of foreign trade operations.

Reform of foreign economic ties has already yielded certain results. Foreign trade firms set up by enterprises and industrial ministries not attached to the Ministry of Foreign Trade have begun to operate. Many producers are now exporting goods themselves through these firms, and are independently buying equipment abroad with the hard-currency earnings accruing to them. Joint companies have started up and are already producing. The Soviet-West German enterprise Krayan in Odessa has begun to build heavy cranes using tractors from dismantled SS-20 rockets.

Large-scale plans for setting up joint firms with American companies are under discussion. Occidental Petroleum is planning to build a petroleum-chemical complex at the huge Tenghiz oil and gas deposit on the eastern shore of the Caspian Sea jointly with the Italian companies Montedison and Enikem and the Japanese company Marubeni (49 percent of the equity capital, invested by foreign participants, will be on the order of $3 billion). Two American companies—Combustion Engineering and McDermott—have signed a protocol with *Minneftekhimprom* (State Department of Petrochemical Industry) on their intention to create joint petroleum and chemical enterprises in Surgut and Tobol'sk in Siberia. Another American company, Pepsico, is preparing to establish a chain of pizzerias in Moscow and a jointly operated factory for fruit juice concentrates, and also to expand a network of bottling plants.

By the summer of 1988, three small Soviet-American joint enterprises had been set up, and around fifty were in the planning stage. At that time, there was a total of forty-three joint enterprises on the territory of the Soviet Union, established with the companies and organizations of seventeen countries, including Hungary, India, Yugoslavia, and fourteen western states. By October 1988, their number increased to 105, by the end of 1988 to 191, and by mid-1989 to 400. In November 1988, an agreement was signed with Japan's Mitsubishi Corporation about the construction of a large petrochemical complex, consisting of fifteen plants, in Siberia near Nizhnevartovsk. The estimated project cost is $5 billion; 30 percent of production is supposed to be sold in the world market.

Some Soviet enterprises and organizations are trying to set up their own companies abroad. The Interindustry Science-Technical Complex Eye Microsurgery, which is headed by S. Fyodorov, plans to set up branches in West Berlin, Jordan, Malaysia, and the Canary Islands.

Needless to say, there are many complications. World markets have not been favorable to us for the past three years. The sharp drop in prices for oil and gas in 1986 considerably reduced our earnings in hard currency, and there was consequently a reduction in the importation of a whole series of products from western and developing countries. During the past two to three years, purchases of consumer goods for freely convertible currency have been sharply curtailed—by as much as fourteen to fifteen times. Imported footwear, clothing, perfume, toothpaste, and coffee have begun to appear less often on the domestic market. As a whole, the Soviet Union's foreign trade turnover in terms of value fell from 142 billion rubles in 1985 to 129 billion in 1987, and increased slightly to 132 billion in 1988.

Added to this problem were the difficulties of the transitional period, when the old mechanism of foreign trade ties was gradually being phased out, and the new one was not yet working at full strength. Enterprises and ministries that have gained the right of access to the foreign market, but which have neither the necessary experience of conducting business nor the qualified personnel, are taking just their first steps and often make mistakes. Business relations with foreign partners are sometimes disrupted, agreements are reached that are professionally crude and poorly thought out, and there are cases of clear overpayment for imported goods. The Izhorsk Machine-Building Plant, for example, recently sold its unique, thick cold-rolled plate at prices substantially below the world price the Soviet Union was paying for regular imports of the same plate. Irrational exchanges also arise from the fact that when an enterprise delivers goods abroad as part of a special barter exchange, it keeps all the hard currency it earns (which is spent in its entirety for the purchase of foreign goods), while for ordinary exports the enterprise receives only somewhere between 10 percent and 30 percent of hard-currency earnings. It is therefore more advantageous for some enterprises to sell their goods abroad at reduced prices, while obtaining surplus payment in goods as a form of barter exchange, rather than to export their products at the normal world price but without any commodity exchange.

The first foreign trade firms and joint companies are running into numerous bureaucratic barriers. Foreign trade firms on the one hand seem to operate on the basis of cost accounting and self-financing, but on the other they are essentially managed by those enterprises and ministries under which they were set up, and they do not have the status of "state enterprise." Foreign trade firms set up by ministries often turn into small "foreign trade bosses," dictating to the subdepartmental enterprises that produce and make purchases abroad. Because of their monopoly position, they become bureaucratic, are not as efficient as they should be, and often lose out on profitable deals. Although the procedure for sending specialists abroad on business has recently been somewhat simplified, it remains excessively complicated.

Joint companies expend too much energy on receiving permission to sell a product on the market of any country and at any price. Sometimes they do not even succeed in getting a price set for their products and for the materials they purchase. For example, a Soviet-Bulgarian enterprise producing electronic equipment for automobiles in Plovdiv, Bulgaria, could not decide for a long time whether it should buy the components it needed in the

Soviet Union or acquire them elsewhere, because the Soviet Ministry of the Automobile Industry was simply unable to set a price for
these components.

Taken as a whole, our difficulties in this area are symptomatic of
a transitional period. The old mechanism of foreign trade ties is
gradually receding into the past, and the new one is just being
formed.   In 1986, the physical volume of our foreign trade
increased by 2 percent in all, in 1987 by 1 percent, and in 1988 by
2.5 percent. Clearly, these problems seriously impede our goals.
However, they are related just to the implementation of decisions
already adopted, and those decisions themselves were essentially
compromises to begin with. Therefore, the great potential benefits
of our new foreign economic strategy are not yet materializing.

IV. PROSPECTS FOR THE RESTRUCTURING OF
FOREIGN ECONOMIC TIES

Both the growth of foreign trade and the creation of joint
companies are now being held back by the inconvertibility of the
ruble. Without such convertibility, as has already been argued, one
cannot expect that Soviet industry will become competitive on the
world market. The new economic mechanism now replacing the
former directive planning system can at best provide for greater
scientific-technical progress within the Soviet Union, but not for
the achievement of world standards of efficiency and quality. To
equal and surpass these standards, we absolutely must build bridges
across the abyss dividing the Soviet economy from the world
economy, and, above all, establish a realistic and single exchange
rate by which producers may exchange rubles for foreign currency
without limitations.

It is often asserted that ruble convertibility is a matter for the
distant future and can only follow a price reform that eliminates
the obvious disparities between domestic prices and world market
prices. However, this is obviously just a pretext. It is perfectly clear
that differences in the structure of domestic and world prices will
not disappear in the foreseeable future. We cannot blindly copy
world market prices either today or in the near future. If, for
example, we take the world market price ratio today between grain

and computers (at a rough calculation, 10 tons of grain for a simple personal computer), then no one in our country would produce personal computers because production costs would now be equivalent on the domestic market to at least 100 tons of grain.

There is, however, a simple method of smoothing out differences in prices on the domestic and world markets, a method others have used for more than a century—customs duties, which we never needed with our supercentralization of imports, and which have stopped playing any kind of a role in Soviet trade. With the help of customs duties, it would be possible within broad limits to regulate the volume and structure of imports when the ruble is convertible. But this would be the regulation of a market mechanism, not its complete replacement by a directed and dictated planning of imports. The control of imports with a convertible ruble by means of changes in customs tariffs is by nature a self-tuning tax regulation of market mechanisms; the advantages of such regulation over all-embracing directive planning of production and prices are obvious.

In short, having established a sensible system of customs duties, we can begin a gradual transition at least to convertibility of the ruble for enterprises (not for individuals), simultaneously granting direct producers broad rights to purchase on the world market.

The introduction of ruble convertibility would at least allow us to calculate our debts and credits, reduce them to a common denominator, and enable us to use the ruble in operations with other countries, including socialist ones. It is hardly rational that trade between two major socialist countries—the Soviet Union and China—proceeds on the basis of barter, because the ruble and yuan are not reciprocally exchanged, so that all calculations are made in Swiss francs, or that the so-called transferable ruble used within the CMEA framework is little more than an instrument of accounting.

Further, it is evidently necessary within the CMEA framework to find ways to make a gradual transition to current prices on the world market, rather than using the actual formula (average for the previous five years). This is a delicate and largely political problem. If current prices were introduced tomorrow into mutual accounting, the Soviet Union would lose the most, because today it sells oil and gas to CMEA countries for higher than world prices, whereas the prices were lower than world prices from 1974 to 1986. A mutually acceptable solution must be sought, because under present practices, trade within the CMEA is not based on principles of economic expediency (buy where a product is cheaper), but on arbitrary administrative decisions. The adoption of world prices for reciprocal computations does not, of course, exclude the creation within the CMEA of special international funds for price stabilization and aid from some countries to others. Again, this would only be a sensible correction to market mechanisms, not a complete replacement by the planning of trade flows from the center.

As long as we have decided to draw foreign firms into our national economy, this policy must be followed unambiguously and consistently. Until now, the matter has gone far too slowly; by the beginning of 1988—one year after adoption of relevant government decrees and a half-year after the first joint company (the Soviet-Hungarian Littara-Volnapak Association in Lithuania for the output of packing materials) began operations—we had roughly thirty joint companies, including seventeen with western countries; by the middle of 1988, sixty-one joint enterprises with reserves amounting to several hundred million rubles had been created; by the beginning of 1989, there were about 200 joint companies; and by mid-1989, there were 400.

This is clearly not the scale we need. We are lagging tens and hundreds of times behind other socialist countries. Since 1979, when China began to follow an "open door" policy, an average of 1,000 have been created annually with the participation of foreign capital, so that their total number is nearing 9,000 and the sum of their investments exceeds $8 billion. About 300 firms in which Chinese enterprises participate now conduct operations in fifty-three countries and have a total capital of $0.5 billion.[11] There are 275 joint companies in Yugoslavia and more than 100 in Hungary.[12] In Poland, there are almost 700 *poloniyniy* companies, (firms owned by Poles who live abroad). Their rapid growth began only in 1982, and now they provide 1 percent of output of all Polish industry.[13]

11. *Sovetskaya Rossiya,* October 1, 1987.
12. *SShA - ekonomika, politika, ideologiya,* No. 3, 1988, p. 62.
13. *Pravda,* September 29, 1987.

In the Soviet Union, as the first year after the creation of joint companies has shown, this process has developed much too slowly, not only because of traditional bureaucratic red tape, but because of the presence of a number of unjustified restrictions that complicate their operation. For example, the lack of ruble convertibility and the requirement of ability to pay their way in foreign currency act as great constraints, as the principal motive for a foreign partner setting up a joint company is access to the large Soviet market. In this regard, it is probably necessary to embark on a certain increase in foreign currency expenditures if we are to receive the necessary return and not resemble the "miserly knight," one who counts kopecks but loses far more at the same time.

The absolute legal requirement to reserve to the Soviet side no less than 51 percent of the capital of companies created jointly with western firms apparently was unfounded. Given that most of the tangible assets of any modern enterprise consist of the value of equipment and technology, and because in most of the projects discussed at present the foreign partner secures precisely these components, the Soviet side often cannot cover its share solely through the land, buildings, and structures. In December 1988, the Council of Ministers recognized the problem with the 51-percent requirement and subsequently abolished it, which a number of socialist states have already done.

It is incomprehensible that we cannot make use of concessionary agreements, which were widespread in our country in the 1920s, or of the possibility of attracting companies completely owned by foreigners. There is a precedent for such agreements—Finland to this day operates the Soviet part of the Saymen Canal and the island of Maliy Vysotskiy, rented to it in 1962.

Moreover, the tax rates established for joint companies are also excessively high—the foreign partner can in effect export only slightly more than half of the profits due him, which is 1.5 to 2.5 times less than permitted by tax laws in the United States, the People's Republic of China, or Yugoslavia. A foreign partner barred from assuming the leadership of a company and excessive regulation in the areas of price formation, management, quality control, and hiring of the labor force also play negative roles.

The idea of creating special economic zones is very promising. By utilizing such zones, China in particular has succeeded in attracting large foreign capital investments in a relatively short time. The successful functioning of these zones is related to their special attractiveness to foreign companies—minimal tax assessment, incentive crediting, a guaranteed supply of power, raw materials, and a qualified labor force at preferential rates.

In general, foreign capital must be actively attracted. If steps already taken do not augur results, new and additional stimulus must be provided. The mountain is clearly not preparing to go to Mohammed, which means that Mohammed must go to the mountain.

We must fundamentally reexamine our policy on the international monetary markets. In January 1988, a branch of the Soviet Foreign Economic Bank in Zurich issued the first bond loan in convertible currency. It was the first, because in the past financial resources were attracted solely in the form of bank credits; free hard-currency resources were only temporarily invested in bonds in order to receive profits. Now 5-percent bonds with a maturity of ten years and a total value of 100 million Swiss francs have been sold to anyone who wants to buy them—banks, corporations, or individuals.

The loan's success, in the opinion of Foreign Economic Bank specialists, exceeded all expectations—all bonds were sold in four days. This direct entry onto the international bond market is unquestionably a desirable change, one which will, in the words of a Swiss banker, go down in world banking history. But we absolutely must move further, so that we ensure that: (1) access to international capital markets ceases to be the monopoly of the Foreign Economic Bank, and (2) all banks and enterprises receive the right to carry on international credit-financial operations in foreign currency.

We do not need to worry too much about whether the access of enterprises to international credit markets will lead to an increase in our indebtedness. The net Soviet debt in convertible currency is very small—on the order of $20 billion at the beginning of 1989, which, by international standards, is considered a very modest amount. The United States, for example, has a clear indebtedness of $500 billion, which, according to predictions, may rise to $1 trillion in the beginning of the 1990s; Brazil is more than $100 billion in net debt, and Mexico only a little less. In general, our position in the world, considering all types and geographical dimensions of indebtedness, is still that of creditor, not debtor. If the ruble becomes convertible, payments from our creditors, issued in rubles or transferable rubles, can in principle be transformed into convertible currency and can be used to liquidate loans made to us by the West.

Many of our larger enterprises, which export products to western countries (the Paton Institute and the Volzhskiy Auto Plant, for example) could already independently obtain loans on international financial markets to expand export production. Guarantees would naturally be necessary, but the Foreign Economic Bank could certainly give them, as our creditworthiness is not doubted in international financial circles. Moreover, a possible increase in the Soviet Union's borrowings is perceived in the West as a perfectly natural phenomenon during the stage of restructuring of all spheres of economic life. To be sure, monetary borrowings must be used sensibly, and loans taken in the West must be accompanied by measures that allow for future receipts of hard currency to repay them.

We should also explore the possibility of using part of our borrowings abroad, as well as using gold and hard-currency reserves to pay for imports or to liquidate loans, and of converting our credits with socialist and developing countries, demonetized in rubles, into hard currency or real and financial assets of Soviet enterprises and organizations abroad. (Proposals of this type—debt-equity swaps—already exist.)

Finally, an essential condition for the effectiveness of our external economic policy is its complete openness. Unfortunately, our situation thus far in this respect is worse than anywhere else. Compared to all countries in the West and to the majority of socialist and developing countries, we are still not publishing regular and detailed statistics on our balance of payments, international investment and indebtedness, gold and foreign currency reserves, quantities of money in circulation and monetary aggregates, and exchange rate coefficients. The absurd secrecy in this area undermines confidence in the Soviet Union on the part of international business and financial circles. Clearly, such "closedness" during a period of openness is an anachronism. If we truly want to become a full-fledged member of the international economic community, we should begin precisely by making public statistical and other data relating to foreign trade and financial and credit ties.

These are only a few basic desirable directions for the further restructuring of our foreign economic ties. Movement along these lines would enable us to participate fully in international economic life and to reap real benefits from the economic internationalization now unfolding.

V. A ROLE FOR THE WEST?

The restructuring of the Soviet Union's economic ties is first and foremost our own business. We are now defining the dimensions of our problems and the need for cardinal reforms. But at the same time, a great deal also depends on the United States, on its inclination toward cooperation and benevolent relations and on its willingness to meet the Soviet Union halfway.

There is an artificial restraint on East-West economic contacts. Political factors—the general instability of the political situation, the linking of economic contacts with political problems, sanctions, embargoes, restrictions on credit, and bans on the export of strategic goods and technology, for example—play a decisive role. Such policies pursued by a number of states are largely responsible for the fact that our economic contacts with the West have not really expanded during the past ten years. While our trade turnover with the West increased from 4-5 billion rubles to 30 billion rubles (including a 2.5 increase in physical volume) during the 1970s, when détente was developing successfully, the trade turnover hardly increased in the 1980s, comprising a total of 30-40 billion rubles ($60-70 billion). In view of this extremely low level of mutual trade—only a few percent of the total foreign trade turnover of western countries—its stabilization at this low level seems artificial. Although the socialist and capitalist states are responsible for 75 percent of world industrial production, their reciprocal trade amounts to only 2-3 percent of overall world trade. The U.S. share in the Soviet Union's foreign trade is only slightly above 1 percent, and the Soviet Union's share in U.S. foreign trade is only 0.5 percent.

U.S. administrations have created artificial barriers in East-West economic contacts: the Soviet Union has yet to receive most-favored nation status, which is, incidentally, standard U.S. trade practice; restrictions on extending credits to our country by the U.S. Export-Import Bank remain in effect; and export controls are often used to create obstacles to mutually advantageous trade, rather than in the interest of national security. The ban on deliveries of equipment to build the "Western Siberia-Western Europe" gas pipeline left an unpleasant aftertaste in the Soviet Union, as well as in many other countries.

Not so long ago, the U.S. government forbade two companies—General Motors and General Electric—from taking advantage of the Soviet proposal to use Soviet rocket-launchers on a commercial basis to send commercial satellites and other nonmilitary objects into space. The Reagan administration took a negative attitude toward Soviet membership in the GATT, the World Bank, and the International Monetary Fund. Such a policy serves neither the interests of the Soviet Union nor the United States. Research by the U.S. Academy of Sciences has shown that efforts by the Reagan administration to hinder the export of high-technology goods to the Soviet Union were generally unsuccessful and cost the American economy $9 billion annually.[14]

Incidentally, the U.S. share in total western trade turnover with CMEA countries is less than 10 percent, and it has advanced less than 10 percent of all credits received by CMEA countries from the West. In trying to dictate its policy line to other western countries, the United States, in effect, crudely interferes in someone else's problems, while claiming to have a decisive voice in places where its relative weight in world affairs does not give it that right.

World socialism, and particularly that in the Soviet Union, is interested not in destabilizing the world economy, not in the disruption of the capitalist economy, and not in the deepening of economic crises—structural or cyclical—but in constructive, equitable economic cooperation, in stable trade relations that exclude outbreaks of protectionism, and in the stability of the world monetary and financial system. Many economic problems have now outgrown the framework of national economies and affect all

14. *The Nation,* December 19, 1987.

countries without exception. Assistance to developing countries, a strategy for making use of limited energy and other raw material resources, the environment, mastery of space, and the world ocean are problems common to all countries, and they require the united efforts of all states, both capitalist and socialist.

Changes in recent years in the sphere of international policy, and particularly in Soviet-American relations, have created a favorable atmosphere for increased economic cooperation between the Soviet Union and the United States, and among other countries with different social systems. The depoliticization of international economic relations is on the agenda, and one hopes that we may count on the mutual understanding of Americans to meet both U.S. and Soviet goals.

VI. EXTERNAL ECONOMIC POLICY AND DOMESTIC REFORM

The role of foreign economic ties in the process of restructuring the domestic economy deserves some mention. In the long run, the Soviet economy should become an integrated part of the world economy. Even in the short run, external economic policy may play a crucial role in the development of internal economic reforms because of the urgent need to increase imports of consumer goods to saturate the domestic market.

The preferable scenario for the restructuring of the Soviet economy is based on the following assumptions:

1. Economic reforms will be radical, not gradual, which implies a fast transition to a market economy, including eliminating obligatory production quotas for the enterprises; replacing rationed supplies of investment goods by wholesale trade; deregulating prices; redistributing economic power away from industrial departments and regional authorities to work collectives; and creating normal conditions for the development of family farms in agriculture in place of huge and inefficient state and collective farms, as well as for the development of co-ops and individual enterprises.
2. The government budget deficit will be financed not by expanding money supply, as is the current practice, but by

internal and external borrowings so that the equilibrium between money demand and the supply of goods will be restored.

3. The appropriate policies and mechanisms for regulating the emerging socialist market will be put into effect (antitrust legislation and competition policy, fiscal and monetary policies, and social policy, for example).

If these steps are followed, perestroika is going to pay for itself in five to seven years, as the efficiency of a new market economy will be considerably higher than that of the present system of overwhelming directive planning.

The current Soviet system is extremely wasteful. Due to enormous losses, a huge gap exists between production and consumption; we need to produce roughly 1.5 times as much as a market economy to provide the same level of consumption and living standards. In the United States, for example, net investment absorbs 6-7 percent of national income, while in the Soviet Union the comparable figure is 25-30 percent. Allowing for differences in the relative size of military expenditure in both countries, the share of a consumption fund in Soviet national income is hardly more than 50 percent, while in the United States it is more than 85 percent.

In other words, if the Soviet economy manages to make a transition to a market economy, and thus reduce the losses to a level of an average market economy, it will be possible, using the same volume of inputs (the same technology, the same labor force, the same amount of investments and resources), to increase living standards by approximately 1.5 times simply because of the better management and improved ability to put resources together in a more efficient way. In the five to seven years it takes to make a transition to a market economy, it is possible to increase considerably the efficiency of the whole system so that the economic restructuring will pay for itself. Thus, the major problem is to obtain the resources needed to finance the costs of adjustment, that is, to finance the government budget deficit without money emission and to increase expenditure for social purposes, such as the social security system and retraining of employees.

Is it possible to meet these costs? The answer is yes, and there is a group of economists in the Soviet Union and in the West that advocates the idea of heavy internal and external borrowings, which may provide the funds needed to finance the transition to a market economy. These economists point to the fact that the internal debt at the moment is negligible (the value of government bonds, held by the population, is less than 10 billion rubles), and the external debt is not great at all. Net Soviet indebtedness in hard currency was approximately $20 billion in the beginning of 1989, and, besides, the Soviet Union is a net creditor toward socialist and developing countries. (These credits are mainly in rubles, so they are not convertible in hard currency, but they do exist, and there may be a way to convert at least some of them into hard currency at some exchange rate, as the ruble becomes convertible).

Those who advocate foreign borrowings also point out that if economic reforms are truly radical, it will be possible to repay the debt (or at least to service it) as the efficiency of the economy increases. For example, the radical reform in agriculture—dismantling of collective and state farms, elimination of *goszakaz* and rationed supply—is going to bring about the considerable increases in agricultural production so that it will be possible to save hard currency (several billion dollars annually), which is currently being spent on food imports.

Borrowings abroad might be used for imports of consumer goods, which would enable the government to bring the consumer market into equilibrium in a short time and to eliminate numerous shortages that currently create not only economic problems, but social and political ones as well. The borrowings might be used to import equipment for health care (a severe shortage of disposable syringes, which contributes to the spread of AIDS, has already caused a public debate on this issue in the Soviet Union) and education, such as personal computers for schools.

In short, foreign borrowing would minimize the costs of transition and allow an efficient market economy without major sacrifices in living standards. This is a desirable and real option, providing that all the outlined measures are implemented simultaneously in a package: radical reforms, strict limits on monetary expansion, creation of regulatory mechanisms for a new type of a market economy, and imports of consumer goods financed by external borrowing. This scenario is the most desirable for the development of the Soviet economy as a whole.

There is, however, another scenario of economic restructuring, one that implies that the reforms will be slow and gradual, not radical, that the government budget deficit will not be reduced substantially and that increases in prices and shortages will persist, and that the government will not be able to apply a coherent set of competition, social, fiscal, and monetary policies.

If these urgent needs are not met, if the government fails to implement the necessary changes, the transition to a new market economic mechanism in a short time and at a low cost will not be possible. The Soviet economy will then enter a painful period of "stop-and-go" policies; government attempts to stimulate the economy and to accelerate the implementation of reforms are likely to lead to increased inflation, income inequality, indebtedness, and so on. At the same time, government efforts to reduce inflation by tightening price controls will impede the progress of economic reforms and delay the transition to the new economic mechanism. This is, in fact, already happening: at the end of 1988, the Council of Ministers, frightened by the acceleration of price increases charged by cooperatives—the newly created independent enterprises in services and industry that operate without a plan—passed a regulation imposing stricter control over co-op prices.

Such "stop-and-go" policies may now be observed in socialist countries that began economic reforms earlier than the Soviet Union. Examples include Yugoslavia, where inflation is running at a rate of several hundred percent, Hungary, China, and Poland, where inflation is over 15 percent and international indebtedness tends to surpass acceptable levels. The Soviet Union, however, does not have to repeat the mistakes of these countries. Although time is running out quickly, the Soviet Union is still able to control the maelstrom of events that threaten to drive the economy into a costly and dangerous period of "stop-and-go" policies.

REFERENCES

Economic Report of the President, 1985.   1986.   Washington, DC: Government Printing Office, pp. 252-374.

McMillan, Carl H.   1987.   *Multinationals from the Second World.* London: St. Martin's Press, pp. 34-39, 91.

Yudanov, A. Yu.   1983.   *Theories of the 'Open Economy': Doctrines and Reality.* Moscow, p. 21.

CHAPTER 5

Reflections on Perestroika and the Foreign Economic Ties of the Soviet Union[1]

BELA BALASSA and MICHAEL P. CLAUDON

Dr. Popov has provided an extremely interesting discussion of the present situation in Soviet foreign trade and outlined a new foreign economic strategy for the Soviet Union in Chapter 4 of this volume. We will briefly summarize his conclusions, with which we are in general agreement. Next, we will examine the preconditions of the proposed changes in terms of domestic economic policy and the measures that may be used to promote exports. Finally, possible implications for CMEA trade and for trade with capitalist countries—particularly the U.S.—will be considered.

Dr. Popov notes that the Soviet Union has not exploited its foreign trade potential. He adds that Soviet trade is still being carried out on the basis of "an archaic, outmoded, and essentially 'colonial' trade structure" that has largely involved exchanging fuels and raw materials for machinery and industrial consumer goods. In reference to the general upgrading and advance of world trade, he notes that the "Soviet Union has so far remained outside these developing worldwide economic processes." Dr. Popov further criticizes the system of import controls, lack of convertibility of the ruble, and the practice of multiple exchange rates in the Soviet economy.

1. This paper was written in response to Vladimir Popov's conference paper, which appears in this volume in a revised form as Chapter 4.

In connection with perestroika, Dr. Popov notes that improvements have been made in giving a number of organizations the right to trade directly abroad and providing possibilities for joint ventures. At the same time, he makes proposals for the development of a new foreign economic strategy in the Soviet Union, which would include: making the ruble convertible while establishing a system of customs duties; easing the conditions of establishing joint ventures and setting up special economic zones; permitting Soviet enterprises to borrow abroad; and making balance-of-payments statistics freely available. The described changes aim to "make the Soviet economy more open, create a modern export potential, give the Soviet producers entry onto foreign markets, and attract foreign firms to participate in projects carried out in the Soviet Union," according to Dr. Popov.

These are worthy objectives, and one can on the whole agree with the policies proposed to pursue them. At the same time, consideration needs to be given to domestic policy measures necessary to support the policies introduced in regard to foreign economic relationships. Also, policies to promote exports will have to be spelled out. Domestic policies will need to change to ensure efficiency in foreign trade and to provide exports of high quality in the Soviet Union. For one thing, without domestic reforms, increases in trade may give rise to welfare losses because prices do not reflect resource scarcities so that high-cost rather than low-cost commodities may be exported. For another thing, domestic reforms are needed to ensure the upgrading of the Soviet export structure.

PRICE-SETTING IN THE CONTEXT OF ECONOMIC REFORMS AND EXPORT EXPANSION

Prices in the Soviet Union do not reflect resource scarcities or conform to consumer demand. The prices paid by consumers are divorced from producer prices, with turnover taxes imposed at variable rates separating the two. Producer prices are based on average costs often of a long period, as there is an aversion to raising prices. Average costs are calculated to include wages and capital costs, which make insufficient allowance for the scarcity of capital; they do not compensate for the use of natural resources. At the same time, there is no linkage between domestic producer prices and world market prices. As Dr. Popov notes, this means that every product effectively has its own exchange rate. In fact, for many products there is more than one exchange rate, because in CMEA trade products are often sold at different prices in trade with different countries.

But how to establish rational prices? Could one set prices centrally that reflect resource scarcities and conform to consumer demand? Some suggested that this could be accomplished by solving on a giant computer a system of equations that would incorporate producer and consumer relationships.[2] This is a chimera. The Soviet Union today has a sophisticated economy with tens of thousands of products, where different prices would need to be set for different product varieties and, as far as consumer prices are concerned, for products sold at different distances from the factory. Furthermore, technology is changing so that past data on production coefficients soon become outdated. Consumer tastes also change, giving rise to variations in demand.

And what about adopting world market prices? Such recommendations have been made for small socialist countries, such as Hungary, which can maximize welfare by adopting world market prices domestically. The Soviet Union has a large domestic market and manufactures products (Lada automobiles, for example) that are not produced elsewhere. However, standardized commodities (petroleum, for example) have a single world market price, and it may be assumed that the Soviet Union cannot affect the prices of the products it imports (wheat provides an exception to this conclusion). World market prices are thus relevant to the Soviet Union, as they indicate opportunities available internationally. The Soviet Union has long been isolated from international markets, however, and a wholesale changeover to world market prices cannot be effected overnight. While for some commodities world market prices can be adopted at an early date, this is not the case for others. In the following, some suggestions are made with regard to pricing under present-day conditions.

2. See, for example, Lange (1985).

The domestic prices of raw materials and fuels should be set on the basis of world market prices. As noted earlier, raw materials and fuels importantly enter into Soviet exports, while other products are imported. Adopting world market prices would permit ensuring specialization according to comparative advantage and economizing with raw materials and fuels. World market prices should also be used for manufactured exports. This means that producers would receive the prices they obtain abroad times the exchange rate. This would contribute to the expansion of exports that are profitable from the point of view of the national economy and would give incentives to producers to seek better prices abroad. In turn, imports of manufactured goods would be sold at prices obtained by adding a tariff to the CIF import price expressed in terms of domestic currency at the exchange rate.

Different considerations should apply to manufactured goods produced at home and sold in domestic markets. These products should be sold at prices that equate domestic demand and supply. This would mean linking consumer prices to producer prices and permitting prices to adjust top demand and supply conditions. Eventually, world market prices would be brought to bear on domestic prices in conjunction with the liberalization of imports. But this will be a long process due to the fact that after several decades of strict import limitations, there is a pent-up demand for imports that cannot be satisfied, because the Soviet Union does not possess the foreign exchange necessary to pay for these imports.

FOREIGN EXCHANGE NEEDS AND CAPITAL INFLOW

Increases in the value of Soviet exports after 1973 resulted in large part from the rise of petroleum prices that brought the export share of fuels from 16.2 percent in 1960 to 47.3 percent in 1986. With the recent fall in petroleum prices, Soviet foreign exchange earnings derived from fuels have declined. Correspondingly, as Table 4-1 in Dr. Popov's paper shows, the ratio of foreign trade to national income decreased in both 1986 and 1987, when exports fared more poorly than imports in both years. At the same time, Soviet manufactured goods are not of world quality that would permit replacing the lost fuel exports.

The Central Committee of the Communist Party of the Soviet Union set out as a target for the quality of manufactured goods to reach 90 percent of the world market level by 1990 and 100 percent by 1993.[3] These targets appear unrealistic if we consider that, according to sources cited by Dr. Popov, 17-18 percent of Soviet manufacturing output is competitive on the world market on quality grounds under optimistic estimates, and 7-8 percent under pessimistic estimates. At the same time, the targets point to the need for the increased importation of machinery to improve product quality. This conclusion is strengthened if we consider the need to replace outdated machinery; reportedly, the average age of machinery in the Soviet Union is twenty years, compared with twelve years in the United States and ten years in West Germany and France.[4]

To increase the importation of machinery under present-day conditions regarding exports, a capital inflow would be needed. The central authorities should seek foreign loans rather than individual firms, otherwise there is the danger of excessive indebtedness, as shown by the example of highly indebted developing countries. Joint ventures offer advantages over borrowing, however, for several reasons. First, there are no interest payment obligations, and transfers of dividends are made from the firm's profits. Second, joint ventures bring in new technology, thereby improving the technological level and the international competitiveness of a Soviet enterprise. Third, joint ventures can export through the marketing channels established by the foreign partner.

In practice, some mixture of foreign borrowing and joint ventures may be envisaged. While the legal and fiscal treatment of joint ventures may be improved further,[5] and the 51-percent domestic ownership limitation has been abolished, the experiences of other countries indicate that the establishment of joint ventures takes time. Nor can it be expected that foreign interests would supply more than a fraction of the Soviet economy's requirements. Correspondingly, there is a need for external

3. *Financial Times,* August 25, 1988.
4. *Ibid.*
5. See Chapter 11 in this volume by Alexander Volkov.

borrowing to provide foreign exchange for the increased importation of machinery. Nevertheless, over time the bulk of the increment in foreign exchange availabilities would have to come from exports. The question then arises: Which commodities could (and should) the Soviet Union export in greater quantities?

THE PREREQUISITES OF EXPORT EXPANSION

We have seen that fuels account for nearly one-half of Soviet exports. Increases cannot be foreseen in regard to fuel exports, in part because of domestic supply limitations and commitment to East Europe, and in part because higher Soviet export volume would create problems with OPEC, as it would contribute to a further weakening of petroleum prices. Supply limitations are also (eventually) apparent in regard to the export of raw materials. Such being the case, the Soviet Union would have to increase the exportation of manufactured goods. In the short to medium run, the best possibilities appear to lie in increasing the export of raw materials and fuels in the processed form. In such exportation, the availability of raw materials and fuels gives advantage to the Soviet Union. At the same time, the technological processes of transforming raw materials and fuels are largely standardized and are either available in the Soviet Union or can be obtained abroad.

The Soviet Union could develop and expand the export of petrochemicals, involving a partial shift from the exportation of petroleum. There are further possibilities for exporting basic chemicals and, eventually, chemical products. Also, nonferrous metals could be exported in the processed form. The Soviet Union could not, and should not, aim at the exportation of labor-intensive products, such as textiles, clothing, shoes, and various simple manufactures. Textiles and clothing are subject to the Multifibre Arrangement, and all labor-intensive products can be exported by developing countries and China, countries that have considerably lower wages than the Soviet Union.

With the upgrading of industry, there are further possibilities for Soviet exports. These lie in the middle range of manufacturing industries, where the level of technological sophistication is

moderately high. Examples are automobiles (but this would require considerable improvements in the Lada, which is presently
exported in small quantities to the West) and relatively simple
machinery and tools. But to substantially increase manufactured
exports, certain conditions have to be met. This requires, first of
all, establishing a realistic exchange rate. The present exchange
rate between the ruble and the dollar is an artificial creation that
does not correspond to the purchasing power of the two currencies
in international markets. Thus, while the official value of the
ruble is greater than that of the dollar, the opposite is the case as
far as the ruble and the dollar exchange rates of Hungary and
Poland are concerned. In fact, 1 ruble was worth 27 Hungarian
forints on June 5, 1987, while the dollar was worth 47.5 forints at
the exchange rate of the Hungarian National Bank. This means
an implicit exchange rate of 1.76 rubles for the dollar against the
official exchange rate of 1.55 dollars per ruble.

The exchange rate should be set to make marginal exports
profitable. Because in the Soviet case marginal exports are manufactured goods, their profit can be assured by calculating the
domestic cost of foreign exchange for manufactured exports and
setting the exchange rate on this basis. Such a method of exchange
rate determination was used in Hungary following the 1968
reforms, except that the average domestic cost of foreign exchange
rather than its marginal cost was calculated. This procedure did
not provide sufficient incentives for exports while necessitating
subsidies for exports that produced foreign exchange at a domestic
cost higher than the average. Increasing the domestic price of
exports will not suffice, however, under present-day conditions
because of pent-up domestic demand for manufactured products.
Also, exporting involves considerable uncertainty, so the fulfillment of the production plan may be jeopardized if exports do not
work out as expected. Finally, exports have high quality requirements that involve a considerable extra effort.

At the same time, foreign exchange has a scarcity value that
exceeds the exchange rate under conditions of import control.
Thus, to encourage export expansion, consideration must be given to
enlarging the scope of the existing foreign exchange retention
scheme for exports, which would involve increasing foreign
exchange allotments to exporters and allocating part of the

allotment to the producers of inputs for export manufacture. The latter point is of particular importance given the difficulties exporters encounter in obtaining inputs for export production in general and inputs of appropriate quality in particular. These difficulties may be obviated if the producers of inputs for export production (indirect exporters) receive a foreign exchange allotment.

One may set a foreign exchange allotment as a percentage of net foreign exchange earnings from exports. This involves deducting from FOB export value the CIF cost of imported inputs as well as the FOB value of materials that would otherwise have been exported. The deduction of exports foregone (for example, that of fuels used in producing petrochemicals for export) is necessary because otherwise the increment in foreign exchange availabilities due to manufactured exports will be overestimated. Subsequently, the foreign exchange allotment can be divided between direct and indirect exporters on the basis of their contribution to net foreign exchange earnings. Foreign exchange allotments could be used to import machinery as well as intermediate products. One may also envisage an auction market for foreign exchange because some firms may not utilize their entire foreign exchange allotments. Such a currency market would ease the foreign exchange shortage under which Soviet firms operate.

It would also be desirable to increase the number of firms that can directly trade abroad. Dr. Popov noted that in 1987 twenty-two ministries and departments and seventy-seven associations, enterprises, and organizations were given the right to carry out export-import operations directly in foreign markets, accounting for 20 percent of exports. This proportion should be increased to ensure a direct contact between producers and foreign markets. In the absence of such contacts, it is difficult to ascertain the changing needs of markets abroad. At the same time, replacing foreign trade enterprises by ministries and ministry departments in carrying out export trade will not suffice. It is the producing enterprises rather than the supervisory organizations that should have foreign contacts. Decentralization in the trade area, in turn, should be part and parcel of decentralization in the overall economic sphere.

DECENTRALIZATION, PROFIT INCENTIVES, AND COMPETITION

The decentralization of decisionmaking is necessary to ensure that supply responds to demand. This is relevant not only at the consumer level, but also at different stages of fabrication. Centralized planning cannot ensure the equalization of demand and supply, in part because of the impossibility of collecting information on all products at the center, and in part because of continuous changes that occur in needs and availabilities. For producers to respond to users' needs, they should aim at maximizing profits that bring the firm's own interests into harmony with the society's interests in efficient resource allocation. Profit maximization involves minimizing costs and catering to demand. Setting production targets from above would interfere with the pursuit of these objectives. To ensure that firms maximize profits, firm managers should be provided with appropriate incentives, which involves basing the managers' bonuses on profits rather than on the subjective judgment of supervisory organizations.

For profit maximization to lead to efficient resource allocation, there is need for greater competition among producers. Competition can be ensured in the Soviet Union, which has a large domestic market that can support a number of efficient-size producers in most industries. This contrasts with the case of small socialist countries, such as Hungary, where the domestic market can support only one or two efficient-size producers in each industry.

Emphasis should be given to the interdependence of rational prices, decentralization, profit maximization, incentives, and competition. For commodities produced domestically, the establishment of rational prices requires equating demand and supply, which, in turn, necessitates the decentralization of decisionmaking and profit maximization by the firm. Managers have to be provided with appropriate incentives to ensure that firms maximize profits. Furthermore, there is need for competition to guarantee that profit maximization leads to the efficient allocation of resources. Expressed differently, under the conditions indicated, the working of the market system in a socialist economy simultaneously ensures efficient resource allocation and the establishment of rational prices.

The described provisions go beyond the measures included in the document approved by the Supreme Soviet on June 30, 1987. The document, entitled "Basic Provisions for Fundamentally Reorganizing Economic Management," represents a halfway house between central planning and market socialism. While it contains a modicum of decentralization, "the basic provisions stress that the economy will continue to be centrally planned and managed as 'a unified national economy complex' directed toward carrying out the party's economic policies" (Schroeder 1988, 56). Also, the possibilities for competition would be limited "by accelerating the ongoing process of amalgamating enterprises into production and science-production associations and creating large new groupings called 'state production associations,' which integrate entities engaged in all phases of the research-production-marketing claim" (1988, 58).[6]

An additional consideration is that rational prices of products presuppose that there are also rational prices for the factors of production. This, in turn, requires establishing markets for these factors where prices equate demand and supply. Thus, markets are needed for capital, labor, and natural resources. For the rational pricing of productive factors, the existing excess demand for these factors will need to be eliminated. Excess demand occurs when the desire of the firm to expand is not checked by financial limitations on the expansion. Utilizing an expression introduced by János Kornai, firms face a "soft" budget constraint in the sense that they can expect their losses to be financed from the government budget. Hardening the budget constraint means making firms fully responsible for the consequences of their actions. Inappropriate actions thus may lead to bankruptcy if losses accumulate as a result. Therefore, one needs the carrot as well as the stick of competition, with firms benefiting from making profits and suffering the consequences of losses.

The discussion so far has pertained to industry. It has been recognized that agriculture also needs a far-reaching transformation to fully utilize its production potential. The recent decision to

6. For a detailed discussion of the Soviet reforms, see Hewett (1988).

lease land to individual farmers for up to fifty years represents an important attempt toward introducing greater efficiency in farming.[7] It is necessary to transform the huge cooperatives and state farms into smaller, profit-oriented units. In this connection, reference may be made to the experience of Hungary, where the operation of profit-oriented units in agriculture has led to a considerable expansion of production. But Hungary is also an example of how a halfway house approach in industry, where continued state intervention limits the full-fledged development of market socialism, has resulted in adverse effects on production and exports.

TRADE RELATIONS WITH OTHER COUNTRIES

What are the implications of policy changes in the Soviet Union for trade relations with other countries? Decentralization in the economic system of the Soviet Union also requires decentralizing trade with the CMEA countries. While at the end of 1987 only 500 of nearly 40,000 Soviet firms established direct links with firms in the CMEA countries (Ivanov 1987), trade on the basis of inter-governmental contracts needs to be increasingly replaced by market relations among firms. In the manufacturing sector, trade may increasingly take the form of intra-industry specialization, which would ensure the exploitation of large-scale economies associated with longer production runs and the use of specialized machinery as firms narrow their product composition.

There are further possibilities for joint ventures among the CMEA countries. As of November 1987, only four joint ventures were created with firms in CMEA countries, and letters of intent were signed for eight others (Ivanov 1987). Yet there are considerable opportunities for joint ventures among firms that use different technologies. In the past, trade and joint ventures among the CMEA countries were limited by the lack of a convertible currency. Because the surplus in bilateral trade between two CMEA countries could not be used to finance a deficit with another CMEA country, there was an incentive to retrench rather than to expand exports.

7. *Washington Post*, August 27, 1987.

As a first step to remedy this situation, a clearing of bilateral balances in CMEA trade should be established. Next, the resulting multilateral balances in CMEA trade should be settled in convertible currencies. In the final step, the currencies of the CMEA countries should be made convertible. At the same time, the requirements for convertibility should not be underestimated. In the absence of balanced trade, with allowance made for the inflow of foreign capital, and sufficient foreign exchange reserves, there is the danger that a run will be created on the currency, precipitating a substantial decline in its value. This danger is especially apparent under present conditions in the Soviet Union, where exports do not appreciably respond to changes in the value of the currency. Thus, domestic policy reforms providing for an elastic supply of exports is a precondition for currency convertibility.

Convertible currencies are used to settle balances in trade with the capitalist countries. But Soviet trade with these countries, as was noted earlier, has been limited by the availability of exports that could compete in their markets. Thus, the first priority is to increase the scope of commodities that are competitive in the markets of capitalist countries. Geographical proximity favors Soviet trade with the European Community. In recent years, this trade suffered from the relatively poor economic performance of the Common Market countries, as well as from limited product availability from the Soviet Union. However, with the completion of the internal market in the EC by 1992, a resurgence of growth is foreseen. Geographical proximity also favors trade between the eastern parts of the Soviet Union and Japan. The question is, though, whether the Soviet Union can compete on the Japanese market in middle-range manufactured products, where Japan is strong competition, as are the East Asian newly industrializing countries.

Many agree that the Soviet Union has limited possibilities to export to the United States because of distance. This statement is true for fuels and raw materials, for which the Common Market countries provide nearby markets. But transportation costs have limited importance for manufactured goods, as indicated by the success of Japan and the newly industrializing countries in the U.S. market. If the Soviet Union could establish a competitive export structure, it should be able to sell in the United States. As noted earlier, establishing joint ventures would help the Soviet export effort. U.S. firms may play a particularly important role, as they have considerable experience with joint ventures in West Europe and in developing countries. At the same time, Soviet exports to the United States are hindered by not enjoying most-favored nation status. This obstacle is likely to disappear with the ongoing changes in the Soviet economy, increased emigration, and agreements on reducing nuclear and conventional armaments.

CONCLUSION

In this paper, we have focused on the policy conditions of changes in Soviet foreign trade. The discussion has centered on price reform, foreign exchange needs and capital inflow, the pre-requisites of export expansion, the interdependence of the reform measures, and trade relations with other countries. We argue that domestic policies need to change to ensure efficiency in foreign trade and to provide exports of high quality. The first prerequisite is the establishment of rational prices. This objective may be pursued by adopting world market prices for raw materials and fuels, having the exporters of manufactured goods receive the prices they obtain abroad, setting the domestic prices of imports at world market prices plus a tariff, and establishing market-clearing prices for manufactured products that are produced and sold domestically.

Eventually, world market prices would be brought to bear on domestic prices in conjunction with the liberalization of imports. This will, however, be a long process, because the pent-up demand for imports cannot be satisfied from available foreign exchange. At the same time, given the limitations of raising fuel and raw material exports, it would be necessary to increase the exports of manufactured goods where quality is a constraint. To upgrade quality there is a need for foreign machinery, the purchase of which would necessitate external borrowing and joint ventures. This would then help to expand exports that will have to provide the bulk of the increment in foreign exchange availability over time. There are possibilities for exporting fuels and raw materials in processed form. The Soviet Union should also seek possibilities in middle-range products, such as automobiles and relatively simple machinery and machine tools. It is at a disadvantage, however, in exporting labor-intensive manufactures.

Establishing a realistic exchange rate is a precondition for expanding the exports of manufactured goods. It would be desirable to increase foreign exchange retention quotas and to allot these to direct and indirect exporters alike. Finally, the scope of firms that directly trade abroad would need to be substantially enlarged.

The decentralization of decisionmaking in foreign trade should be accompanied by decentralization in the domestic economy, to be accompanied by the introduction of the profit motive and competition. In fact, rational prices, decentralization, profit maximization, incentives to managers, and competition are interdependent, and they will have to be pursued simultaneously for efficient resource allocation. Improvements would need to be made in the conditions under which agriculture operates. Decentralization of the economic system also requires decentralizing trade with CMEA countries. At the same time, the expansion and rationalization of this trade would require the clearing of bilateral balances and the settlement of multilateral balances in convertible currencies, with the currencies of the CMEA countries eventually also becoming convertible.

Geographical proximity favors Soviet trade with the Common Market countries. Nevertheless, once a competitive export structure is established, there will be possibilities for exporting manufactured goods to the U.S. market. In the meantime, joint ventures with American firms hold considerable promise, and such agreements should be pursued vigorously, even if current laws need to be changed to ensure foreign interest.

REFERENCES

Hewett, Ed A. 1988. *Reforming the Soviet Economy.* Washington, DC: The Brookings Institution.

Ivanov, Ivan. 1987. "Restructuring the Mechanism of Foreign Economic Relations in the USSR." *Soviet Economy* 3, 3: 207.

Lange, Oscar. 1985. "The Computer and the Market." *Comparative Economic Systems: Models and Cases.* Ed. Morris Bronstein. Homewood, IL: Richard D. Irwin.

Schroeder, Gertrude E. 1988. "Gorbachev's Economic Reforms." In *Gorbachev's New Thinking.* Ed. Ronald D. Liebowitz. Cambridge, MA: Ballinger Publishing.

The Implications of East-West Economic Cooperation for Market Economies

PETER MURRELL

This chapter examines the implications of expanded East-West trade for market economies. In addressing this topic, the paper examines some common assumptions about the nature of modern economies, the causes of the problems of the socialist economies, and the nature of likely solutions to these problems. These common assumptions are quite representative of the conventional wisdom that guides, and has guided, policies in East Europe. By reflecting on the implications of the assumptions and by considering some of the most basic differences between socialist and market economies, one can begin to see clearly some of the future possibilities for East-West trade.

To understand the nature of future possibilities, one must begin by seeking an explanation for the present trade behavior of the socialist countries. Only by understanding the central determinants of socialist economic behavior can one hope to predict the

The research for this paper was partially supported by a grant awarded to the University of Maryland by the Pew Charitable Trusts. I would like to thank Barbara Hopkins for excellent research assistance.

An earlier version of this paper was prepared as a comment on the papers of Alexander Volkov and Vladimir Popov, which were presented at the Geonomics conference on "Prospects for and Implications of Greater East-West Economic Cooperation" in September 1988. I would like to thank the participants at the conference, whose comments helped me revise this paper.

effect of changing international economic relations on trade. Only if one comprehends the nature of the changes that socialist countries must implement to improve trade performance can one understand whether the present reforms and improved East-West economic relations will have any strong effect on the western economies.

ASSUMPTIONS BEHIND POLICY CHOICES IN SOCIALIST ECONOMIES

Here, I reflect on some common underlying assumptions that have guided policymaking in socialist countries for much of the last forty years.

The Primacy of Heavy Industry

A key facet of socialist economies rests on the implicit assumption that economic progress can only be attained by concentrating a country's resources on the development of heavy industry and the investment sector, with the consequent neglect of light industry, consumption goods, and services. This emphasis also is found in present Soviet policy, where the initial phases of the present reform seem to be concentrated on devoting even more resources than previously to the machine-building sector (Aganbegyan 1987).

Such an emphasis consigns much more than half of present-day economic activity to malign neglect. It represents a Dickensian view of the nature of modern industry that is far removed from fact. A cursory examination of the basic statistics of economic life in the developed economies would show that food processing is as important as chemicals, restaurants and hotels are as important as metallurgy, and retail and wholesale distribution is much more important that machinery.[1] In the United Kingdom today, exports of services are as important as exports of all types of machinery (United Kingdom 1989). If policymakers ignore sectors such as

---

1. The information given here reflects statistics on value added in the 1980s obtained from United Nations (1986).

services and light industry because these activities do not conform to a specific vision of economic progress, then the economy loses the chance to develop vast areas of activity that seem to be central elements of economic success in the most advanced countries.

The Obsession with Science

In current Soviet writings, one frequently encounters the notion that the application of scientific knowledge at its highest levels is essential to economic success.[2] One almost feels that "science and technology" are one word, with the two concepts conceptually indistinguishable.

Nobody would dispute that the use of scientific and technological knowledge is an important ingredient in economic success. However, one feels on reading the papers of many East European economists, and on examining the statements of top policymakers in the socialist countries, that there is no serious thought given to the notion that the economy's use of science must be commensurate with the needs and abilities of the country in question. Nor is serious thought given to the notion that new ideas do not always emerge from the scientific-technological elite. Put simply, in most economies, a large proportion of economic progress does not come from the application of the latest scientific advances. New "technologies" are often far removed from hard science—for example, the organization of "fast-food" restaurants and the "Toyota" production method are both revolutionary technologies unconnected to hard science.[3]

Apart from the possible squandering of resources, the obsession with science has the effect of limiting the scope of new ideas that can be considered for implementation in the economy. This emphasis on science slights the importance of product design, pro-

2. See, for example, Aganbegyan (1987) and Logimov (1987).
3. On the Toyota production system, see Abegglen and Stark (1985). Also known as the just-in-time method (a term that carries too narrow a meaning), the application of the Toyota production system is presently revolutionizing world automobile production. Interested readers should consult the papers of MIT's International Motor Vehicle Program.

duct variety, organizational changes, and marketing innovations, which rarely emanate from the scientific community.

This emphasis on science is misplaced for at least three reasons:

1. Even in the most developed economies, the application of science does not seem to provide the most powerful explanation of economic success. Dennis Mueller has been examining the most consistently profitable large firms and their industries in the United States in the postwar years. Of the 1,000 largest firms, the three most profitable were producers of cosmetics, domestic appliances, and apparel. The three most profitable industries produced glass products, hats, and shoes (Mueller 1986, 34-35, 43). In his results, there seems to be no tendency for the most R&D-intensive industries to be the most successful. Moreover, in terms of sheer size in the economy, there is no reason to emphasize the scientific sectors: U.S. value added in electrical and electronic goods does not exceed that in food and tobacco; U.S. value added in drugs and medicines is less than that in beverages.

2. The former point is only amplified by recognition of the fact that the socialist countries of East Europe are not at a stage of development where one would expect them to have a comparative advantage in the most scientific sectors. The middle-income countries do not make their success in such sectors: the Spanish value added in electrical and electronics is only half that in food and tobacco, and the Spanish value added in drugs and medicines is only half that in beverages; for a country such as Greece, the corresponding ratios are one-third.[4]

3. As is acknowledged by Soviet economists (Aganbegyan 1987), any supposed failure of the socialist countries is not to be found in the amount of resources that is presently allocated to science. The socialist countries already devote a very large share of their resources to science and to the process of technological change in the industries in which science is most important. In some of these industries, there have been some remarkable successes. More emphasis on science is not needed. What is needed is more reflection on why the past devotion to science has been

4. For verification of these points, see United Nations (1987).

successful in some sectors and not others. Subsequent sections of this paper provide some thoughts on this point.

Focus on Cooperation

The third implicit assumption is the notion that all cross-national organization can take place effectively through cooperation.[5] This view overlooks what might perhaps be the most significant change in the world economy in the postwar years: the rise of the multinational corporations. The increasing significance of these entities in the world economy cannot be overemphasized, as Table 6-1 attests.

Theoretical reasoning and empirical evidence tell us that cooperation between sovereign entities cannot replace the activities of multinational corporations in all economic sectors. The essence of these corporations is that they replace market exchange by hierarchy. In some spheres of activity, where outcomes are very hard to predict and where the establishment of a relationship makes each party vulnerable to the other's actions, arm's-length exchanges might not be efficient, or even feasible. That multi-nationals play a particularly important role in some sectors can be seen in Table 6-2.

Moreover, it seems clear that cooperation is no substitute for hierarchy. I have made some rough calculations of the importance of foreign capital in Yugoslavia, which bars foreign control, and some market economies, which allow foreign majority-owned affiliates. These figures show that foreign-owned capital is eight times more important in Portugal than Yugoslavia, twelve times in Greece, thirty-five times in Austria, and 100 times in the Netherlands.[6] Furthermore, this nonequivalence of cooperation and hierarchy applies particularly to the sectors in which foreign direct investment occurs, as the figures in Table 6-3 attest. As is evident from Table 6-3, the Yugoslav share of foreign direct

5. Between the date of the first presentation of this paper in September 1988 and its finalization in July 1989, laws have been passed in East Europe and the Soviet Union that acknowledge the need for foreign majority ownership. At the time of writing, the practical effect of these laws is still unknown.
6. The relevant data are from OECD (1986).

investment seems to be low in food processing, machinery, and electrical sectors. The explanation for the situation in food processing can perhaps be found in similar types of emphases in policymaking to those discussed above. That is certainly not the case for the high-tech, heavy-industrial machinery, and electrical sectors. The explanation for these sectors is presented in a later section of this paper.

Focus on Resource Allocation

The last emphasis results from a sin of omission rather than commission. Nowhere in the ideas of Soviet policymakers is thought given to one of the most important dynamic forces in modern economies: the continuing creation of new institutions. There seems to be an implicit assumption that radical change can occur simply by radically reallocating resources among existing institutions. What this approach ignores is the fact that much dynamism comes from new firms—the Sonys and the Apples—and from firms that change their sphere of activity—the Hondas and the Xeroxes. A policy that focuses on the planned reallocation of resources will not avail itself of this form of dynamism.

DETERMINANTS OF COMPARATIVE ADVANTAGES
IN SOCIALIST ECONOMIES

Implicit in the comments made here is a specific view of the way in which the structure of socialist systems determines their trade behavior (and indeed their overall economic performance). That view has been laid out—and tested against trade patterns—in a recent book by this writer (Murrell 1989). I would like to adumbrate some of the ideas of that book, because those ideas, in combination with the emphases identified above, can go a long way to explain past socialist trade behavior and to identify the dilemmas that the socialist economies presently face.

The essence of the views to which I subscribe is that technological progress is the central ingredient of economic

Table 6-1. Shares of the Majority-Owned Affiliates of Multinational Corporations in the Exports of Some Industrializing Countries[a]

Country	Date	Share (%)
Belgium	1975	43
Brazil	Late 1970s	40
France	1975	25
Singapore	Late 1970s	90
South Korea	Late 1970s	30
Spain	1975	51
Taiwan	1976	30

a. The figures for European countries cover manufacturing exports only.

Sources: The data for non-European countries are from World Bank (1987) and Lee and Liang (1982). The data for European countries are from Dunning and Cantwell (1987).

Table 6-2. Shares of the Majority-Owned Affiliates of Japanese and U.S. Multinational Corporations in the Exports of Specific Sectors of Industrializing Countries

Sector	Share of Multinationals in Exports (%)
Basic Metals	7.0
Chemicals	19.1
Food	3.6
Electrical and Electronic Goods	47.0
Nonelectrical Machinery	31.3
Transportation	19.3

Source: Blomstrom, Kravis, and Lipsey (1988).

success. I must emphasize that by the term "technological progress" I mean a very broad category of changes—organizational, marketing, new goods, and new designs, as well as new processes. (I would like to contrast this broad notion of technological change with the one that leads to the phrase "scientific and technological advances.") Compared to the implementation of such changes, all other factors impinging on economic performance pale into insignificance. In particular, this view downplays the importance of efficiency in the static allocation of resources, which is the centerpiece of neoclassical economics, of which the market socialist model is an integral part.

To think about the elements of economic systems that affect the ability to implement technological change, it is particularly useful, especially in the context of foreign trade, to distinguish three types of goods. The names of the goods are taken from the economic theories that best describe the factors that explain why specific countries specialize in the production of the goods.[7]

Ricardian goods are ones in which natural-resource content is very high. To a rough approximation, the production and export of these goods is determined by the beneficence of nature. Obvious examples are bananas, crude oil, and wine.

The characteristics of *neoclassical* sectors are to be understood largely as relative ones in contrast to the properties of goods in the third category. Neoclassical sectors have standard well-known technologies that are relatively easily transferable. In such sectors, the production of radically new goods is not an important phenomenon. Moreover, quality, to the extent it varies, can be relatively easily determined; sales and service by the manufacturer are not crucial to the buyer. Technological advances in neoclassical sectors might be important, but the advances build upon a large stock of existing knowledge and are most usually in the form of new processes, whose economic effects can be estimated with a tolerable degree of accuracy. If that is the case, the transfer of new technology can be accomplished at arm's length through licenses, purchases of plant, or cooperative agreements. Neoclassical sectors

7. The idea for this categorization came from Hufbauer and Chilas (1974). The differences between their classification and mine mainly center on the economic theories used to describe the third categories of goods. Hufbauer and Chilas use product-cycle theories and I use Schumpeterian notions.

Table 6-3. Sectoral Shares of Foreign Direct Investment

| | Percentage Shares | | |
Sector	Yugoslavia	Turkey	All LDCs[a]
Chemicals	24.7	21.5	24.4
Electrical, Electronics	2.3	8.8	13.1
Food	5.5	16.3	11.2
Machinery	4.9	14.0	14.7
Metals	29.2	8.8	5.6
Transportation	23.2	15.8	8.4
Wood/Paper	4.4	2.4	6.5

a. U.S. multinationals only.

Sources: OECD (1982, 1983); U.S. Department of Commerce (1981).

are usually the more traditional sectors in which large firms dominate. Obvious examples are steel, basic chemicals, shipbuilding, and even automobiles. In summary, the determinants of success in neoclassical sectors are well known and largely understood. Hence, the model of rational decisionmaking in the presence of known constraints can be applied with a tolerable degree of accuracy.

Schumpeterian sectors are ones in which the process of change is better characterized by an evolutionary model rather than by the neoclassical paradigm of maximizing rational agents. A variety of factors can make a sector classifiable as Schumpeterian, and to some extent these factors can vary across sectors independently of each other. In Schumpeterian sectors, the technological and organizational characteristics of successful firms are less well understood, perhaps because the sector is new or going through some radical restructuring. New products are very important, and these might be significantly different from existing ones, thus making their value difficult to estimate. For these reasons, technology is difficult to transfer at arm's length, because prospective buyers cannot estimate the economic value of the technology. Reputation for quality and after-sales service might be important ingredients in selling goods, and this reputation cannot be easily transferred to other organizations.

The ingredients of an economic system that lead to an economy having successful Schumpeterian sectors are very different from those that promote neoclassical sectors. In Schumpeterian sectors, uncertainty about the character of successful decisions and the radical nature of change mean that an economic system must be open to ideas from outside any specific sector. This is especially the case in view of the fact that existing institutions are often resistant and blind to the new. Entry of new firms and existing firms from outside the sector is essential to economic success in Schumpeterian sectors.

When knowledge of the ingredients of success is limited, an economic system must choose the most successful decisionmaking units through an evolutionary process. Exit and entry will be fundamental elements of this process. Moreover, because the arm's-length transfer of the ideas promoting success is difficult, the system must be open to rapid growth of successful organizations. The success of the organization itself must determine the speed of its growth, because previous success is the most important guide to the fitness of its organizational structure, choice of technology, or type of product. In the Schumpeterian sectors, the system must allow organizations themselves to determine the speed with which they conquer new territory, or indeed die out. In the modern open international economy, both of these elements of Schumpeterian success—entry and exit and spread of new ideas by the expansion of existing organizations—lead to one very important conclusion: receptiveness to multinational corporations is absolutely essential to economic progress. Obvious examples of Schumpeterian sectors are machinery and consumer electronics, but specialized sectors of many traditional industries could also be examples—apparel when style is important, or simple manufactured products when new marketing techniques or methods of quality control constitute the technological innovation.

DETERMINANTS OF EAST-WEST TRADE PATTERNS

In Table 6-4, I present very rudimentary information on the most important sectors of manufacturing industry. Two sets of characteristics are noted in the table. First, I give my judgment on whether a sector is best classified as Ricardian (R), neoclassical (N), or Schumpeterian (S). This judgment is based on a variety of information—whether technological change in the sectors is process- or product-oriented, the degree of product differentiation, whether entry of new firms is significant in the industry, and the extent to which intra-multinational corporation trade is significant in the sector. The last two items of information are summarized separately in columns (2) and (3) because they are so pertinent in any discussion of the systemic features of the socialist economies. Of course, the quality of information in the table is very crude and must be viewed from that perspective. The table serves solely to present the implications of the above discussion in the simplest way.

The second set of factors noted in Table 6-4 is the emphases that, as I have commented above, seem to be implicit in the economic policy of the socialist countries during the last two decades or longer. Again, the information presented in Table 6-4 is very simple, summarizing essentially the popular image of the sector— whether it produces consumer goods, whether it has that Dickensian quality of being "heavy," and whether it has an image of being "high tech."

Despite the quality of information, the composite picture from Table 6-4 is striking. For the socialist countries, there is a very bad fit between the sectors that the policymakers want to emphasize and those for which the system is best suited. The Schumpeterian sectors are not ones in which socialist countries will have a comparative advantage because of systemic characteristics—the lack of entry and exit, the difficulty that successful organizations have in expanding their activities into different sectors and different regions, and the nonacceptance of multinational corporations. Moreover, many of the neoclassical sectors—food processing, textiles, apparel—are neglected because the image (and I stress the word image, in contrast to substance) of the sectors is not one that catches the eye of policymakers. Apart from Ricardo goods, whose production is at least partially determined by the presence of specific endowments, the sectors in which the socialist countries find themselves able and willing to concentrate their efforts are basic chemicals, processing of fuels, and basic metals. Thus, one has a prediction of the sectors in which the socialist countries will specialize. As all will be aware, this prediction fits the facts on East-West trade extremely well.

THE EFFECTS ON THE MARKET ECONOMIES OF LIMITED REFORMS OF THE SOCIALIST ECONOMIES

I return to the basic question that was assigned to me by the conference organizers: What will be the effects on the market economies of attempts to expand East-West trade? The answer to this question must necessarily come in two parts, depending on whether or not one assumes a radical change in policy on the part of the East European countries. First, let us assume that the reforms take the economies no further than, say, the Hungarian system over the last twenty years. Then, I would argue that the attempts to expand East-West trade have few implications for the market economies, because these attempts would fail. Why? At least three reasons are clear:

1. If the above analysis is correct, market socialist reforms do not address the central problems of the socialist economies. Schumpeterian theory predicts that the dynamism of important sectors of the economy arises from the creation of new institutions and the selection process that the market provides. With their emphasis on the incentives of managers, price reforms, and decentralization of decisions within the existing institutions, market socialist reforms do not change by one iota the behavior of the socialist economies within the Schumpeterian sectors.

2. At present, there are no serious attempts in the socialist countries to provide the type of environment that is required by multinational corporations—an intervention-free atmosphere in which control is in the hands of the parent company. The present tortuous negotiations and the long delays in setting up

Table 6-4. Predicting the Sectoral Concentration of East-West Trade

	(1) Ricardian Neoclassical, or Schumpeterian	(2) Entry Is Not Crucial	(3) MNCs Are Not Important	(4) Heavy Industry	(5) Investment or Intermediate Sector	(6) High Tech	(7) Shares in Trade of Middle-Income Countries
Raw Materials	R	Yes	Yes	Yes	Yes	No	2.8
Fuels	R/N	Yes	Yes	Yes	Yes	Yes	14.9
Basic Chemicals	N	Yes?	Yes	Yes	Yes	Yes	5.3
Basic Metals	N	Yes	Yes	Yes	Yes	Yes	9.5
Food	R/N	Yes	Yes	No	No	No	8.5
Beverages	N	Yes	Yes?	No?	No	No	1.9
Textiles	N	Yes?	Yes?	No?	No?	No	3.5
Apparel	N/S	Yes?	Yes/No	No	No	No	2.6
Wood/Paper	N/S	No?	Yes/No	Yes?	No?	Yes/No	2.1
Transport	N/S	No?	Yes/No	Yes	Yes/No	Yes/No	8.6
Specialty Chemicals	S	Yes?	No	No	No?	Yes	1.8
Nonelectrical Machinery	S	No	No	Yes	Yes	Yes	8.3
Electrical, Electronics	S	No	No	Yes/No	Yes/No	Yes	10.1
Other							20.4

Notes: A "No" means that a sector has characteristics that would make one predict that the socialist countries do not have a comparative advantage in the sector.

The information is intended to convey a five-point scale—Yes, Yes?, Yes/No, No?, No—indicating the proportions of sub-sectors within the major sectors that have the indicated property.

Column (2) is based on information on the degree of entry in the sectors in the United States.

Column (3) is based on information on the importance of intra-MNC trade in the sector.

Column (6) is based on information on R&D/Sales and Patents/Sales.

Column (7) lists the average trade percentages within the sectors for the United Kingdom, Belgium, Ireland, and Greece. For the information used for columns (2), (3), and (7), see Murrell (1989, chap. 4).

new joint ventures are not simply the results of bureaucratic inertia. They are quite predictable if one uses current theories of internal organization. In the sectors in which the multinationals are common, it is so difficult to judge the value of what these companies offer that it is impossible to reach any satisfactory cooperative agreement. That is exactly why cross-border hierarchical organization is needed and why cooperation is no substitute.

3. The sectors in which the comparative advantage of socialist economies lies are exactly the ones in which the market economies have been, and will be, most protectionist. Neoclassical sectors have mature technologies, and they are therefore more likely to have had time to develop the strong coalition of interest groups that lobbies for protection. These sectors are the ones whose goods are homogeneous. Hence, the parties threatened by imports are readily identifiable. The neoclassical sectors are also the ones that are in relative decline in the advanced economies. Therefore, job security is an important issue.

For all these reasons, any expansion of East-West trade at present is likely to meet with increased protectionist sentiment simply because the socialist economies specialize in those sectors in which protectionist sentiment is most rampant. The most extreme conclusion that could be derived from the above is that the attempted expansion of East-West trade will have few implications for the market economies. Even if market socialist reforms were carried out, and even if the socialist countries were given the same general trading status as analogous market economies, East-West trade would not expand dramatically.

PREREQUISITES FOR FUNDAMENTAL SHIFTS IN EAST-WEST TRADE

If the socialist economies are to increase their participation in the international economy, then fundamental changes must occur. Let us list those changes, beginning with the most palatable:

1. The emphasis on sectors that seem "high tech" or investment-oriented must be diminished. There is no reason, apart from image, why there cannot be an expansion in trade of the products of light industry or of the consumer goods sector. I would presume that this expansion can occur without a large change in organizational structure. However, I do have reservations about the extent to which policymakers are willing to sacrifice their interest in high-visibility projects. (Witness the Concord in the U.K. and France and the high-capital intensity of the projects undertaken in the poorer Yugoslav regions.)

2. The socialist countries must take a more pragmatic attitude toward the operations of the multinational corporations. The figures presented above show just what a force these corporations are in the affairs of modern market economies. Those figures also show that the multinationals are even more important in the very sectors that policymakers in the socialist countries want to emphasize—electronics and engineering. The biggest question mark over the implementation of such a policy is whether political leaders can accept the perceived loss of sovereignty that is involved in attracting the multinationals. (Is any East European leader willing, as were the socialist leaders of France and Spain, to fawn over the representatives of the Disney company to attract Disney World to their country?)

3. Although I regard this as unlikely, the socialist economies must accept the fact that economic success cannot be secured solely by allocating resources within an existing set of institutions. The future is highly uncertain, and any economy needs to experiment with alternatives, needs new institutions constantly created that might just be better-fitted to a new environment, and needs a mechanism by which the better-fitted are able to grow very quickly and compete for the domain of the less productive entities. Whether a system with such properties can be constructed under socialism remains to be seen.

One of the papers presented at the Middlebury conference remarked that what is needed for the socialist economies is "planned expansion of cooperation." I disagree. Hierarchy, as the multinational corporations show, is a valuable form of economic organization and can be superior to cooperation in many cases. Which of the many types and forms of hierarchies are most appropriate for the various sectors of a modern economy cannot be judged *a priori*, but must be based on the observed merits of each. Thus, instead of planned expansion of cooperation, I would suggest "chaotic competition between hierarchies."

REFERENCES

Abegglen, James C., and George Stalk, Jr. 1985. *Kaisha: The Japanese Corporation.* New York: Basic Books.

Aganbegyan, Abel. 1987. "Basic Directions in *Perestroyka.*" *Soviet Economy.*

Blomstrom, Magnus, Irving B. Kravis, and Robert E. Lipsey. 1988. "Multinational Firms and Manufactured Exports from Developing Countries." NBER Working Paper. Cambridge, MA.

Dunning, John, and John Cantwell. 1987. *IRM Directory of Statistics of International Investment and Production.* Basingstoke,UK: Macmillan.

Hufbauer, Gary C., and John Chilas. 1974. "Specialization Among Industrial Countries: Extent and Consequences." In *International Division of Labour Problems and Perspectives.* Ed. Herbert Giersch. Tubingen: Mohr.

Lee, T. H., and Kuo-shu Liang. 1982. "Taiwan." *Development Strategies in Semi-Industrial Economies.* Baltimore: The Johns Hopkins University Press.

Logimov, Vadim P. 1987. Remarks in the "Panel on Growth and Technology in *Perestroyka.*" *Soviet Economy.*

Mueller, Dennis C. 1986. *Profits in the Long Run.* Cambridge, MA: Cambridge University Press.

Murrell, Peter. 1989. *The Nature of Socialist Economies: Lessons from East European Foreign Trade.* Princeton, NJ: Princeton Univ. Press.

OECD. 1982. *Foreign Investment in Yugoslavia.* Paris: OECD.

———. 1983. *Foreign Investment in Turkey.* Paris: OECD.

———. 1986. *Trends in International Direct Investment.* Paris: OECD.

United Kingdom, Central Statistical Office. 1989. *Annual Abstract of Statistics.* London: HMSO.

United Nations. 1986. *National Account Statistics, 1984.* New York: United Nations.

———. 1987. *Industrial Statistics Yearbook, 1985.* New York: United Nations.

United States Department of Commerce. 1981. *U.S. Direct Investment Abroad, 1977.* Washington, DC: Government Printing Office.

World Bank. 1987. *World Development Report.* Washington, DC: World Bank.

CHAPTER 7

Integration Reform: New Horizons for the CMEA and East-West Economic Relations

JOZEF M. VAN BRABANT

The age of perestroika has brought about a set of policy parameters for the Council for Mutual Economic Assistance (CMEA)[1] that differs markedly from that prevailing just a few years ago. This paper analyzes the new horizons for relations with the West, with an emphasis on economic matters.

Section I lists a number of recent seminal changes in Soviet policy that in time may transform the horizons for intra-CMEA and East-West relations. Section II highlights the most important recent developments in the Soviet foreign trade and economic management systems. In Section III, the discussion shifts to the CMEA organs, policy objectives, and integration mechanisms that appear to be related to ongoing transformations in the Soviet Union and in several other CMEA members. Section IV accents a few priorities in relations with the global economy, especially developed market economies (DMEs), that are chiefly of Soviet domestic concern. This section also discusses many of the issues

---

The views expressed here are my own and do not imply expression of any opinion whatsoever on the part of the United Nations Secretariat.

1. The CMEA consists of full members, associate member (Yugoslavia), cooperants (eight developing countries and Finland), and observers (other socialist countries, developing countries, and representations from international organizations). In what follows, I shall confine myself to the active European members of the CMEA as defined in Footnote 2.

related to Soviet participation in international economic organizations. Section V looks more closely at Soviet involvement with the General Agreement on Tariffs and Trade (GATT). Section VI provides a brief perspective on the agreement recently signed between the two economic blocs in Europe. Section VII deals with some aspects of global economic security. The paper concludes in Section VIII with a few observations on what may be in store for East-West relations, particularly with reference to Europe as a whole.

I. EMERGING CHANGES FROM PERESTROIKA

Developments in the Soviet economy and international political perceptions of the Soviet leadership since early 1985 have signaled a plethora of changes that in time may radically alter the Soviet economy as a typical centrally planned economy (CPE). This change is bound to affect the other CPEs, the interaction of these countries within the CMEA context, and within the global economy, and the fact that the group has essentially remained at the fringes of global economic relations in the postwar period. Four problem areas bear on the theme of this paper.

First, potentially radical changes in Soviet society, including in economic affairs, call for more growth-oriented policies, with the accent now clearly on the quality of economic development rather than on the sheer rise in physical output of goods and services. These shifts amount to setting priorities, including: (1) the loosening of Soviet dependence on export revenues from fuels and raw materials; (2) bolstering the Soviet Union's position in markets for manufactures; and (3) deliberately shifting Soviet import priorities with a view to exploiting more fully comparative advantages, particularly in nonfood consumer goods and in technologies that may significantly enhance the growth of the economy's factor productivity. This sentiment has contributed to a much more favorable attitude toward participation in international economic relations.

Second, the ambience of perestroika has been exerting direct and indirect effects on relations among CMEA states due largely to the emulation of perestroika policies in several other CMEA members, particularly in East Europe.[2] This is not to mean that Soviet reform sentiments have been *the* most critical determinant of the reassessment of economic policies and the reorganization of planning and other institutions in East Europe. Indeed, predisposition toward reform in some of the smaller CPEs has itself exerted a powerful influence on the evolution of Gorbachevian thinking at least since March 1985! Nevertheless, the ambitious and vast scope of Soviet societal reform has created a new impetus to East European economic policies. Indirect effects have manifested themselves chiefly through Soviet preferences regarding the reconstruction of the CMEA as a regional economic organization, as well as through the priorities with respect to socialist economic integration (SEI), issues examined more fully in Sections II and III.

Third, Soviet perceptions of the key components of predictable and sustainable international economic relations have undergone noticeable modifications. These have moved the leadership toward seeking greater involvement in the global economy. One key concern has been how the Soviet economy could gain a faster growth path, partly through the importation of western technology, without incurring a substantial external debt. But it stems also from the apparent desire of the reform-minded administration to assume greater responsibility for world economic affairs. This change may in part reflect concerns about the stature of the second most powerful country in conceiving, directing, and modifying the global framework. The shifts that have emerged to date include overtures to international economic organizations, most notably the GATT; new initiatives in the United Nations regarding global security, especially international economic security, the policing role of that organization, the United Nations' function as an honest broker in global affairs, and internal administrative and other reforms; the surprising ease with which long-standing obstacles to some form of association with the European Communities (EC) were recently resolved; and,

2.   East Europe here is defined as comprising Bulgaria, Czechoslovakia, the German Democratic Republic (GDR), Hungary, Poland, and Romania. At times I shall use the concept also to include the Soviet Union when the context makes it clear that I have this wider notion in mind. East Europe and the Soviet Union constitute the active European members of the CMEA. Albania is formally still a full CMEA member, though it ceased active participation in 1961.

of course, a variety of proposals on nuclear disarmament, lower-keyed defense postures more generally, and resolving or sharply easing regional conflicts that, earlier in the decade, measurably and abruptly soured relations between East and West.

Finally, whereas the East-West rift since World War II has been driven predominantly by the bilateralized political, economic, and societal rivalry between the Soviet Union and the United States, one can detect in recent months several instances in which Soviet leaders appear to be casting a more multi-sided, realistic view of both Asia, including China and Japan, and West Europe, particularly the EC. There is also a slowly emerging reappraisal of Soviet involvement with the Third World.

II. PERESTROIKA AND SOVIET FOREIGN TRADE

Even before the momentous radical reform that Mikhail S. Gorbachev outlined at the Central Committee Plenum in June 1987, the Soviet Union announced it would introduce a major change in its foreign trading system, effective January 1, 1987. Envisaged was a decentralization of decisionmaking in foreign trade in favor of approximately twenty ministries and seventy manufacturing firms—energy and most raw materials were specifically and intentionally excluded from this devolution for obvious reasons. Not only were these enterprises and ministries to be free to trade directly on foreign markets, they also would be held financially accountable for their transactions. Soviet authorities were willing to grant these organizations a certain measure of autonomy in pricing to establish links between domestic and foreign trade prices by enacting internal conversion coefficients (similar to shadow exchange rates of the Soviet *valuta* currency in terms of domestic currency), to provide them with foreign currency credits, and to implement foreign currency retention quotas. It subsequently also led to the creation of a new superministry—the Commission for Foreign Economic Relations, of which the former Ministry of Foreign Trade forms only one part—expanding the tasks of the *Vneshtorgbank* (Bank for Foreign Trade) and renaming it *Vneshekonombank* (Bank for Foreign Economic Relations).

Furthermore, the Soviet Union announced that it would foster direct enterprise relations with CMEA partners as well as with the market economies (MEs) with a view to establish joint ventures. A joint venture law was formulated by early 1987, revised in October of the same year, and updated once again in late 1988. Clearly, Soviet authorities intended to utilize joint ventures as a gateway to obtaining foreign currency by boosting convertible currency exports; to generate inflows of high technology not obtainable through commercial channels, possibly for lack of financial resources; and to access capital funds and technical expertise from DMEs. Whether these priorities would blend in with those held by western partners is a different matter. The latter's interest in a joint venture would presumably be geared primarily by concerns about expanding local markets partly on the basis of relatively low-cost, skilled, and rather highly reliable labor. If these *a priori* notions hold, the commonality of priorities is exceedingly narrow and shallow. Nonetheless, the formation of joint ventures has moved ahead much faster and far more pragmatically than could have been anticipated. Perhaps most surprising has been the willingness of the Soviet authorities to revise joint venture legislation when it proved to be a hindrance to fostering deals.

Has the foreign trade reform to date shown any measurable success? It is clear that the implementation of market-based foreign trade and joint ventures has been much more difficult than had originally been anticipated. But such an outcome could have been predicted, because both the external and the internal partial decentralization environments were far from conducive to ensuring success. These constraints would presumably remain as long as the system prevents genuine wholesale trade with flexible domestic prices and dependable exchange rates. But if domestic preconditions change, as is already envisaged, the scope for foreign trade reform may well soon be transformed and serve as a multiplier for even greater change.

Finally, in February 1986, it was made clear that the Soviet Union would not forever condone the CMEA's "armchair administration" and endless committee deliberations Gorbachev chided so scathingly at the 27th Party Congress of the Soviet Union. The implicit and explicit changes mentioned above would involve not only the CMEA as a regional organization, but also the priorities governing intra-CMEA economic relations, the instruments and institutions utilized to advance regional cooperation, and the longer-term strategic goals sought by the CPEs.

III. RENEWAL IN THE CMEA?

Since the preparations for the June 1984 CMEA economic summit[3]—the first since April 1969—there has been considerable agitation for enacting profound changes in the CMEA and SEI, particularly among the European members. These emerging shifts, conceptually or otherwise, can be grouped conveniently under three main themes. First, there has been a broad-based debate about revamping the institutional and organizational setup of the CMEA with a view to rationalizing the bureaucracy, streamlining the mechanisms through which issues are handled, and rendering the deliberative organs more effective. As was made clear at the 27th Party Congress, transforming the CMEA into an effective regional organ that contributes to the enhancement of SEI ranks very high on the Soviet policy agenda. Second, the ultimate purposes of SEI and means (institutions, instruments, policy coordination, and structural macroeconomic policies) to pursue it were to be reexamined comprehensively. Finally, the institutional and instrumental framework within which day-to-day matters affecting SEI can be enhanced was to be the focus of probing inquiries, including how it was to relate to reform initiatives in other CPEs.

These three themes have been debated at the highest policy-making levels, including the recent two CMEA economic summits (held in June 1984 and November 1986), most Council Sessions held since 1983, and the numerous sessions of the Central

---

3. This is known officially as the "Conference of First Secretaries of Communist and Workers' Parties and of the Heads of Government of the CMEA Member Countries." This gathering convenes intermittently on grave issues affecting fraternal relations among Communist Parties. When they do so mainly to deliberate about economic issues within the CMEA alliance, I shall dub the meeting "an economic summit" or simply "summit" if no confusion is possible.

Committee Secretaries in charge of economic affairs.[4] Although a consensus is only slowly emerging, some important decisions have already been implemented, while others are in the process of being carried out.   There are, however, important issues that continue to be debated within the CMEA,[5] including those emanating from the failure to move ahead swiftly with the SEI program endorsed in December 1985 on scientific-technical cooperation.[6]

A few words about the 1985 SEI program, its objectives, and its initial implementation attempts are warranted.   The impetus behind the goal of SEI came from the CMEA's disappointing economic performance of the early 1980s, continuing imbalances in many CPEs, and lackluster progress with SEI since the abrogation of the earlier debate on SEI in the mid-1970s (Brabant 1987a, 64-67).   These factors also served as the impetus for the 1984 CMEA economic summit, which, among other things, worked out a comprehensive program for CPEs to invigorate their pace of technological progress.   Some measures were enacted quickly, including the identification of the so-called "head" or "lead" organizations (*golovnaya organizatsiya*),[7] designed to foster cooperation among economic agents from various CMEA countries.

4. This last group has emerged as perhaps the second highest, if informal, organ of the CMEA. It essentially came into its own in connection with the tortuous preparation of the CMEA summit in 1983-1984, which after many delays was finally convened in June 1984. Since then, it has played a critical role in propagating "new thinking" in the CMEA in preparation of summit meetings and Council Sessions.

5. An apt illustration may be gleaned from the commentary of the various national Central Committee Secretaries in charge of economic affairs provided after their recent meeting (Budapest, June 1-2, 1988).

6. The full title reads: *Comprehensive Program to Promote the Scientific and Technological Progress of the Member Countries of the Council for Mutual Economic Assistance up to the Year 2000.* It was published in all nine Communist Party papers of December 19, 1985. I abbreviate it here to *Scientific-technological Progress.*

7. Although the "notoriety" of these organs, particularly in consequence of the suspicions raised by western observers, stems from the initial attempts to breathe life into *Scientific-technological Progress,* they had in fact been called into existence, at least on paper, in the 1972 document that lays down the basic organizational, methodological, and legal foundations of scientific-technological cooperation (STC). The document is called: *Organizatsionno-metodicheskiye, ekonomicheskiye i pravovyye osnovy nauchno-tekhnicheskogo sotrudnichestva stran-chlenov SEV i deyatel'nosti organov SEV v etoy oblasti.* It is reproduced in CMEA 1977, pp. 328-86. I shall abbreviate it here as *Osnovy.* The passus on the head organization is on pp. 342-43.

On the whole, 1986 proved to be a disappointing year insofar as bilateral agreements covering the technological progress were concerned. Overall economic performance was disappointing as well. Reasons for the Council's difficulties in implementing *Scientific-technological Progress* included worsening interfirm relations; great reluctance, and limited ability in any case, to engage in common capital formation in the CMEA; the fact that *Scientific-technological Progress* was endorsed after the five-year plans for 1986-1990 had been formulated; the problem of reconciling decentralized decisionmaking by central planning organizations; and the setbacks incurred during the earliest stages of the implementation of the new five-year plans.[8]

These circumstances led to the sudden convening of the 1986 economic summit, shortly after the annual meeting of the Council Session. Vigorous discussions on the reorganization of the CMEA and the prospective policies and instruments of SEI have been under way since.

In many ways, the 43rd (Moscow, October 1987) and 44th (Prague, July 1988) Council Sessions were a revelation as well as a disappointment—a disappointment because the meetings failed to resolve a number of critical problems of SEI that have been on the policy agenda for many years. The debates at the Sessions were nonetheless informative in a number of respects. First, they confirmed that the November 1986 summit meeting had been very critical in charting potential CMEA policies. In fact, in some ways the 44th Session held in Prague in 1988 might be elevated to an exalted position heretofore exclusively reserved for the April 1969 summit. Recall that it was only then that the very concept of SEI was finally adopted as the paramount objective of CMEA cooperation and was placed as such at the top of the policy agenda, including the elaboration of *Integration Program*.[9] The 44th Session made a number of tentative recommendations that are bound to exert a major influence on the course of SEI in the years ahead.

8. For a discussion of the systemic and policy-induced aspects of these problem areas, see Brabant (1988a).
9. The full title reads: *Comprehensive Program for the Further Extension and Improvement of Cooperation and the Development of Socialist Economic Integration by the CMEA Member Countries.* The original Russian version is reproduced in Tokareva (1972, 29-103).

The CMEA Organization

The last two Council Sessions agreed, apparently unanimously, to reform the organizational structure of the CMEA. Proposed changes involve abolishing organs that have not performed well; consolidating units that have in effect duplicated one another; retrenchment of the civil service; and generally giving less emphasis to the day-to-day planning of production and distribution in favor of medium- to long-term strategic charting of the key directions the CPEs should explore for meaningful structural change. These objectives are similar to the intentions of perestroika, with the Soviet variant providing the major impetus for change. One of the aims here too is to separate the objectives and instruments of central planning for structural change from the day-to-day economic decisionmaking at both the micro- and macroeconomic levels. Some reforms were already carried out in early 1988. Ikonnikov (1988) reports, for example, that nineteen of the formal CMEA organs, particularly the Conferences and Standing Commissions, were abolished or transformed into Committees of the Executive Committee. Of the thirty-six official organs in place in October 1987, many were abolished, replaced, or superseded by newly created ones; only twenty-four official organs reportedly remained in early 1988.[10] For reference, Figure 7-1 presents the official CMEA organs as of late 1988.

In further changes, a sizable portion of the international civil service of the CMEA was cut or is slated to be redeployed in the home countries. The goal seems to be to reduce staffing by about one-third, or roughly 600-700 individuals.

The aforementioned changes are part and parcel of a more sweeping reform of the CMEA organization and personnel, including the specialized or affiliated CMEA organs. The 44th Council Session welcomed these changes, called for further vigorous restructuring, and mandated additional changes to orient the activity of the CMEA and its associated organs "toward seeking,

---

10. By my count, there should have been forty organs that were reduced to twenty-eight by early 1988. I can square these data with Ikonnikov's only by leaving out the Session and the Institutes as being perhaps organs that he did not consider to be among the *predstavitel'nyye organy*. But that is at best arbitrary.

substantiating, and determining strategic and conceptual solutions for scientific-technical problems."[11]

The Role of the Developing CPEs in Integration

There was widespread agreement at the 43rd Council Session in Moscow—though assent in some cases was rather reluctant—to rechart assistance policies to CMEA developing states, particularly Cuba, Mongolia, and Vietnam. All agreed that past economic and technical development assistance efforts on the part of the European CMEA members had not been as effective as they should have been. Disenchantment was evident for both recipient and donor.

Although details are lacking, the preparation of a special development assistance program has apparently been moving forward at a satisfactory pace, as noted at the most recent (June 1-2, 1988) meeting of the Central Committee Secretaries in charge of economic affairs. Even so, the program was said to be primarily in the area of involving these peripheral CPEs more closely in SEI, particularly production specialization and cooperation.

Three separate drafts of comprehensive economic cooperation with each of the non-European members were presented in Prague. Once agreed upon and harmonized into one common policy stance, it will become part and parcel of the new SEI strategy (see subsequent section). The basic objective is to integrate these countries more fully into the CMEA edifice through concrete agreements on production cooperation and specialization, placing STC on more than a gratuitous basis, and further commercialization of their economic interactions with the CMEA. Some forms of assistance to the non-European countries will continue to be provided by the developed membership on a gratuitous basis, however. The programs also contain relatively extensive lists of specific projects to be commissioned.[12] But the donor countries have already made it clear that a number of those projects "require clarification as regards construction deadlines, assessments of the

---

11. Speech by Lubomir Strougal, as reported in *Rudé Právo*, July 6, 1988, p. 4.

12. Georgi Atanasov reported that Bulgaria would be prepared to participate in "71 of the total 178 actions envisaged in the specific comprehensive programs" (*Rabotnichesko delo*, July 6, 1988, p. 6).

Figure 7-1. The CMEA Organization in Late 1988

| Council Session |

| Executive Committee |

Planning   Engineering   STC   Electronization
Foreign Economic Relations   Agrocomplex   Fuels & Raw Materials

| Secretariat |

| Standing Commissions |

Electrical & Nuclear Energy   Currency & Finance   Metallurgy   Statistics
Chemical Industry   Legal Affairs   Environment   Light Industry
Transportation   Standardization   Postal and Telecommunications

| Institutes |

Economic Problems   Standardization

Source: "RVHP - nová struktura orgánu." *Svet Hospodárství* 106: 4, 1986.

economic expediency of individual projects, and measures to ensure that they produce returns as soon as possible."[13]

Toward a New Integration Strategy

In addition to the effort to assist developing-country CMEA members, it was agreed in Moscow to work out a new SEI strategy for the period 1991-2005. Efforts to set forth such a new integration program have been on the debating table since the early 1980s. Nothing had been laid down, however, until the debates following the 1986 economic summit. This resolved that it would be useful to take a fresh look at SEI objectives, policies, instruments, and basic institutional supports. This program, tentatively entitled "Collective Concept of the International Socialist Division of Labor for the Years 1991-2005," was slated to be presented as an advanced draft to the Prague Session in 1988. Its major objective was stated to be laying the foundations for a unified economic market, at least for the European CMEA members.

The newly conceived collective concept of the international socialist division of labor (ISDL) should ensure the "transition to a qualitatively new level of cooperation" in the coming years. In addition to reiterating well-tested forms of SEI and strengthening planning in laying down guidelines for medium- to long-term development, the new program should foster efficiency in the various forms of cooperation, chiefly by transparent economic means. It was expected to endorse a more comprehensive use of commodity and financial relations in all CMEA affairs.

A draft was debated in Prague—although Central Committee Secretaries in charge of economic affairs, who met June 1-2, 1988, in Budapest, had strenuously objected to its excessive blandness and generality—but it has not yet been published. The Secretary of the CMEA clarified that the new concept focuses on accelerating technological progress, intensifying production, broadening production specialization, and integrating more fully the non-European CMEA members. It also singles out the main branches, chiefly engineering and electronics, and pays attention to the use

13. From Ryzkov's speech, as reported in *Pravda*, July 6, 1988, p. 4.

of raw materials, social issues, and cooperation in environmental protection.[14]

The idea to create a unified CMEA market was first mooted by the Soviets in Moscow. At the Prague meeting, it was endorsed by all, except Romania, and placed at the core of the new ISDL concept. Its adoption on the eve of the 40th anniversary of the CMEA may be symbolically significant. But the communiqué is very carefully worded and masks some of the more impassioned presentations, including one by Ryzkov. He noted that this market aims at:

> . . . ensuring a high degree of uniformity of economic conditions, the relatively free movement of goods, services, manpower, and finances among our countries' economic organizations, and the unified macroeconomic regulation of economic processes—regulation based on a coordinated policy—are a matter for the remote future. But we must keep this prospect in mind even now. For us the unified market is not a fashionable slogan but an important guideline for the development of the integration process.[15]

On the Mechanisms of Integration

Directly related to the proposed SEI program is a set of major decisions concerning the precise mechanism of SEI as it relates to the broader reform process in key CPEs. Gaining concurrence on this matter at the two Sessions and since has been much more complex than on any other issue. Although in Moscow there was apparently broad agreement on the need to revise key elements of planning and monetary-financial cooperation, members were divided on a number of critical economic issues, including the introduction of a modified form of limited regional convertibility; multilateralism in trade and payments; the determination of unified exchange rates; the revision of the price-formation mechanism; the linking of domestic and CMEA trade prices and in turn closer with world market, or at least East-West, prices; and enhancing the role of capital movements within the CMEA. The

14. Interview with Mr. Vjaceslav V. Sycěv, as reported in *Rudé Právo*.
15. The communiqué is in *Isvestiya*, July 8, 1988, pp. 1 and 4, and the speech is reported in *Pravda*, July 6, 1988, p. 4.

Session also emphasized the need to reinvigorate the implementation of *Scientific-technological Progress* by improving the economics of interfirm relations and elaborating the organizational prerequisites for such forms to contribute measurably to SEI. It was stressed that guidance rules, instruments, and institutions should facilitate microeconomic decisionmaking. The measures proposed include settlement of accounts for selected transactions, implying some highly limited form of intraregional convertibility.

The Soviet proposal envisages the introduction of a peculiar form of currency convertibility inasmuch as it would be limited in three respects. First, convertibility would presumably be confined to the most important forms of exchange within the limits set by direct enterprise relations and provided for by the formal and other provisions of *Scientific-technological Progress*. Second, it would be restricted to intraregional transactions, such as forints against zlotys, but not zlotys against dollars. Finally, the envisaged variant of convertibility would be introduced gradually, starting in 1991, over a period of at least ten years. Agreement in principle on this particular point was reached in Moscow by seven members, with the GDR, Romania, and Vietnam dissenting.

In the meantime, some of the member countries have made more rapid progress with this part of the CMEA reform agenda than they had originally anticipated. In early 1988, Bulgaria, Czechoslovakia, Mongolia, and the Soviet Union concluded some bilateral agreements[16] with the goal of moving ahead with this type of convertibility beginning in January 1989 (September 1988 in the case of Bulgaria-Czechoslovakia). It is unclear whether the other members that concurred on moving toward limited convertibility (Cuba, Hungary, and Poland) will soon introduce similar measures.

A minimum requirement for convertibility is that some class of transactions can be cleared anonymously and automatically, and

16. As of the date of writing, even this limited four-way circuit continues to be incomplete. The Soviet Union has apparently concluded agreements with all members listed, and Poland also is scheduled to join very soon. Bulgaria and Czechoslovakia have signed an agreement, and Czechoslovakia is slated to sign another one soon with Poland (Vetrovsky and Hrinda 1988). But I have no evidence of these two countries having come to terms with Mongolia on the issue of limited convertibility. Both have indicated, however, that agreement with Poland is imminent.

that some provisions enable surplus countries to mobilize their assets. Well-placed Soviet officials have hinted that their proposal envisages the automatic and anonymous clearing of selected transactions conducted by enterprises, and there is as yet no ceiling on the aggregate volume of transactions that can in principle be settled automatically and anonymously. Instead, all of the properly identified types of transactions will be conducted at local currency prices negotiated between partners on the basis of the Bucharest pricing principles. However, the clearing of accounts will take place as for all other transferable ruble (TR) transactions. In case the enterprises utilize local prices, the amounts invoiced will first have to be translated into proper TR values by way of internal adjustment coefficients. Some observers have indicated that the 1973 joint investment coefficients might now be invoked.[17]

In recognition of the lack of realism of the above-mentioned conversion rates, for example, Czechoslovakia and the Soviet Union have settled on a conversion rate of 10.4 koruny per TR, which implies a sharp depreciation of the koruna, because the official commercial exchange rate is 8 koruny per TR. But this de facto devaluation is considerably less than what would have prevailed under the joint investment agreement of 1973. At that time, partners agreed to convert domestic to official currency at the rate of 2.25, or a devaluation from 8 to 18 koruny per TR (Brabant 1987a, 218-20). I have no evidence to affirm that the members will preserve symmetry, so the devaluation of the Soviet domestic ruble vis-à-vis the external ruble (which is nominally equal to the TR) would be identical to that implied by the koruna devaluation. But there need not be symmetry even in bilateral relations, owing to the fact that the price systems in each CPE are different among themselves, and hence against the TRP network. If that were to prevail, the cited rate would imply only a very marginal devaluation of the ruble in terms of the TR—from 1.2 to 1.3.

Perhaps the greatest flaw in the proposal, if the above reading of events is accurate, is that convertibility is not really at stake. The

17. For details, see Brabant (1987a, 218-30); *Svet Hospodárství* 88: 2, 1988; and Vetrovsky and Hrinda (1988). A detailed discussion of the rates presently available can be found in Brabant (1988d).

major shortcoming of all previous attempts to introduce genuine multilateralism in the CMEA has indeed been that regular TR surpluses cannot be mobilized in the short run. Furthermore, there is as yet no multilateral agreement as to which bilateral exchange rates will be utilized. Inasmuch as there is no possibility to convert bilateral imbalances, the Ryzkov proposal is essentially concerned with facilitating simple settlements of decentralized transactions. Without some "stick" to enforce convertibility and to ensure its steady expansion, this laudable step forward is likely to remain just a constructive initiative without follow-up. The proposal is bound to get bogged down very quickly by the serious problems of incompatible domestic prices, the disarray in TRPs, and imbalances in the aggregate deliveries being offset against the regular trade accounting executed by the International Bank for Economic Cooperation (IBEC). One may therefore legitimately question whether interfirm relations will lead to a further Balkanization of bilateralism. Perhaps the continued pragmatism of external trade and foreign policy stances exhibited by Soviet leaders in recent years also may soon be applied in formulating a more transparent, revised version of the convertibility proposal. Such an amended proposal, even if it were to be applied only to two or three CMEA members bent on forging ahead, could demonstrate the possibilities of market-type criteria for enhancing SEI.[18]

The links of the reformed mechanism to the aforementioned new SEI program, as well as specifications on both, should have been the particular focus of the 44th Council Session. The Prague Session emphasized the need to have a mechanism in support of more intensive forms of economic development and integration. For that, the role of the economic tools of management must be improved, the function of cooperation through the coordination of national economic plans must be modified, and firms are now to play a much more significant role in the day-to-day pursuit of SEI. A particularly critical role in enhancing interfirm relations based on economic incentives falls onto the TR and TRPs. These and other elements of the refurbished economic mechanism of SEI are

18. The possibility of this subgroup of countries forging ahead was first grasped at the 43rd Session. It was underlined once again, even if it were to involve only a few countries, at the recent session of the Central Committee Secretaries in charge of economic affairs.

to be firmly in place in time for the introduction of the next medium-term plans in 1991. An unusual item on the agenda was the creation of socialist multinationals centered around key national firms. The Soviet Union declared that it was "prepared to study thoroughly [this idea] with those partners who are interested."[19] The suggestion had earlier been endorsed at the June meeting of the Central Committee Secretaries in charge of economic affairs.

On the Future Role of Planning and Plan Coordination

The 43rd Council Session gave little substantive attention to the need to better coordinate each member's economic plans and to provide supports at the regional level for direct enterprise relations. The GDR and Romania, as exemplified by the speeches at the 43rd Council Session delivered by Willy Stoph and Constantin Dascalescu, respectively, stressed the paramount role of plan coordination in one case to foster scientific-technological coordination and in the other to ensure prompt deliveries of adequate volumes of critical fuels and raw materials. These policy stances stand in shrill contrast to the role accorded to these instruments by the commentators of the other CPEs. Improving plan coordination was also debated in Prague, but in a limited way and only by the GDR and Romania. As Ryzkov stated, the new SEI mechanism should amount to:

> . . . a model of cooperation that, while preserving the forms that have proved valid, would be based on the criteria of efficiency, on the ever-increasing role of commodity-money relations and econo-mic instruments, and on engaging the countries' economic organi-zations in all areas of cooperation on a broad scale.[20]

Against this backdrop, expectations regarding the follow-up Council Session in 1989—as they were for the 44th[21]—are very high, particularly because the CPEs will be commemorating the

19. Only Ryzkov apparently raised it in Prague (*Pravda*, July 6, 1988, p. 4).
20. Speech reported in *Pravda*, July 7, 1988, p. 4.
21. Maciej K. Krzak (1988, 5) referred to it as the "summit of the ten."

40th anniversary of their organization. Not only must drafts on attitudes toward the developing-country CPEs and the new concept of long-term SEI be further refined, but the CPEs have also committed themselves to clarify details on the new SEI mechanism and its institutions and to further streamline the organizational structure of the CMEA. The future will be exciting, though one should not harbor illusions that a change in SEI can be implemented quickly.

Organizationally, the CMEA institutions do not as yet possess an international civil service staff dedicated to the ideals of SEI and imbued with a spirit to move forward with integration that derives from the economics of "new thinking" as it relates to regional cooperation. Even if these obstacles can be removed, there remains the paramount role of the symbiosis between domestic and regional reforms. If domestic reforms require moving forward for at least ten to fifteen years, the process of revamping the CMEA edifice is bound to take at least as long. Moreover, raising a generation of enterprise managers that will set its economic horizon against regional or global boundaries is not something that can be accomplished overnight.

IV. THE SOVIET UNION, THE WORLD ECONOMY, AND INTERNATIONAL ORGANIZATIONS

Shortly after the Soviet Union indicated it would seek reforms in its foreign trade organization, a note from the Soviet Council of Ministers dated August 12, 1986, was presented to the Director General of GATT. In it, the Soviet Union requested permission to take part as an observer in the then upcoming multilateral trade negotiation round in Punta del Este (Uruguay).[22] This *démarche*

22. Note that the Soviet Union did *not* request observership in the GATT as such. The distinction may be subtle but is nonetheless significant, as the Soviet Union may have been testing the waters that provide the ebb and flow of multilateral economic organizations. Requesting observership in the GATT would have gone a step beyond the one actually explored. Having been denied permission to participate in the Uruguay Round on the instigation of major Contracting Parties, the Soviet Union could conceivably apply for observership in the GATT, if circumstances favored such a move, without having to glance back at a formal diplomatic faux pas.

should not have been all that surprising, given that several high-level Soviet spokespersons earlier in the year had indicated that the Soviet Union had an interest in seeking some form of GATT participation and eventually an association with some Washington monetary institutions, including the International Monetary Fund and the International Bank for Reconstruction and Development (IBRD) and its affiliates (the World Bank), as well as other international financial organizations.[23] Tentative feelers regarding Bretton Woods institutions have been sent out, but Soviet spokespersons officially deny that the Soviet Union would seek some form of association with the IMF and the World Bank prior to a "fundamental" reform of the international monetary system. The latter should bring about a more stable exchange rate system, an "ideal" reserve currency rather than one based on national currencies that are by definition subject to domestically orientated monetary policies, and the elimination of veto power even in principle.[24]

Soviet intentions regarding the global economic framework should be examined. This is because the integration of the Soviet economy and Soviet participation in organized international economic relations *might* require and even facilitate discussions about reforming the global trading and financial frameworks.[25] Indeed, it might signal Soviet willingness to share part of the responsibility—and perhaps the burden—of maintaining stability and growth in the world economy through synchronization of macroeconomic policies, however discordant such policies in MEs and CPEs are likely to remain. Finally, it might create a new attitude on the part of the Soviet Union, and perhaps the socialist group as a whole, toward the North-South dialogue and

23. Including the Asian Development Bank, which the Soviet Union joined as an observer in 1987.

24. Soviet spokespersons realize that voting is not such a key issue in the Bretton Woods institutions, because most decisions are first reached through broad consensus. But the threat of a veto hangs over every potential issue, and hence Soviet interest in removing even that possibility.

25. I emphasize this in full awareness of the fact that the Soviet Union, or any other major socialist country for that matter, has not always constructively participated in international organizations. There is thus a largely political, but also administrative, fear—perhaps a presumption?—that the Soviet Union would join only to foment political controversy that might stifle the pragmatism of these organs.

responsibility for shouldering the burden of maintaining a minimum pace of development in the developing countries (DEs). Whether these changes can materialize within existing institutions, in new ones, or within the scope for U.N. deliberations is addressed in Section VII.

Given the chance for these changes, the curt refusal to entertain Soviet observership at the Uruguay Round is regrettable. Admittedly, the request as much as the denial was political in nature. Nonetheless, it should be recognized that there was a logic to the GATT request and the possibility of seeking closer association with multilateral economic organizations. First, in connection with the reform of the foreign trade system announced in mid-1986, it was logical for the Soviet Union to explore ways of "normalizing" relations with other countries, which would have provided greater flexibility for the economic agents granted autonomy in trade negotiations. But the eventual impact could have been much more profound, because there is evidence that "participation in the GATT and economic reform feed on each other" (Patterson 1986, 203). Furthermore, the foreign economic environment in early 1986 was unusually adverse, partly because of the sharp drop in oil prices, which placed severe constraints on pursuing the reform with the vigor that had been called for at the 27th Soviet Party Congress. The modernization of engineering sectors was selected as the pivot of the new 1986-1990 Five-Year Plan and the broader-based economic reconstruction envisaged by Mikhail Gorbachev. The marked shortfall in investment activity during the first full year of perestroika due to foreign economic developments may have made it imperative to broaden the scope of Gorbachev's strategy or at least to implement its requisite policies faster.[26]

By prematurely short-circuiting Soviet overtures to observer status at economic meetings, western governments may have curbed, perhaps inadvertently, Soviet confidence in the support the Soviet

26. Clearly, negotiations about accession would realistically have taken several years. The direct advantages accruing from membership could therefore have alleviated the short-run problems of the Soviet economy only in a minor way, if that. The interpretation that following up on the Soviet Union's request would have helped to "bail (it) out now that it has economic problems" (Dirksen 1987, 229) is without merit. But the initiative as such, even if in the end it would have been aborted, could have yielded immediate indirect effects in terms of "goodwill" and related intangibles.

Union could gain from international economic relations as they relate to the restructuring of the domestic economy. If western leaders are genuinely interested in Soviet reform, the response to the GATT feelers was most regrettable. In some contrast, the warm reaction to the more recent Soviet request to join the Multifibre Arrangement[27] can be interpreted as an implicit admission of the faux pas in August 1986. There are several reasons for this position that deserve attention.

First, it is questionable diplomatic practice to dismiss out of hand an overture in international economic relations without at least ascertaining and evaluating what precisely is at stake. This is particularly important when these areas of potential interaction have been strained for so many years by conditions that do not easily lend themselves to compromise without incurring a political cost.

Second, from an economic point of view, seeking to include the CPEs in the GATT has always been a contradiction in terms. The foundations of the trade framework of these countries rests on principles that are at considerable variance, if not wholly incompatible, with those that form the backbone of the GATT. Given the absence of market-type price signals and supporting institutions in the Soviet Union, it would have been useful to clarify what the Soviet Union intended to undertake in terms of domestic and trade reforms.

Third, when such an unusual announcement is issued by a major "outsider" to the global economic framework, the insiders need to explore which key aspects of its economic policies, policy instruments, and institutional supports the outsider would be willing to revise to strengthen its case to become part of the framework. This need not necessarily have been brought up immediately in terms of GATT "entrance fees"—chiefly the trade-off offered by the Soviet Union in return for most-favored nation (MFN) tariff concessions by the Contracting Parties. The technically complex issue of accession trade-offs, including broader aspects of commercial policy, could have been broached at a more appropriate time. A cogent argumentation of why the Soviet Union requested accession would have been very illuminating; the

27. As reported in the *New York Times,* August 28, 1987, pp. D1 and D3.

argument in favor of exploring the possibilities for GATT member- ship is compelling because the Soviet step was not apparently pre- ceded by the usual diplomatic efforts designed to sound out major partners about the chances of eliciting a favorable response.[28]

At the same time, exploration would have given the Soviets information about how prepared the western community is to modify important pillars of its multilateral trading system.[29] As is known, the international trading region has been crumbling in recent years into multiple systems that are only poorly interlinked, partly due to the so-called new protectionism of the 1980s. Major and minor shifts in trade policy may be required not only to accommodate countries that have traditionally excluded themselves from the GATT approach, but also to make the "global" trade system sufficiently flexible to allow wider participation.

Finally, the curt refusal to entertain the Soviet request may undermine whatever aspirations GATT has for universality (Kennedy 1987, 25). Although this point may appear to conflict with the second one, the two provide only a paradox that derives from the point of departure one may wish to take in seeking to regulate world trade. If, as some contend, "there is more to be gained by full and universal participation in the international discussions of economic affairs than there is by the exclusion of certain states" (Jackson 1969, 777), then the stance adopted in 1986 was shortsighted and does not augur well for bringing the Soviet Union into the global fold.[30]

28. Diplomatic channels were not even activated in an "informal way." This was particularly unusual in view of the well-known opposition for decades of U.S. interests to freeing up East-West trade from some of its political, strategic, and security shackles. Also, ever since the Soviet Union first approached the GATT, reportedly in late 1982 (interview material and Pankin [1986]), the GATT Secretariat has instructed Soviet emissaries to sound out first the key Contracting Parties. This *démarche* reportedly made in the past in response to GATT counsel was not repeated in 1986, however.

29. It is, of course, perfectly possible that the rebuff provided an indication that the western community—or perhaps mainly the United States?—is not at all prepared to entertain any change in the global trading framework. I am not yet sufficiently cynical to subscribe to this reading of events, however.

30. There are, of course, a host of other issues pertaining to policy coordination that could usefully be reexamined. See Artis and Ostry (1986) for a succinct run- down of some of the key problems.

V. THE SOVIET UNION AND OTHER CPEs IN THE GATT

One can realistically anticipate the Soviet Union's application for association to the GATT in the near future.[31] The many complex issues that are bound to crop up at that time could usefully be examined now so that the international community will be ready to tackle the special problems of negotiating Soviet accession. One set of tasks involves taking stock of the experiences of the CPEs in the GATT—to assess whether the CPEs have been satisfied with their participation in the GATT, whether they have obtained what they thought they had negotiated, and what avenues are available to improve their positions in the global trade framework. The other set of tasks refers specifically to the shortcomings and limitations of the GATT as an "organ" for regulating global trade by way of tariff concessions, and to the opportunity for rethinking the GATT due to requests for accession of major partners in world trade, such as China and the Soviet Union.

On the Fundamentals of the GATT Approach

The foundations of the GATT are reciprocity, nondiscrimination, transparency, and safeguards in international trade. A major objective of postwar trade negotiations was to reduce trade protection to *ad valorem* tariffs as much as politically feasible, with the goal to restrict divergences between domestic and foreign prices to the tariff and normal factors of time and place. The global trade order built after World War II sought to remove all forms of quantitative restrictions and to reduce tariffs through negotiations. In other words, nondiscrimination among all actors in the global economy—domestic as well as foreign, excepting the uniform external tariff to be negotiated away—was itself conditioned by the underlying assumption of the GATT tariff system that trade is conducted by private firms whose actions are guided by commercial, profit motives. Such an environment was expected to yield prices justified solely by commercial considerations.

---

31. Well-placed Soviet policymakers contend that such a request will be lodged before the end of 1990.

These objectives are, of course, perfectly compatible with the functioning of ideal MEs. The expansion of trade on a non-discriminatory basis and the reduction of tariffs as the paramount guides to bolstering trade would be impaired if private or state-sponsored monopolistic organizations were permitted to inhibit trade through discrimination. This follows from the difficulty of ensuring "free" market access and of restricting the operations of such firms to economic motives, given the potential influence of the state in the economy in general and state-controlled economic organizations in particular (Hartland-Thunberg 1987).

Among the myriad economic factors that hamper CPE participation in the GATT framework, their inability to satisfy the reciprocity test poses formidable conceptual and practical problems. Prices in CPEs by definition rarely are only a result of commercial factors or true economic scarcities, and economic decisions regarding the trade-offs between domestic and foreign supply are routinely derived from economic *and* a host of other factors. As a result, the GATT is fundamentally ill-equipped to cope with the CPEs, and requests of CPEs for accession to the GATT have been handled pragmatically.

GATT Provisions and the CPEs

The GATT has no specific provisions for CPEs other than its stipulations on state trading monopolies, that is, exceptions from the ME framework. Under GATT rules, such firms are expected to behave as much as possible like their private commercial counterparts and to enjoy a degree of protection as large as that agreed upon for the product group relevant to the monopoly. If applied to the CPE in this way, tariff negotiations must be concerned primarily with the setting of internal wholesale price levels and their structure, along with the special type of trade pricing prevailing within the CMEA.[32] This would entail

32. This peculiar trade price system emerged in good measure in conjunction with the creation of the CMEA in January 1949. But it needs to be stressed that the ensuing, rather peculiar, price determinants built upon pricing practices instituted in relations among the CPEs soon after the end of World War II. For details, see Brabant (1987b, 63-88).

discriminatory treatment of CPEs, for no domestic or regional pricing regulations are explicitly imposed upon other Contracting Parties. Furthermore, such negotiations would be very complex by virtue of the fact that prices in CPEs do not clear markets, thereby making it difficult to assess the real degree of protection.

For these and other reasons, it has been difficult to use the GATT as a framework for reintegrating CPEs into the world economy. In addition, the GATT has been unable to play a significant role in increasing East-West trade. In fact, this important aspect of intersystemic relations has not become the responsibility of any international organization, and it is doubtful that there is any organization in place that could be entrusted with it (Vernon 1979). Furthermore, the experiences of those CPEs that have been in the GATT since the 1960s have not been as trouble-free as had been anticipated, because the CPEs have not fully benefited from MFN status for a number of reasons. And finally, trade among the CPEs, even when GATT members, by and large has been ignored.

Earlier Accessions of the CPEs

The fundamental problems of integrating CPEs into the global trading framework were on the agenda of GATT debates on several occasions. The successive requests for accession first as observer, in some cases as an associate member,[33] and later as full member (Hungary, Poland, Romania, and Yugoslavia), led to many theoretical and practical questions. The responses were thoroughly pragmatic. For Poland and Romania, reciprocity was based on the granting of MFN status by MEs (with some restrictions chiefly on the part of the United States) in exchange for a commitment to increase imports from the Contracting Parties by a fixed percentage. Although not formally agreed upon, these conditions also apply to Cuba and Czechoslovakia—both founding members—as a

---

33. Associate status in fact implies that commercial relations between Contracting Parties and the STC can be conducted in conformity with the rules of the GATT to the extent possible under the STC's economic system. It also enables the country to participate in various organizational bodies of the GATT, including tariff negotiation rounds (Kostecki 1979, 25).

matter of policy rather than as per negotiated agreement.[34] The accession of Hungary was handled very differently, chiefly because it claimed, as Yugoslavia had earlier and Bulgaria and China are currently invoking, that its economic reform envisaged multi-tier tariffs that would eventually fully reconcile the difference between domestic and trade prices. These accessions were negotiated with special provisions, either the full import quota commitment (but with some modifications, notably on the degree of MFN treatment[35]) or by participating under special, limited arrangements.

The experience of the CPEs in the GATT indicates that the trade-off between quantitative import commitments and ME tariffs has not been very satisfactory for either the CPEs or MEs (Kostecki 1979). For one, the targeted import commitments had not taken into account the great inflation of the 1970s, the shifts in the commodity composition of trade, exchange rate fluctuations, global recessions, substantial price shocks, or the adjustment problems that the CPEs and many other countries had to face in the 1980s (Patterson 1986). From the point of view of the CPEs, the Contracting Parties preserved all too many quantitative restrictions, and some MEs have accorded MFN treatment only on a conditional basis.

Global Trade Issues and the Role of the CPEs

Being in essence a contract without members, the GATT is without the necessary institutional tools to anticipate, identify, and address problems in a systematic manner (Hartland-Thunberg 1987, 93). This is unfortunate not only for resolving CPE participation. It applies also in coming to grips with a great number of other issues: the specific problems of the newly industrializing countries (NICs) and the DEs more generally; structural change; graduation rules; the competitive export of unemployment; agricultural protectionism; nontariff barriers; and East-West economic issues,

34. After the February 1948 coup, Czechoslovakia became a CPE, but that development has been studiously put aside in GATT diplomacy except in relations with the United States. Likewise for Cuba since it made its decision more toward CPE status in 1962.

35. Note that this was foreseen in the Havana Charter (see Brabant 1988b).

to name only a few. Since the Tokyo Round, the GATT has been victimized by what Gadbaw calls the "Balkanization of international trade policy" (Gadbaw 1984, 38) in the form of a proliferation of "mini-GATTs," each having somewhat different decisionmaking and enforcement mechanisms, about which nobody seems to be happy. There is, as a result, a *prima facie* need for a comprehensive reassessment of the functions of the GATT in the international trading system and a concerted effort to improve the institutional mechanism for decisionmaking, rule development, dispute settlement, enforcement, and the coordination of national policies affecting trade. The world needs an institution that can reflect and cater to the interests of all nations that participate in a multilateral trading system by serving as a permanent forum for the international discussion of trade policy topics, as well as one that can reconcile a multitude of present and emerging trading problems through persuasion and mutual accommodation.

Many observers of the GATT continue to suggest that a formula based partly on access commitment and partly on undertakings of equal treatment might well be used more generally and more multilaterally as a means to integrate the CPEs into the global trade system. Thus, a special trade-off of tariff concessions on the part of MEs against some import commitment by the CPEs (with escape clauses such as those embedded in the bilateral access and participation agreements) could be easily elaborated. Such a protocol would essentially reflect the interest of countries in the expansion of trade by removing quantitative restrictions inherited from past nonaction or neglect, as well as those superimposed under the escape clauses, and preserve the inherent mercantilist bent of the GATT (Wolf 1987).

While it would be unproductive to seek accession of the Soviet Union, or China for that matter, on the basis of a slight ad hoc modification of the rules and regulations of the GATT, there are at least seven reasons for a reconsideration of traditional trading arrangements, taking into account the potential needs of CPEs.

First, the economic importance of East-West economic relations should not be underestimated. Clearly, there are marked asymmetries. One is manifested in the fact that, judging by any reasonable measure of trade shares and trade participation, this largely intra-European trade is comparatively much less important for the West than for the East.[36]   This asymmetry is likely to continue to prevail for as long as the CPEs refrain from engaging themselves more fully and more automatically in the global economy.   Even so, it bears to note that the burgeoning East-West trade of the late 1960s and early 1970s was dominated by large transnationals.   Effective reciprocity could foster exports by ME firms that cannot afford the investment required to "warm up the market," as the transnationals succeeded in doing so well.   The fact that in the past decade or so some small- to medium-sized enterprises have succeeded in becoming close trade partners of CPEs simply underlines the considerable potential that remains unexplored at this juncture.

Second, the acrimony over East-West trade and finance within the Atlantic Alliance suggests that taking some aspects of East-West economic relations out of the purely political realm would be constructive.   East-West economic relations could usefully be brought under more international control than is the case today by narrowing national security considerations to just that, which might not be an easy task.

Third, whenever participation in rule- or code-making is likely to be useful to all participants, there is every reason to facilitate its emergence.   This would be especially the case for CPEs that are prepared, to paraphrase Harriet Matejka (1982), to make state trading much more the "object" than the "instrument" of commercial policy.   Such a shift in emphasis by CPEs should be reciprocated in the trade policy stances of major MEs.

Fourth, to the extent that one grants credibility to the economic reforms under way in the Soviet Union, it would be helpful to seek ways and means of buttressing this process.   At the very least, one should do everything possible to avoid deliberately harming this societal transformation, the intentions of which are unprecedented in scope and depth.

Fifth, there would appear to be sufficient reason today to reiterate Gerschenkron's evaluation of the Soviet Union's role in

36. But it is not really irrelevant on the margin, as was demonstrated in the mid-1970s, for example, when East European demand provided some significant prop to the faltering level of economic activity in West Europe.

world economic affairs forty years ago: "Russia's reintegration into the world economy is of such a stupendous moment" (Gerschenkron 1947, 624) that a discussion of the potential of a newly conceived ITO is worth entertaining, even if in the end the Soviet Union, as in 1947, were to decide against joining.

Sixth, East-South economic interaction so far has not been very extensive or sufficiently dynamic over a sustained period of time to make the CPEs count in the aggregate trade prospects of the South, which has been unfortunate for both sides. A number of DEs have complained, on occasion bitterly, about the inadequate financial and trade support, let alone development assistance, provided by the CPEs. Providing an institutional framework for increasing East-South economic intercourse within a global trade framework might go a long way toward solidifying the foundations for meaningful change.

Finally, a radical change in the Soviet approach to economic decisionmaking is bound to have an impact on its major trading partners in East Europe, and hence on the CMEA as a whole.[37] It is crucial to bear in mind that the Soviet Union is *the* key member of the CMEA; its joining the global trade framework is bound to elicit bandwagon effects that affect the functioning of the CMEA economic mechanism (see Brabant 1987a, b, c) and the way in which the members interact.

Economic Reforms in CPEs and the Trade System

If the Soviet Union were to succeed in its aim to link domestic wholesale and foreign trade prices in a manner that is acceptable to those championing "free markets," a significant milestone would have been set toward evaluating how CPEs might exchange preferences for ME tariff concessions. Modified CPEs might still conduct trade through firms that enjoy a considerable monopoly over certain import or export products, but state trading is likely to remain very important due to the nature of property relations.

37. I am ignoring the potential effect on the other full members of the CMEA (Cuba, Mongolia, and Vietnam). But shifts in formal and indirect integration mechanisms will only marginally affect these non-European CPEs, as stressed recently in Abolichina, Bakoveckiy, and Medvedev (1987, 139).

Regardless of whether the international community in the end decides to opt for transforming the GATT or for replacing it with an ITO-like institution, the CPEs cannot in the short run be expected to diversify their trade, abandon their bilateralism overnight, or introduce drastic shifts in their trade patterns either by commodity or by partner, or both, within a brief period of time. An acceptable proposal must therefore be tailored to present and foreseeable needs (see Brabant 1987d), including stipulations regarding the purpose of the proposed transition. For this change to be productive, agreement by the international community on guidelines for the transition phase is critical. It is even more important to resolve such principles as preferences for DEs, transition phases in regional integration schemes, graduation rules, the role of the newly industrializing DEs or NICs, the regulation of the trade of the transnationals, and many more.

With respect to CPEs, there is the need for at least three such amendments.[38] First, it has been hypocritical for years to maintain that all traded goods, not to mention services, are dealt with equally in the existing, ostensibly multilateral, trading world. The examples of steel, automobiles, semiconductors, textiles, and agricultural products suffice to support my proposition. It might therefore be constructive to elaborate some *modus vivendi* on the maximum degree of "natural" protection, and in which form such national preferences might be acceptable to all major actors. Such natural protection could be agreed upon for areas of "national security"—minimum levels of domestic food production at whatever cost springs to mind here.

Second, it is incorrect to maintain that all members of the GATT benefit symmetrically from any set of conditions that Contracting Parties may agree upon. Geographical or systemic differentiation needs to be explicitly recognized to accommodate the CMEA on an equal footing with the protection and regulation envisaged by ME integration schemes.

Third, the international economic scene since the 1970s offers little evidence that domestic prices of imported goods are set equal

38. I can only repeat what Frank Holzman has said so eloquently: [Because] "I am an economist rather than a lawyer, political scientist, or politician, my proposals are very general and should be viewed as judgments and sentiments based on economic analysis" (Holzman 1974, 219).

to their landed import price converted at the official exchange rate plus the tariff and domestic distribution and profit margins. As the instability of the dollar in the 1980s has so amply demonstrated, domestic prices of imported goods are frequently "managed" by the exporting firm or its affiliates, certainly in the short to medium run. CPEs, it could be argued, act in a similar way when their trading companies operate on the basis of commercial principles.

The aforementioned features invite the identification of comparable attributes in CPEs, especially a growing autonomy of CPE trading companies and their entitlement to "manage" their own profits. The link between domestic wholesale and trade prices would therefore emerge only "on average," but clearly on the basis of commercial decisionmaking by largely autonomous companies. Of course, tariffs would play an integral part in these modified economies and could be made the subject of international negotiations about MFN treatment. In addition, subsidies and taxes imposed by governments to further certain societal preferences would have to be tolerated. It is critical that CPE governments commit themselves to transforming such preferences to *ad valorem* taxes and subsidies within an agreed period of time.

It would be a mistake to regard these changes as the erosion or abandonment of the state monopoly of foreign trade and payments (MFT) in the Soviet Union or any other CPE.[39] It is possible that the MFT can become an object of foreign economic policymaking— that is, the macroeconomic steering of foreign trade and payments by indirect instruments as well as potentially far-reaching controls over trade and foreign exchange strategies. There is certainly room for greater clarity on the realistic reform intentions and how to take into account "gradualism" in considering Soviet accession to the GATT (Patterson 1986, 203).

During the transition phase, reciprocity could be based on the commitment of the CPEs to giving increasingly more attention to commercial decisionmaking by autonomous enterprises, to making explicit government preferences that influence the setting of

39. Kennedy (1987, 34) posits this as a precondition for GATT accession, but I believe this misconception stems from treating the MFT solely as an instrument. The same kind of shortsightedness appears in his call (p. 35) for the abandonment of central planning as a precondition for joining the GATT.

domestic retail prices relative to wholesale and trade prices, and to setting clear guidelines for how trading companies are expected to assist with maintaining some desirable degree of domestic price stability through the management of profits. Once these conditions are agreed to, the prime justification for reciprocity should be found in ensuring that the fundamental link between domestic and trade prices be as tight as possible based on accepted principles and CPE commitments. This avenue should be explored as much as possible, because import commitments would be inconsistent with the spirit of the major economic and trade reforms presently under way. As Herzstein (1986, 389) has noted with regard to negotiations with China, the precedent for using import commitments, their incompatibility with the reforms now under way, and the rigidities and market foreclosures they leave in place could not be resolved by a modified import commitment scheme. For such trade to flourish, the benefits to be derived must be superior to their associated costs. Improving stability and restoring multilateralism in global trade, which should also be key concerns of the Soviet Union (Ceklin 1987; Pankin 1986), can only benefit the GATT Contracting Parties.

Clearly, these and related matters would have to be the object of intensive trade negotiations that might take years to bear fruit. In that sense, the overture offered by the Soviet Union in mid-1986 was a missed opportunity to embark on a fundamental rethinking of the international trading system. At the very least, it could have facilitated real decisionmaking once the Soviet Union requested to join the pillars of organized international economic relations.

VI. THE CMEA-EC FRAMEWORK AGREEMENT: MORE THAN DIPLOMACY?

After fifteen years of negotiations about the establishment of formal diplomatic relations between the EC and the CMEA, both sides signed an agreement on June 25, 1988, in Luxembourg. The joint declaration, drawn up in no fewer than seventeen authoritative versions, states essentially that the two sides "will develop cooperation in areas which fall within their respective spheres of competence and where there is common interest." This is decidedly a meager result of the protracted negotiations on normalizing relations between the two parts of Europe.

Apart from its obvious diplomatic and political dimensions, one may well question whether the framework agreement really matters, especially because it is no more than a simple statement of mutual recognition. As Willy De Clercq, the EC Commissioner for External Relations, noted, the accord represents "a great change in attitude" and will contribute to East-West "détente."[40]

Perhaps the most important immediate consequence is that the framework agreement enables individual CMEA countries to sign bilateral trade agreements with the EC. The Soviet Union appears to be keen on concluding such an arrangement in the very near future, and so encouraged the framework agreement as a necessary preliminary step. In fact, even before the signing of the agreement on June 25, Bulgaria, Czechoslovakia, the GDR, and the Soviet Union informed the EC Commission that they wished to establish diplomatic relations with the Community. The other CMEA members are expected to follow suit very soon. Creating such a link has been a desirable option for a number of CPEs, including Czechoslovakia, Hungary, and Romania, for quite some time. Czechoslovakia and Hungary rapidly concluded their agreement, and Romania renegotiated the special arrangement first signed in 1983.

To be sure, the EC's formal treaty powers are limited strictly to commercial policy as traditionally understood, hence the reference in the framework agreement to the "respective spheres of competence." All other types of international economic relations, including credits, technology, the environment, information, and so on, remain in the jurisdiction of the EC member governments. The same is true for the CMEA members, even for commercial policy.[41] Even so, especially now that the EC governments have resolved to move toward a truly unified European market by 1992, one can anticipate greater harmonization of these other

---

40. The text of the agreement and De Clercq's comments are quoted from *European Community News*, 1988: 16, pp. 1-2.

41. The EC Commission utilized this for many years as a pretext to refuse to come to terms on an agreement with the CMEA on the ground that it might reinforce Soviet control over East Europe—a rather weak argument.

components of international economic relations to come to the fore in the years ahead.

The next step is the elaboration of bilateral trade and cooperation agreements. These agreements initially will be confined to extending to the CPEs some form of MFN treatment, perhaps even more favorable quota allotments for some products, more circumspect treatment in the EC's imposition of protectionist steps, and other such trade-enhancing measures. If the CPEs can capitalize on these overtures through effective shifts in their export supply in EC markets, they might begin more productive economic and other interactions with the EC.

In viewing the potential impact of the EC-CMEA agreement and follow-up bilateral agreements, the observer should move beyond the purely commercial aspects of these protocols. It might indeed be highly useful to take a fresh look at the fundamental issues of the politics and history of East-West relations. In endorsing the EC-CMEA agreement, both sides have obvious political aims that transcend the purely reciprocal economic incentives. They even go beyond the purely European aspects of the agreement. West Europe has been firmly entrenched in the Atlantic Alliance. Although the DMEs share a number of common political goals, national/regional security interests, and military concepts on strategy and defense, there may now be greater room for West Europe to affirm itself more self-consciously than it has done over the past few decades.

VII. TOWARD GREATER ECONOMIC SECURITY

There appears to be growing sentiment among policymakers that, generally speaking, there is presently greater insecurity in international economic relations than in recent memory. Expressions of such feelings have been aired by national governments, at intergovernmental and regional institutions and gatherings, and in many meetings of organizations that have formed the pillars of international economic relations since World War II. The perceived insecurity has many dimensions, ranging from the potential and actual use of economic force as an overt weapon of foreign policy, sharp fluctuations in international trade prices, and the rise of protectionism, to a feeling of loss of control by national policymakers over the international dimensions of their respective economies.

Some of the aforementioned phenomena may have emanated from the fluctuations and instability inherent in an inter-dependent global economy. The perceived insecurity in the last two decades or so derives largely from the rapid growth of global interdependence at a time of economic and financial integration. The multilateral approach to international economic affairs exemplified by international organizations created after World War II has increasingly been questioned. Indeed, policymakers have allowed key aspects of the institutional mechanisms put in place after World War II to erode or to be replaced by less formalized and controlled mechanisms. Equally as important is the increasing loss of control of policymakers over national and international economic affairs because of sharp changes in national economic institutions and a disregard for some of the key agreements that were designed to regulate international relations in the postwar period.

These and other developments have led to several calls for examining ways and means of enhancing international economic security (IES). Because the concept of national security has for the most part been dealt with in military and strategic terms, IES is often seen as an alternative to ensuring security by merely military means. There is obviously a strategic dimension, but a broader view would be useful, as IES conceptually has several dimensions that have no links at all with military or strategic concerns.

Even if confined to its strategic context, individuals and government spokespersons calling for enhancing IES can hold very different views as to which parts of the strategy should be emphasized. There are at least three views: (1) the resources mobilized for economic and military preparedness, including in selecting partners for economic cooperation; (2) the existence of an actual or perceived threat to some vital aspect of a country's livelihood, such as food or energy security; and (3) the generation of new ideas regarding the better organization of international economic relations so as to promote peace by averting armed confrontations.[42] Discussions on what causes insecurity are even less prone to yield broader international or national agreement.

The quest for IES is an inevitable consequence of the increasing economic interdependence of states, primarily through foreign trade, but also through direct foreign investment, other types of international capital mobility, and international labor flows. The integration of a national economic system into the world economy, while widening the range of economic opportunities, makes a country vulnerable to more or less serious disruptions caused by developments in other countries, beyond its own jurisdiction and control. The closer the economic links between countries, the wider the range of measures that can have such consequences.

The collective search for security is being recognized as the search for common security, indicating that the security of one state cannot be enhanced at the explicit expense of another state's security. Collective security, in other words, is seen not as a zero-sum game, but as a positive-sum game. Many of the challenges arising from asymmetrical vulnerabilities, diversity of actors, and so on, are salient, because states depend on trade and financial relations with each other, yet they carry risks. Some risks stem from potential adverse economic developments abroad or from political conflicts in other parts of the world that result in the disruption of trade routes or foreign markets and sources of supply. Others are associated with the possibility that foreign governments will make decisions, adopt policies, or pass laws that have adverse economic consequences for one's economy.

The postwar international economic order had been aimed at averting the kind of disorder that developed in the 1930s by managing interdependence through international economic and financial institutions, particularly the GATT and the IMF. These organizations were conceived at a time when the developmental concerns that came to the fore in the late 1950s and later were only a subsidiary issue in the policy debate. Furthermore, these organizations did not include the CPEs. By design, but also as a

---

42. The recent discussion of the creation of an "International Economic Security Council" in the context of the United Nations is an example of this use of the security metaphor.

result of later preoccupations, these organizations were fundamentally aiming at the trade and financial problems of DMEs. Some modifications were introduced to permit accession of DEs and some CPEs, but the fundamental philosophy of these institutions has not really thus far been reappraised in any comprehensive manner.   Both groups tried to enhance their economic security by fostering greater economic, financial, and technical integration among themselves.   In addition, many countries have undertaken efforts in the United Nations, notably in UNCTAD, to improve the international economic environment for DEs.   There also have been other ways in which countries have cooperated in recent years, ranging from simple exchanges of information to agreeing upon certain common economic objectives, methods to go about them, and rules to reduce the level of conflict and uncertainty.   Note that these forms, including contractual ones, have not depended on countries accepting binding commitments in the name of an overarching "collective economic security" objective.

Perhaps more important are issues that stem from systemic economic insecurity.   Vulnerabilities here arise not from national actors or contractual arrangements among sovereign states, but from the working of the global economy as a whole.   Systemic economic security has to do with the rules and behavioral norms needed to monitor and reduce the vulnerabilities generated by economic policies or decisions that have systemwide reverberations.   Such an approach is necessarily associated with a redefinition of the precepts of national sovereignty to attempt to understand global hazards.   Examples are a change in a key lending rate or a supply shock from abroad.

The principal weaknesses of postwar international economic organizations are their inability to prevent—or at least to come to grips with—deep recession in the world economy, an ongoing debt crisis of major dimensions, powerful protectionist tendencies, great fluctuations of exchange rates, large payments imbalances, and the collapse of commodity prices.   The key institutions around which international economic relations have centered were originally not designed to avert or even to come to grips with the major economic shocks of the 1970s and their aftermath in the 1980s.   In addition, these institutions failed to change as the bipolar world that prevailed following World War II became more complex.

The ultimate importance of IES is to offer a more meaningful conception of security than the one sought by military means. A renewed commitment to maintaining openness, to providing timely and adequate information, and to equal treatment in international affairs might provide a useful start. It would be instructive to reappraise the mandate given to the United Nations at its inception. Article 1 of the Charter leaves no doubt about the organization being called upon to become "a centre for harmonizing the actions of nations in the attainment" of achieving "international co-operation in solving international problems of an economic, social, cultural, or humanitarian character."

In connection with institutionalized forms of international order, the international community could attempt to bring about greater universality. One subject to be discussed is whether systemic differences remain too great for meaningful participation of CPEs in multilateral organizations such as the GATT or the IMF. The debate on fostering greater IES "across the systemic divide" (North-South, East-West, and East-South) could usefully envisage the implications of the guidelines for formulating macro- and microeconomic policies and of the reshaped institutions and instruments that the CPEs set for their agents. At this crucial formative stage, the international community, rather than rejecting overtures of certain CMEA members, could start a constructive dialogue and communicate to the countries the minimum terms for a meaningful accession to any of the existing international economic organizations.

Alternatively, special bodies might be better suited to identify ways of reducing very marked transaction costs and making things more businesslike. Such special organs might more easily accommodate regimes that recognize the primacy of the CMEA for most of its member countries, while at the same time encouraging mutually reinforcing modifications in policies, institutions, and development strategies. Also, the experience of many DEs in the recent debt crisis makes it essential to consider ways of avoiding such financial instability in the future, while nonetheless ensuring capital flows in amounts appropriate to and compatible with development potential. Another subject of special concern to

DEs is how to enhance South-South trade to make up for the low-growth period of the industrial economies that is expected to persist for some time.

Key aspects of any acceptable concept of IES revolve around the creation of more transparency, stability, predictability, and reliability in international economic relations. Such a development would require that the interests of states with different socioeconomic systems, stages of development, and size be adequately recognized and given fair attention. The existing global, regional, and sectoral arrangements need to be reviewed in light of the changing requirements of global economic interdependence.

VIII. CONCLUSION

At the very least, economic integration depends on the vigorous pursuit of perestroika, not only in the Soviet economy, but by the CMEA as a whole. A critical determinant will be the Soviet Union's perception of its role and responsibility in global economic affairs and global security affairs. That is not to deny an equivalent responsibility on the part of western partners, who could usefully reevaluate their collective strategy on how to do business with the socialist world.

If new attitudes were to evolve in both the East and the West, we might be justified in looking forward to a world that would not only be safer and saner, but would also be a world in which ideological differences would not be allowed to jeopardize economic and political cooperation. If this were to occur, a new Europe could emerge—the first time continentwide peace might be restored since the Vienna Congress in 1815.

REFERENCES

Abolichina, Galina A., Oleg Bakoveckiy, and Boris I. Medvedev. 1987. "Sushchnost' i novyye formy sotsialisticheskoy integratsii." *Voprosy ekonomiki,* No. 1: 129-40.

Artis, Michael, and Sylvia Ostry. 1986. *International Economic Policy Coordination.* London: Routledge & Kegan Paul, for the Royal Institute of International Affairs.

Brabant, Jozef M. van. 1987a. *Adjustment, Structural Change, and Economic Efficiency—Aspects of Monetary Cooperation in Eastern Europe.* New York: Cambridge University Press.

——. 1987b. *Regional Price Formation in Eastern Europe—On the Theory and Practice of Trade Pricing.* Dordrecht: Kluwer Academic Publishers.

——. 1987c. "Economic Reform and Monetary Cooperation in the CMEA." Paper prepared for the Workshop on Financial Reform in Eastern Europe, held at the Istituto Universitario Europeo, San Domenice di Fiesole (Firenze), October 12-16, 1987. Issued by the World Bank in late 1988.

——. 1987d. "The GATT and the Soviet Union—A Plea for Reform." *DIESA Working Paper Series,* No. 6.

——. 1988a. *Economic Integration in Eastern Europe—A Reference Book.* Manuscript.

——. 1988b. "Planned Economies in the GATT Framework—The Soviet Case." *Soviet Economy,* No. 1: 3-35.

——. 1988c. "Regional Integration, Economic Reforms, and Convertibility." *Jahrbuch der Wirtschaft Osteuropas—Yearbook of East-European Economics* 13, 1.

——. 1988d. "Wither the CMEA?—Reconstructing Socialist Economic Integration." Paper presented at the AAASS meetings in Honolulu, Hawaii, November 18-21.

Cheklin, Vladimir N. 1987. "SSSR i GATT." *Vneshnyaya torgovlya,* No. 7: 37-39.

CMEA. 1977. *Osnovyye dokumenty Soveta ekonomicheskoy vzaimopo-moshchi —tom 2.* Moscow: SEV Sekretariat, 3rd edition.

——. 1986. *Kursom nauchno-tekhnicheskogo progressa — 41-oe (vneocherednoye) zasedaniye Sessii Soveta ekonomicheskoy vzaimopo-moshchi.* Moscow: SEV Sekretariat.

Dirksen, Erik. 1987. "What if the Soviet Union Applies to Join the GATT?" *World Economy*, No. 2: 228-30.

Gadbaw, R. Michael. 1984. "The Outlook for GATT as an Institution." In *Managing Trade Relations in the 1980s —Issues Involved in the GATT Ministerial Meeting —1982*. Eds. Seymour J. Rubin and Thomas R. Graham. Totowa, NJ: Rowland and Allenheld, pp. 33-49.

Gerschenkron, Alexander. 1947. "Russia and the International Trade Organization." *American Economic Review*, No. 2: 624-42.

Hartland-Thunberg, Penelope. 1987. "China's Modernization: A Challenge for the GATT." *The Washington Quarterly*, No. 1: 81-97.

Herzstein, Robert E. 1986. "China and the GATT: Legal and Policy Issues Raised by China's Participation in the General Agreement on Tariffs and Trade." *Law and Policy in International Business*, No. 2: 371-415.

Holzman, Franklyn D., ed. 1974. "East-West Trade and Investment: Past and Future Policy Issues." In *Foreign Trade Under Central Planning*. Cambridge, MA: Harvard University Press, pp. 192-239.

Ikonnikov, Igor. 1988. "Sovershenstvovaniye struktury SEV." *Ekonomicheskoye sotrudnichestvo stran-chlenov SEV*, No. 2: 20-21.

Jackson, John H. 1969. *World Trade and the Law of the GATT*. Indianapolis, IN: Bobbs-Merrill.

Kennedy, Kevin C. 1987. "The Accession of the Soviet Union to GATT." *Journal of World Trade Law*, No. 2: 23-39.

Kostecki, M.M. 1979. *East-West Trade and the GATT System*. London: Macmillan, for the Trade Policy Research Centre.

Krzak, Maciej K. 1988. "Idziemy nierownym krokiem." *Zycie Gospodarcze*, No. 29: 5.

Matejka, Harriet. 1982. "Trade-Policy Instruments, State Trading and the First-Best Trade Intervention." In *State Trading in International Markets — Theory and Practice of Industrialized and Developing Countries*. Ed. Maciej M. Kostecki. London: Macmillan, pp. 142-60.

Pankin, M. 1986. "SSSR i GATT: perspektivy vzaimodeystviya." *Ekonomicheskaya gazeta*, No. 49: 23.

Patterson, Eliza R. 1986. "Improving GATT Rules for Nonmarket Economies." *Journal of World Trade Law*, No. 2: 185-205.

Shiryaev, Yuriy S. 1988. "SEV: sovremennaya strategiya ekonomicheskogo i nauchno-tekhinechesko sotrudnichestva." *Izvestiya akademii nauk — seriya ekonomicheskaya*, No. 1: 3-17.

Tokareva, Praskov'ya A., ed. 1972. *Mnogostoronnoye ekonomicheskoye sotrudnichestvo sotsialisticheskikh gosudarstv — sbornik dokumentov*. Moscow: Yuridicheskaya literatura, 2nd ed.

Vernon, Raymond. 1979. "The Fragile Foundations of East-West Trade." *Foreign Affairs*, No. 5: 1035-51.

Vetrovsky, Jiri, and Vasil Hrinda. 1988. "Zuctovani primych vztahu v narodnich menach CSSR a SSSR — rubl a koruna." *Hospodarske Noviny*, No. 15: 3.

Wolf, Martin. 1987. "Differential and More Favorable Treatment of Developing Countries and the International Trading System." *The World Bank Economic Review*, No. 4: 647-68.

CHAPTER 8

The CMEA's Dilemma: More Intra-CMEA Trade or More Trade with the West?

MICHAEL MARRESE

INTRODUCTION

By understanding four trends, the dilemma of more intra-CMEA trade or more trade with the West is resolved in favor of more trade with the West. The four trends that support this conclusion are: Soviet perestroika (restructuring); the growing problems within the Council for Mutual Economic Assistance (CMEA);[1] the deepening of East Europe's economic crisis; and the decline in Soviet terms of trade. Section I of this paper addresses Soviet perestroika from a Soviet perspective, while Section II examines the same phenomenon from a Hungarian perspective. In Section III, the CMEA's growing problems and East Europe's deepening economic crisis are discussed. Section IV covers the decline in Soviet terms of trade and the East European response to that decline.

My special thanks go to Alexei Kvasov and Martin Spechler for their valuable advice, to IREX for funding my 1986-1987 research visit to Hungary, and to the Hudson Institute and Northwestern University for financial assistance. I am very grateful to Scott Johnson, Thomas Maycock, and Lauren Wittenburg for their outstanding research assistance, and to Paula Nielsen for her excellent word processing. All remaining errors are my full responsibility.

1. In this paper, CMEA will refer to the Soviet Union and the East European CMEA countries: Bulgaria, Czechoslovakia, the GDR, Hungary, Poland, and Romania.

Finally, the conclusion in Section V offers an overall evaluation of the aforementioned trends that leads to alternative paths for CMEA reform, each of which points toward more trade with the West.

I. SOVIET PERESTROIKA FROM A SOVIET PERSPECTIVE

Mikhail S. Gorbachev has recognized that the Soviet Union must be technologically and organizationally transformed to achieve the productivity levels and quality standards of advanced western countries.[2] Support for some sort of change has been widespread because Soviet leaders and the Soviet people have recognized the decline during 1970-1985 in the rates of growth of national income, industrial output, agricultural output, fixed assets commissioned, investment, employment, labor productivity, per capita real income, and foreign trade turnover.

Although there has been less agreement on the slowdown's causes, the following views of Tatyana I. Zaslavskaya have been influential in convincing Gorbachev of the need for broad-ranging radical reform by arguing that the economic slowdown is rooted in the "inability of this system to make provision for the full and sufficiently effective use of the labor potential and intellectual resources of society" (Zaslavskaya 1984, 88). The term *uskoreniye* (acceleration) has been a prominent part of this broad-ranging view of reform. Well before the radical reform is to be fully implemented, *uskoreniye* is expected to reverse declining growth rates, encourage innovation, change economic institutions, and revitalize the population (the human factor).[3] The economic aims of *uskoreniye* are to be achieved simply by tapping the creative energy of the Soviet people, increasing discipline, and implementing minor policy changes.

Glasnost (a public airing or increased public openness) has become an important component of both *uskoreniye* and the reform process. From an economic viewpoint, glasnost has been used to convince the population of the need for radical economic reform, to encourage citizens to be publicly critical of mistakes made by enter-

---

2. See, for instance, Gorbachev (1987).
3. This discussion follows Hewett (1988, 306-43).

prises and local governments, and to promote increased public accountability of high-level bureaucrats, party officials, and managerial personnel. Other attractive aspects of glasnost have included new cultural opportunities and an increase in artistic freedom.

The promise of democratization has been another element in unleashing the human factor. Under Stalin, people fulfilled their job-related responsibilities partly out of fear. Since Stalin, material incentives and equity-promoting policies—such as a narrowing of wage differentials, profit leveling among enterprises, and the virtual absence of dismissal from one's job—rather than fear have increasingly motivated people.[4] These equity-promoting policies created a great deal of economic security for Soviet citizens; however, this economic security is expected to be severely reduced by the proposed perestroika. Therefore, democratization in the form of greater worker participation in decisionmaking is being designed to lessen this loss of security by increasing employees' control over their own economic destiny.

The concepts of acceleration, openness, and democratization have been part of Gorbachev's campaign to win support for perestroika since his accession to power in March 1985. However, it was only during the June 1987 Plenum that a clear outline of the proposed radical economic reform was published.[5]

Ed A. Hewett (1988, 349-50) concludes that the *Basic Theses for the Radical Restructuring of the Management of the Economy* rest on four essential principles:

> First, and most important, the Soviet economy will still be a centrally planned economy. But planning will focus on only the most important variables of national importance, leaving all operational decisions to lower levels. Planners will use economic instruments to control economic activity, eschewing any resort to micromanagement through direct commands to individual enterprises.
>
> Second, it will be a system in which success and failure for enterprises and for individuals will be determined impersonally,

4. Profit leveling occurs when the more productive enterprises are taxed more heavily than enterprises of average productivity to subsidize low productivity enterprises.

5. *"Osnovnyye polozheniya korennoy perestroyki upravleniya ekonomiki"* (*Basic Theses for the Radical Restructuring of the Management of the Economy*), *Pravda*, June 27, 1987.

ording to publicly specified, and inviolable, rules based on
onomic—not political—criteria . . . .

The third principle follows from the first two: enterprises in the new
system have the right to their autonomy in operational decisions. In
part this is the obverse of the prohibition against micromanagement
by the center. But far more important is the fact that if enterprises
are to be held responsible for their success and failure, they must be
able to make their own decisions without the interference of any
outside authority, whether it be party or government, local or
national. Outside interference provides the enterprise with the
justification to argue for exceptions.

That leads to the fourth and final principle: individual workers will
exercise control over management so that they can participate in the
decisions that lead to the success or failure of the enterprise.
Without that right, the failure of the enterprise is only a failure of
the state-appointed management, which provides the workers with
the excuse they need to argue for exceptions.

These four principles are based on the fundamental belief that
increased enterprise authority, accountability, and self-reliance in
an environment conditioned by the center's sensible financial
regulation are *all that are necessary* for economic efficiency.[6] Essentially, Soviet reformers have reached the same conclusions that
Hungarian reformers held in the 1960s, namely that the negative
features of central planning can be eliminated by replacing
centrally determined plan targets and supply allocations for
enterprises with a market-guided system based on profit sharing
for enterprise managers and workers. In this model, central
authorities would guide the market along lines consistent with
central preferences via control of taxes, subsidies, interest rates,
access to credit and foreign currencies, import licenses, and
foreign exchange multipliers.[7]

6. The "center" (or equivalently, central authorities) includes the Council of
Ministers, branch ministries, functional ministries, and the various levels of the
Communist Party. These institutions have a great deal of influence on enterprise
decisionmaking.
7. Central preferences refer to decisions about either plan targets or financial
variables (taxes, subsidies, et cetera). Such decisions do not come from maximization of a social welfare function, but rather are the end product of bargaining
among central decisionmakers.

Two facets of the Soviet implementation of radical reform disturb economists both inside and outside the Soviet Union. First, there has been an unwillingness to permit market-determined outcomes to hinder fulfillment of the center's priorities. For instance, the elimination of annual centrally determined mandatory plan targets for enterprises may well occur, yet GOSPLAN (State Planning Commission), ministries, and republican authorities will be able to demand that enterprises fulfill "state orders" (*goszakazy*) to ensure that the government's priorities are not neglected. In addition, each medium- and large-size enterprise will receive five-year control figures (*kontrolnyye tsifry*) that describe the center's expectations for that enterprise in terms of value of output, foreign exchange earnings, technical progress, and the social services provided to all employees (Hewett 1988, 329). Another example appears in the government's new policy toward private and cooperative activity. This policy permits full-time state employees in their spare time, and those with a valid reason for not being state employees (pensioners, housewives, and students), to form cooperatives to improve the supply of consumer goods and services. This official realm of cooperative activity has been explicitly constructed to avoid any significant drain of labor from the state sector. A final example of the center's unwillingness to trust market outcomes comes from the introduction of new wage rates and salaries in the material branches of industry—a process that is to be completed by 1990.[8] This aspect of radical reform consists of *wage-setting by central authorities* in which basic wage and salary rates form a larger portion of take-home pay than previously; skill differentials are being widened; greater scope is being given to offer bonuses based on individual and enterprise performance; and enterprises must finance their own wage increases.[9]

Second, the radical reform has neglected thus far the fact that competitive pressure is needed to combat monopoly power and to encourage Soviet firms to produce more efficiently, to invest more wisely, and to innovate. There are two sources of competitive pressure: domestic competitiveness via "easy entry" into profitable

8. For details, see *O sovershenstvovanii* (1986) or Chapman (1988).
9. Administrative wage reform is occurring in all other areas of the economy as well.

industries and foreign competitiveness in the form of imports. Easy entry into profitable industries may be possible at an advanced stage of Soviet economic reform, when the problems of capital accumulation and capital mobility have been solved, though domestic competitiveness should be expected to be weak in the Soviet manufacturing sector for the next several decades.[10] Meanwhile, using competitive imports to put pressure on enterprises has not received much attention from the Soviet leadership.[11]

Given the Soviet reluctance to trust the market and to endorse competitive pressure, it is not surprising that foreign trade reform has been modest. Three changes in Soviet foreign trade decision-making occurred during 1986-1987: the formation of the State Commission for Foreign Economic Relations; new regulations allowing greater opportunities for joint ventures; and an expansion of direct foreign trade rights from complete supervision by the Ministry of Foreign Trade to shared supervision by the Ministry of Foreign Trade, twenty branch ministries, and about seventy enterprises (Hewett 1988, 342). The State Commission for Foreign Economic Relations is expected to coordinate the Soviet Union's foreign trade policy and to ensure that the center's interests are fulfilled. The new regulations for joint ventures do not address the major disadvantages associated with foreign investment in the Soviet Union, namely the inconvertibility of the ruble, the type of access a joint venture will have to inputs, and the extent of control a joint venture will have over output, marketing, and pricing decisions. The expansion of direct foreign trade rights is deceptively small because the Ministry of Foreign Trade retains control over all foreign trade organizations responsible for trade in fuels, food, and raw materials, and because CMEA trade is still conducted via

10. Currently, domestic competitiveness would be nonexistent in most of the manufacturing sector because of manufacturing's highly concentrated industrial structure and the existence of a seller's market for most manufactured goods (partly due to the population's huge reserve of purchasing power). Because economies of scale have not played such a large role in the development of the construction sector, agriculture, and retail trade, it would be easier for domestic competitiveness to develop in these areas.

11. This statement is consistent with the author's discussions with Soviet economists and with a reading of *Osnovnyye polozheniya* or *Osnovnyye napravleniya* (1986). See also Hewett (1988, 352).

bilateral barter between government-level negotiators.[12] My interpretation of these limitations is that most nonsocialist trade in machinery, equipment, means of transportation, and industrial products is not controlled by the Ministry of Foreign Trade;[13] in fact, only 10.7 percent of Soviet exports to nonsocialist countries and 28.8 percent of Soviet imports from nonsocialist countries (Table 8-1) would not have been controlled by the Ministry of Foreign Trade in 1985.[14]

Such modest foreign trade decentralization is to be expected until the Soviet economy has reformed its price system. A market-oriented Soviet price system is a prerequisite if enterprises are to have control over decisions regarding inputs, outputs, and markets; have direct access to foreign markets and foreign currencies; and face prices that are actively connected to prices on foreign markets. In addition, the tremendous distortions between relative domestic prices of tradeables and the corresponding foreign trade prices need to be eliminated if the ruble is to be convertible.

However, the current Soviet perspective concerning price reform is neither domestically nor internationally market-oriented. Certainly the statements of Nikolay Petrakov, Chairman of the Interdepartmental Council on Problems of Price Formation of the Academy of Sciences of the Soviet Union and of the State Committee for Prices, suggest that there are enough distortions in the current system from a strictly domestic point of view to keep price reformers quite busy. The changes Petrakov sees as necessary for price reform are offered in three recommendations (Petrakov 1987, 137-40). First, relative wholesale prices of products from the extractive and manufacturing sectors should be based on the average cost of the marginal producer or on shadow prices generated by large mathematical programming models rather than on average

12. See Marrese (1988a) for details of intra-CMEA trade negotiations.
13. Non-CMEA socialist trade is generally conducted via bilateral clearing that requires the supervision of the Ministry of Foreign Trade. A portion of Soviet trade with socialist countries is conducted in freely convertible currencies or freely convertible commodities (usually oil), and consists almost entirely in trade of hard goods that is supervised by the Ministry of Foreign Trade.
14. According to the official ruble/dollar exchange rate, these percentages translate into 4.2 percent of all Soviet exports and 11.2 percent of all Soviet imports. However, the ruble is seriously overvalued (Marrese and Vanous 1983, 56-60); these overall trade percentages are, therefore, much too low.

sectoral costs (the current practice). Second, wholesale prices of new machinery embodying technological progress should be based on preliminary estimates of the engineering effectiveness of the new machinery. These estimates should be determined in negotiations between the buyer and seller of the new technology. Third, wholesale prices should provide enough profit so that the set of individual enterprises within a single sector can develop at the planned rate of growth for that sector. These recommendations fail to specify a role for CMEA prices or world market prices and imply that the center can influence prices so that the planned rates of sectoral growth can be met.

The proposed Soviet price reform also calls for increases in the retail prices of food and housing and decreases in the prices of goods in excess supply (certain types of clothing, household products, electronic equipment, and furniture). The general expectation is that the price reform coupled with greater differentiation in salaries will produce much greater variance in the standard of living among individual households. In addition, prices for inter-enterprise transactions are expected to be based on bilateral agreements between producer and purchaser—these are the so-called contract prices.

Let us return to the fundamental innovation of the proposed economic reform, namely enterprise independence in the form of increased enterprise authority, accountability, and self-reliance. The desirability of such independence rests on the actions of the center, the general rationality of the economic environment, and enterprise incentives.

The center intends to influence enterprise behavior via norms, state orders, and control figures. Norms refer to financial regulators such as the process of forming prices, rules concerning taxes and subsidies, interest rates, exchange rates, and to instructions concerning profit retention and the distribution of retained profits into funds for bonuses, collective consumption, and investment. Norms could possibly differ among industrial branches, between sectors, and over geographical regions. State orders would be redundant if it were possible to set norms so that all of the center's "top priorities" could be met. However, such perfection is not anticipated, and state orders will serve as a means of guaranteeing some stability as the economy ends its reliance on mandatory,

Table 8-1. 1985 Commodity Composition of Soviet Exports and Imports
By Groups of Countries
(In Percentages)

	Exports			Imports		
	All[a]	SOC[b]	NSOC[c]	All	SOC	NSOC
Machinery, Equipment, Means of Transportation	13.6	16.6	8.9	37.2	47.5	21.0
Fuels & Electric Energy	52.8	50.0	57.2	5.3	1.8	10.8
Ores, Concentrates, Metals & Products Thereof	7.5	10.2	3.3	8.4	4.9	13.9
Chemical Products, Fertilizers, Rubber	3.9	3.8	4.1	5.0	2.9	8.3
Timber, Pulp, Paper & Products Thereof	3.0	3.0	3.0	1.3	0.4	2.7
Textile Raw Materials & Semi-Finished Textiles	1.3	1.9	0.4	1.7	0.3	3.9
Food Products & Raw Materials for Food	1.5	1.6	1.3	21.2	18.0	26.2
Industrial Products	2.0	2.1	1.8	12.4	15.3	7.8
Unspecified Products	14.4	10.8	20.0	7.5	8.9	5.3
Total	100.0	100.0	100.0	100.0	100.0	100.0

a. All = all countries.
b. SOC = socialist countries.
c. NSOC = nonsocialist countries.

Source: Vneshnyaya torgovlya SSSR v 1985 g. (Foreign Trade of the USSR in 1985). Moscow: Finansy i statistika, 1986, pp. 8 and 18.

enterprise-level plan targets. Control figures will inform each enterprise of the center's overall expectations for it, not just the center's top priorities.

Norms are supposed to remain unchanged for five-year periods to avoid the disincentives associated with the ratchet effect and to force enterprises to face hard budget constraints. As long as norms do not respond ex post to enterprise performance, each enterprise will realize that success depends on its efforts, not on its attempts to receive special considerations from supervisory authorities.

The general rationality of the economic environment depends on the effectiveness of the norms with respect to static efficiency, dynamic efficiency, and exploitation of potential gains from trade. If norms are relatively uniform across industries, sectors, and geographical regions, and consistently express the center's preferences, then these norms will encourage static efficiency as defined by the center's preferences. If enterprises have access to capital, say by bidding for investment funds, and capital mobility is high, then these norms will encourage dynamic efficiency. If enterprises are allowed to trade on any domestic market or on any foreign market at prices related to those prevailing on these foreign markets, then these norms will encourage enterprises to exploit gains from trade.

Enterprise incentives refer not only to carrots such as attractive profit-sharing rules and sticks such as the threat of bankruptcy and unemployment, but also to an economy that has become more monetized. Thus, if the center constructs rational norms, state orders, and nonobligatory control figures, and if enterprises face strong incentives to act effectively from static, dynamic, and trade points of view, then enterprise independence will help the Soviet economy to reach the productivity levels and quality standards of advanced western countries.

II. SOVIET PERESTROIKA FROM A HUNGARIAN PERSPECTIVE[15]

As mentioned earlier, Hungarian economic reform during 1968-1979 was based on the assumption that the implementation of

---

15. This section follows material from Marrese (1988b).

central preferences via indirect regulation would lead to a higher level of efficiency than the implementation of those same preferences via detailed mandatory plan targets. Central preferences did not radically change in 1968. The economic system was still supposed to guarantee job security, stable prices, and a socially acceptable distribution of income. Previously existing institutional characteristics—such as ministerial appointment of enterprise management, central control over all but minor investment decisions, administrative wage and price regulation, profit leveling among enterprises, and government-negotiated CMEA trade obligations—remained intact. Consequently, the Hungarian leadership wished to obtain greater efficiency, yet to sacrifice neither equity nor any other central preference. Hence, Hungary embarked on its reform with widely incompatible central preferences. This gave Hungarians at all levels of the decision-making hierarchy tremendous latitude in justifying their behavior in the sense that while most any enterprise or ministerial achievement could never meet all of the objectives inherent in the incompatible set of several preferences, it could meet the objectives of some subset of central preferences. The fact that enterprise or ministerial agents could prove that the demands placed on them were impossible to reach, yet were willing to reach some subset of these demands, led to the bureaucratic bargaining that undermined the effort to reform the economy via indirect regulation.

In fact, Hungary's reformed system was unable to achieve efficiency within the constraints imposed by central authorities. Hungarian policymakers during 1968-1979 contributed to reform failures by demonstrating an unwillingness to trust markets, ignoring the positive attributes of competitive pressure, making the transition to the guided market system as painless as possible for bureaucrats, enterprise managers, and workers, and being overly optimistic about the efficiency-generating attributes of limited enterprise independence. It is no wonder that the Hungarians are skeptical about the medium-term prospects of radical reform in the Soviet Union.

The way in which most Hungarian economists evaluate the implementation of Soviet radical reform can be seen in János Kornai's criticism of initial Hungarian reform efforts. Kornai distinguishes between the Hungarian state-owned sector (state-owned firms in industry, construction, transportation, communication, and trade plus state-owned farms) and the nonstate sector (agricultural cooperatives, household farming, private farms, nonagricultural cooperatives, the formal private sector, the second economy, and combined private-state ownership). The state-owned sector, according to Kornai, operates in an atmosphere of dual dependence, depending vertically on the bureaucracy and horizontally on its suppliers and customers. Vertical dependence refers to the rules of entry and exit, the selection of top management, and the prices, wages, credit conditions, taxes, and subsidies a state-owned firm will face. Vertical dependence dominates horizontal dependence, which refers to a state-owned firm's autonomy with respect to determination of its outputs and inputs. A firm in the nonstate sector, though not free from bureaucratic control, does not rely on the paternalistic assistance of the state for growth and survival, but must pass the market test (Kornai 1986, 1694-1710).[16]

Kornai (1986, 1729-30) goes on to explain how the initial reform efforts were fundamentally naive:

> The naive reformers searched for a reasonable line of separation between the role of the bureaucracy and the role of the market. Many of them thought that such a separation line could be drawn like this: "simple reproduction" (in Marxian terms) regulated by the market and "extended reproduction" by the planners. In other words, current production controlled by the market and investment by the planner. It turned out that this separation is not viable. On the one hand, the bureaucracy is not ready to restrict its activity to the regulation of investment. On the other hand, the autonomy and profit motive of the firm become illusory if growth and technical development are separated from the profitability and the financial position of the firm and are made dependent only on the will of higher authorities.
>
> The pioneer reformers wanted to reassure all members of the bureaucracy that there would be ample scope for their activity. Their intention is understandable. The reform is a movement from "above," a voluntary change of behavior on the side of the controllers and not an uprising from "below" on the side of those who are controlled. There is, therefore, a stubborn inner contradiction in the

16. For statistical evidence, see Kornai and Matits (1984, 1987).

whole reform process: how to get the active participation of the very people who will lose a part of their power if the process is successful. The reassurance worked too well in the Hungarian case; the bureaucracy was not shattered . . . .

The naive reformers were concerned with the problems of the state-owned sector and did not spend much hard thought on a reconsideration of the nonstate sectors' role. It turned out, however, that up to the present time, it has been just the nonstate sectors that have brought the most tangible changes into the life of the economy.

In my opinion, conflicts stemming from divergent interests seem to underlie Kornai's explanation of the naivete of the scheme "central preferences → center's financial regulation of enterprises → efficient outcomes." These can be viewed as occurring among four hierarchic levels: (1) members of the Central Committee and the Council of Ministers; (2) members of branch and functional ministries, banks, and economy-wide agencies and committees; (3) managers of enterprises, state farms, and cooperatives along with the trade union leaders and members of local government; and (4) workers and consumers.

The problem of divergent interests with respect to reform has been seen most clearly among the two coalitions responsible for regulating the economy—one from level (1) and the other from level (2). Each coalition of decisionmakers has reflected the diverse opinions of many interest groups. Therefore, internal and external conflict within and between coalitions has flourished—as would be the case in any heterogeneous society. However, there also has existed an awareness that a stable consensus concerning economic priorities should be reached to promote rapid and effective decisionmaking. The central question for economic reform is whether such consensus will lead to a distribution of resources based on "bureaucratic rules of thumb" or on "market outcomes."

Clearly, a national objective function and a commonly perceived set of constraints would contribute greatly to the formation of consensus able to accept market outcomes. Instead, the diversity of opinion in these two coalitions yields too many national goals alongside too many constraints. Decisionmakers in level (1) strive for growth of national income, a steady rise in per capita consumption, faster incorporation of technical progress, importation of needed technology and raw materials, increased labor productivity, and better investment decisionmaking. The constraints are no less formidable: maintenance of institutional stability within the political-economic hierarchy, equilibrium of domestic demand and supply, full employment, a relatively low inflation rate, fulfillment of CMEA obligations, and adherence to various restrictions concerning income distribution.

The absence of a national objective function, in itself, is not fatal. If profitability, for instance, would be accepted by each interest group as the means through which conflicting priorities are to be resolved, then the absence of an objective function may simply be a sign of the game-theoretic nature of reality. Game theory rarely specifies an overall objective function, but it concentrates instead on the interaction of different agents. However, the highly monopolistic industrial structure and the complex tax and subsidy system in Hungary have prevented profitability from serving in this mediating role because Hungarian prices have not been good measures of scarcity.

The priorities implicit in a national objective function would also be unnecessary if all interest groups had the same preferences for the economy's development, either because of a unifying socialist consciousness or a hierarchically consistent incentive system. Either would result in successful decentralization and would thus eliminate the need for maximization of an explicit objective function. However, neither has occurred nor is likely to occur. All levels of the Hungarian hierarchy have different priorities. Members of level (1) are concerned with the overall well-being of the economy and their status; members of level (2) concentrate on the well-being of their own institutions and their status; members of level (3) focus on lifetime income, benefits, and security; and members of level (4) maximize individual utility.

Inconsistencies among incentives arise because the national interest often does not coincide with branch or enterprise interests. For example, from a national point of view, every enterprise should reveal its honest anticipation of the completion time and benefit stream associated with each project for which it seeks centrally allocated investment funds. From an enterprise point of view, its productive capacity is crucial for its ability to bargain with the center for special firm-specific treatment; hence, it should obtain investment funds even at the "cost of being overly optimistic" about its investment potential. The inconsistency arises because the actual opportunity cost of investment funds for an enterprise is much lower than the value the center places on these funds.[17]

The widespread practice of determining firm-specific regulations for state-owned firms is directly related to the diversity of preferences on each decisionmaking level and to the absence of either a well-working price system or an explicit objection function. Such a situation permits the priorities of each interest group to be represented in terms of selected goals subject to selected constraints. Moreover, each interest group tends to maximize its own subset of goals relative to unique perceptions of shadow prices because no national shadow price system exists. The interaction of such divergent means of measuring tradeoffs results in a failure to evaluate national tradeoffs in any consistent manner.

Consequently, Hungarian skepticism about Soviet perestroika is founded on experience that indicates that administrative financial guidance of enterprises deteriorates into enterprise-specific bureaucratic bargaining.

On a more practical level, Hungarians realize that the Soviet radical reform can achieve impressive micro success yet still suffer from macro failure. Again, Hungarian experience is eye-opening.

The dimensions of a micro success have included:

1. the tremendous variety of activity in the legal second economy that has resulted in dramatic improvements in the food supply, privately constructed housing, services available to the population, and the assortment of consumer goods (mostly clothing);
2. a multitude of ways of encouraging the merger of first-economy and second-economy interests, such as supportive policies for agricultural private plots and the opportunity to organize economic working groups in industrial enterprises;
3. the decision to allow agricultural cooperatives and state farms to engage in nontraditional industrial, trade, and construction activities;

17. See Kornai (1980) for an exhaustive discussion of soft budget constraints, which is an enlightening way of discussing firm-specific treatment of enterprises.

4. new forms of private-sector activity, such as increased opportunities for private shop rental, organizing restaurants on a contract basis, and encouraging the growth of small, non-agricultural cooperatives;
5. industrial production systems (or technically operating production systems) in agriculture that have created competitive conditions that have stimulated rapid technological diffusion;
6. a significant increase in work intensity and a lengthening of work; and
7. the gradual pluralization of Hungarian life—economically, culturally, and even politically.

There are three primary reasons for Hungarian micro success. First, Hungary has had no other choice than to release the full energies of its people in a much less planned manner, because Hungary has had a very poor endowment of natural resources and thus has had to rely more heavily on the world market than, say, the Soviet Union. Hungary's opportunities for extensive development were exhausted long ago, and Hungarian leaders and economists have been disillusioned with the relative advantages of a system of centralized economic management. Second, opportunities to accumulate large, visible differences in individual income have served as a means of stimulating individual productivity. Third, substantial investment in consumer-oriented industries has provided the population with a desirable array of products.

Yet to achieve these dimensions of micro success, previously important central preferences had to change. A new managerial elite and a new entrepreneurial elite have emerged in Hungary, while Marxist-Leninist ideology and the Hungarian Socialist Workers' Party have become less important. People have less leisure time and have exhibited deteriorating health, increased tension, and greater alcoholism. Finally, a much less egalitarian distribution of income and wealth has become the norm.

Accompanying Hungary's micro success has been its macro failure, the dimensions of which are well known:

1. slow growth of national income;
2. large debt to the West;
3. inefficient domestic utilization of energy and raw materials;

4. a low level of competitiveness on world markets due to short-sighted government policies;

5. a much weaker relative position in the world economy today than in 1970;

6. poverty among pensioners; and

7. inflation.

The reasons for macro failure are complicated. On one level, the macro failure is due to the soft budget constraints that enterprises face (Kornai 1980, 1986). On another level, one may cite a variety of external and internal factors. The external factors include declining terms of trade from 1973 to 1986; world market interest rates in real terms that have been much higher than Hungarians anticipated; the worldwide increase in agricultural protection and the continual implementation of the green revolution in developing countries; CMEA institutional characteristics, such as inconvertibility of the transferable ruble (TR), that have inhibited intra-CMEA trade, product specialization, and technological transfer; and Soviet import requirements that have discouraged Hungarian development of commodities that would be competitive on the world market (Marrese 1986b, 1988). Internal factors center on poor economic policymaking in areas of wage regulation, investment policy, foreign trade—such as short-sighted investment credits used to stimulate exports—and price-tax-subsidy policy.[18]

The costs of macro failure are clear: a thoroughly dissatisfied population, emigration of some of the most talented young people, and a backward production and trade structure.

A reasonable question at this point is whether other East European economists and policymakers evaluate medium-term prospects of radical reform in the Soviet Union as skeptically as Hungarians do. I think the Czechs, East Germans, and Poles—all of whom have designed economic reforms and are acquainted with the associated difficulties—are as skeptical as the Hungarians.[19]

18. See Kornai (1988) for a comprehensive list of references; see also Marrese (1980, 1981a, 1981b, 1982, 1983, and 1986a).

19. The Czech reform that began in the mid-1960s was cut short by Soviet intervention. The GDR's economic experiment lasted from the mid-1960s to the early 1970s and was abandoned voluntarily. The Polish reform started in the early 1980s and is still evolving.

III. THE CMEA'S GROWING PROBLEMS

CMEA countries have not fully exploited the potential gains of intra-CMEA trade and have not become integrated into the international economy because of institutional obstacles, including government-level rather than enterprise-level trade negotiations; settlement mostly in inconvertible transferable rubles (TRs); bilateral balancing of overall trade; use of restricted contingency lists to facilitate bilateral barter of one country's commodities for another country's commodities; and incentives that often fail to promote specialization and technological cooperation among member countries. The net result is that the trade patterns and technological transfers of CMEA countries are outmoded in today's world. East European and Soviet enterprises are not integrated into international capital markets, nor do they cooperate among themselves or with multinational corporations as closely as do western firms. Since the pace of technological transfer and inter-firm production cooperation has increased during the last two decades, and enterprises are the primary conduits for these activities, the economic disadvantages of CMEA membership also have been growing.

Evidence of the growing economic disadvantages are the following negative trends that have plagued CMEA countries since 1970:

1. sharp declines in economic growth and in productivity increases;[20]
2. increasing technological backwardness of manufactured goods;
3. rigidities in domestic and CMEA institutions that have hindered product specialization, technological transfer, multilateral trade, and exploitation of gains from bilateral trade;
4. the predominance of bureaucratic interaction rather than market interaction in each country, which has created rigid production and trade structures; and
5. a much weaker relative position in the world economy.

Due to these problems, a consensus has developed within the CMEA that CMEA reform is necessary.

---

20. See, for instance, Alton et al. (1988) for GNP and industrial production comparisons among East European countries.

IV. THE DECLINE IN SOVIET TERMS OF TRADE
AND THE EAST EUROPEAN RESPONSE

The Soviet Union's ruble terms of trade with the East European members of the CMEA stagnated in 1986, declined by 5.5 percent in 1987, and underwent another 5 to 6 percent drop during the first ten months of 1988.[21] Moreover, this trend is expected to continue during the next three years.

The flipside to this deterioration is an improvement in the terms of trade of Bulgaria, Czechoslovakia, the GDR, Hungary, Poland, and Romania vis-à-vis the Soviet Union. The response of East European countries to these developments is an important indication of East Europe's willingness to exchange its manufactured goods for Soviet manufactured goods. This willingness is directly related to the topic of this paper: More intra-CMEA trade or more trade with the West?

To analyze the issue of more intra-CMEA trade or more trade with the West, it is necessary to understand the asymmetry in the Soviet-East European pattern of trade, the separability of each East European country's trade with respect to the Soviet Union, the rest of the CMEA, and the West, and the negative consequences of this separability.

The asymmetry in the Soviet-East European pattern of trade has meant that East Europe has been much more dependent on the Soviet Union as an export market for its manufactured goods than vice versa, and that East Europe has been much more dependent on the Soviet Union as a source of imported fuels, ores, minerals, and metals than vice versa. The following evidence from Hungarian data provides a picture that is typical for all of East Europe. During 1974-1986, 64.8 percent of Hungary's exports to the Soviet Union were manufactured goods (categories 1 and 2 of Table 8-2), while only 24.6 percent of Soviet exports to Hungary were manufactured goods. Simultaneously, 4.4 percent of Hungary's exports to the Soviet Union were fuels, ores, minerals, and metals (categories 3 and 4 of Table 8-2), while 58.4 percent of Soviet exports to Hungary were composed of similar items.

21. *PlanEcon Reports* III, 27-28: 13, July 9, 1978; IV, 32-33: 2, August 1988; IV, 41: 6, November 4, 1988.

Until now, CMEA trade has grown so quickly because the Soviet Union has subsidized East European countries primarily by being a net exporter of fuel and nonfuel raw materials at prices *below* corresponding world market prices and by being a net importer of manufactured goods at prices *above* corresponding world market prices. The Soviet Union has traded with East Europe at such disadvantageous terms of trade to secure military, strategic, political, ideological, and special economic benefits from individual East European countries. Without these subsidies, East European countries would have aligned their economies more closely to West European and world market needs rather than Soviet needs.

One cost of CMEA economic integration caused by the above mentioned institutional obstacles to intra-CMEA trade is the failure of efforts by CMEA countries to develop manufactured goods that can be exported to both the CMEA market and to developed capitalist countries. Indeed, this has lead to a separability in the approach that East European countries have taken toward trade.

For example, in Hungary, separability has meant that its foreign trade decisions have rarely been based on an evaluation of trade opportunities across all trade partners, but rather on partner-specific priorities. More specifically, Hungary's trade partners may be categorized into these primary groups: the Soviet Union, the rest of the CMEA (RCMEA), and the rest of the world (ROW). Hungary's priority in the Soviet market has been to maximize imports of fuels and raw materials obtainable for TRs and at intra-CMEA foreign trade prices (FTPs). In trade with ROW, Hungarian priorities have been dominated by the goal of reaching $-export levels consistent with timely repayment of Hungary's $-debt. Finally, Hungary's trade with RCMEA has been driven by the mutual exchange of manufactured goods that have not been highly valued on western markets. Production of these manufactured goods has been maintained partly to prevent unemployment and partly because these goods have served as substitutes for goods that otherwise would have been imported from the West.

Before we discuss the negative impact that separability has had on Hungary, it is important to demonstrate that Hungary's foreign trade strategy has been unsuccessful since the early 1970s. The first piece of evidence is that Hungary's overall (both $ and TR) terms of trade steadily declined from 1973 to 1986. In comparison to

Table 8-2. Pattern of Hungarian Trade By Commodity Categories
and Trade Partners
1974-1986

	USSR	GDR	CZECH	POLAND	RSOC[a]	ECAP[b]	OCAP[c]	DEV[d]
CAT	Hungarian Category j Exports to Market m as a Share of Total Hungarian Exports to Market m							
1	46.7	55.3	45.3	44.3	41.5	7.8	18.3	38.6
2	18.1	11.0	16.8	15.6	13.6	21.2	43.4	16.0
3	0.6	0.7	1.5	1.8	3.3	11.5	0.1	1.4
4	3.8	5.8	5.1	12.3	12.3	12.5	7.8	13.0
5	4.0	1.9	3.6	4.7	12.5	10.2	5.8	8.1
6	0.8	1.0	3.5	1.0	2.2	1.4	1.0	2.9
7	0.7	2.9	1.7	3.1	4.3	9.9	1.7	2.0
8	7.4	5.6	8.8	6.7	4.4	7.4	3.5	8.2
9	14.3	9.8	11.4	7.4	5.5	17.1	16.8	9.8
10	3.6	6.1	2.3	3.1	0.5	1.0	1.6	0.0
	Hungarian Category j Imports from Market m as a Share of Total Hungarian Imports from Market m							
1	22.3	62.0	49.3	48.2	30.3	32.8	34.4	0.8
2	2.3	14.4	16.0	12.7	19.4	8.6	9.4	7.3
3	43.5	3.9	7.3	13.0	7.4	2.2	1.5	28.8
4	14.9	2.9	7.5	9.6	7.9	9.6	5.0	5.6
5	6.4	10.3	6.3	4.8	13.5	23.7	16.8	4.0
6	0.8	1.7	5.8	3.2	3.3	3.9	1.0	0.2
7	9.1	2.6	2.9	3.3	5.3	15.2	27.6	29.1
8	0.2	0.1	0.8	0.2	3.0	1.1	3.3	19.6
9	0.3	1.3	1.0	2.7	8.4	2.4	1.0	4.6
10	0.2	0.9	3.0	2.3	1.5	0.5	0.1	0.0

1. Machinery & Equipment (CTN 1)
2. Industrial Consumer Goods (CTN 9)
3. Fuels (CTN 20-23)
4. Ores, Minerals, Metals (CTN 24-27)
5. Chemicals (CTN 30-35)
6. Building Materials (CTN 40-42)
7. Nonfood Raw Materials (CTN 50-53, 55-58)
8. Animals, Cereals & Food Raw Matls (CTN 60, 70-72)
9. Food & Food Products (CTN 80-84)
10. Beverages & Tobacco (CTN 85)

a. RSOC = Rest of Socialist Countries: Albania, Bulgaria, Kampuchea, Cuba, Mongolia, Romania, Yugoslavia, North Korea, Vietnam, and the PRC.
b. ECAP = European Capitalist Countries.
c. OCAP = Other Capitalist Countries.
d. DEV = Developing Countries.

Source: Külkereskedelmi Statisztikai Évkönyv (Hungarian Foreign-Trade Statistical Yearbook, hereafter referred to as *KSE*), annual volumes from 1974 to 1986, from tables dealing with Hungary's trade organized by two-digit CTN categories.

nineteen other developed capitalist and socialist countries for the period 1973 to 1986, Hungary experienced the third sharpest decline in terms of trade (after Australia and Greece). In comparison to Austria, when each country's terms of trade is set equal to 100 in 1980, Austrian terms of trade were 112 in 1973 and 105 in 1986, whereas Hungarian terms of trade were 120 in 1973 and 88 in 1986 (Marrese 1988a, 35-36).

Another sign of the failure of Hungarian foreign trade strategy comes from a comparison of the foreign trade performance of European CMEA member countries and Yugoslavia during 1981-1986. Hungary suffered the worst drop in $-terms of trade among these eight countries, and Hungary's net debt grew 61.3 percent during this period—a dismal record relative to that of the other seven countries.[22]

At this point, it seems reasonable to presume that the separability discussed here resulted not from Hungary's ability to follow comparative advantage better than most other developed countries, but rather from the Hungarian leadership's willingness to meet short-term pressures without sufficient regard for long-run efficiency. Now let us take a closer look at the negative consequences of separability.

First, separability has been related to stagnation in Hungary's export structure by adding tremendous complexity to foreign trade policymaking (Marrese 1988a). Hungarian leaders have used this complexity as an excuse to espouse priorities with the Soviet Union, RCMEA, and ROW that have been short-run in nature. In other words, Hungary has adopted policies that support a continuation of the status quo to take advantage of implicit subsidies or to meet $-export targets or to utilize domestic manufacturing capacity. Two signs of stagnation appear in Table 8-3: ten out of the first eleven most highly valued exports for 1986 were ranked in the top thirteen in both 1976 and 1981; and the top twenty-five exports for 1986 contributed 40.7 percent to Hungary's total 1986 export earnings, 36.5 percent in 1981, and 34.7 percent in 1976.

Second, none of Hungary's top exports of machinery and equipment have sold well simultaneously in the USSR, RCMEA,

22. See Marrese (1988a, 33) or *PlanEcon Report* III, 36-37-38: 5, 23, and 26, September 17, 1987.

Table 8-3. Hungary's Top Exports: Rank and Share
of Total Hungarian Exports
(In Descending Order of 1986 Rank)

Description	Quantity Measure	1986 Rank	1981 Rank	1976 Rank	Percentage of Total Hungarian Exports		
		(In Value Terms)			1986 Export Share	1981 Export Share	1976 Export Share
Buses	Pieces	1	1	1	4.49	3.85	5.01
Parts for Road Motor Vehicles	Tons	2	7	6	3.12	2.40	2.13
Crude Oil & Petroleum Products	–	3	11	60	3.04	1.41	0.36
Cereals	Tons	4	3	8	2.86	2.90	1.83
Packaged Medicine	–	5	6	3	2.77	2.45	2.44
Rolled Steel	Tons	6	4	2	2.42	2.59	4.47
Raw Meat	Tons	7	2	10	2.15	3.36	1.74
Part-Products of Road Motor Vehicles	Pieces	8	8	13	1.99	1.68	1.45
Slaughtered Poultry	Tons	9	5	5	1.96	2.52	2.16
Leather & Artificial Leather Footwear	1,000 Pieces	10	9	7	1.72	1.62	2.05
Pharmaceutical Raw Materials	Tons	11	12	11	1.52	1.17	1.56
Basic & Press-Matter Plastic Materials	Tons	12	29	–	1.28	0.66	–
Plant Protectives	Tons	13	28	51	1.12	0.67	0.42
Canned Vegetables	Tons	14	20	17	1.09	0.86	0.89
Bottled Wine	Hectoliters	15	16	14	0.99	0.97	1.25
Fruit	Tons	16	10	9	0.99	1.53	1.80
Incandescent Lamps	1,000 Pieces	17	19	19	0.92	0.87	0.83
Aluminum Products	Tons	18	45	26	0.89	0.49	0.72
Electric & Magnetic Measuring Instr.	–	19	64	69	0.85	0.36	0.32
Special Measuring Instr.	–	20	52	*	0.84	0.40	0.25
Canned Fruit	–	21	25	34	0.78	0.68	0.64
Finished Cotton & Cotton-Type Textiles	Sq. Meters	22	23	*	0.76	0.77	0.11
Knitted Outer Garments	Tons	23	30	25	0.73	0.66	0.72
Metallurgical & Remelted Aluminum	Tons	24	13	18	0.73	1.16	0.87
Canned Meat	Tons	25	44	31	0.69	0.50	0.70
Total					40.70	36.53	34.72

* Rank lower than 75.

Source: KSE (1976, 163-242; 1981, 179-255; 1986, 159-219).

and ROW during any one year. Let us say that an export is widely sold if its trade intensity coefficients with respect to the USSR, RCMEA, and ROW are equal to or exceed 0.5.[23] Using Table 8-4, we see that raw meat, plastics, canned fruit, cotton textiles, and canned meat were widely sold in 1976; part-products of road motor vehicles, plastics, plant protectives, canned fruit, cotton textiles, and canned meat exhibited this characteristic in 1981 and 1986; and an additional category, knitted outerwear, was widely sold in 1986. This has not been the case for machinery and equipment: buses have been exported predominantly to the USSR, electric and magnetic measuring instruments along with special measuring instruments to both the USSR and RCMEA, and incandescent lamps to ROW (Tables 8-4 and 8-5).

These observations demonstrate the separability of Hungary's markets for its manufactured goods and are consistent with the following conclusions drawn from a survey of twenty large Hungarian manufacturing enterprises and nine Hungarian foreign trading organizations:

1. TR-export capacity for Hungarian manufactured goods has done nothing to generate Hungarian $-exports.
2. TR-exports of Hungarian manufactured goods have required $-exports as inputs and therefore have contributed significantly to Hungary's $-debt.
3. All but high-tech TR-exports of Hungarian manufactured goods are relics of a bygone development strategy, and their persistent presence is a distressing sign of the stagnating influence of CMEA institutional characteristics.[24]

---

23. In this paper, a trade intensity coefficient is defined as the ratio of the Hungarian exports (imports) of a given commodity going to (from) a particular market (USSR, RCMEA, or ROW) divided by the share of all Hungarian exports (imports) to (from) that market. For example, the 1986 trade intensity coefficient for Hungarian exports of buses (ranked number 1 in Table 8-4) to the USSR is 69.9 + 33.9 = 2.06; to RCMEA is 26.3 + 21.2 = 1.24; and to ROW is 2.7 + 44.9 = 0.06 (all figures from Table 8-4). Thus, Hungarian buses sold well in the USSR and in RCMEA, but not in ROW.

24. See Inotai (1986b), Pártos (1986), Rácz (1986a, 1986b), Réti (1986), and Török (1986), or a summary of these articles in Marrese (1988b).

It is important to emphasize that these conclusions are not based on the unsupported speculation of a few reform-minded Hungarian economists, but are representative of the opinions of the vast majority of managers of large Hungarian manufacturing enterprises.

Third, stagnation was also present among imports. Among the twelve most highly valued imports for 1986, eleven were in the top eighteen in both 1976 and 1981 (Table 8-6). Moreover, the top twenty-five imports for 1986 were responsible for 39 percent of Hungary's total 1986 import bill, 35.1 percent in 1981, and 34.5 percent in 1976. This stagnation among imports reflects the rigidity in Hungary's production structure, which is connected to the previously mentioned short-term nature of Hungary's foreign trade priorities.

Fourth, Hungary has not shown a willingness to increase its dependence on the Soviet Union for imports of machinery and equipment or industrial consumer goods. As is evident in Tables 8-6, 8-7, and 8-8, Hungary's import dependence on the Soviet Union has increased over time with respect to crude oil and petroleum products, natural gas, plastics, parts for road motor vehicles, chemical fibers, raw cotton, black coal and anthracite, and hot-rolled semi-finished steel products. Simultaneously, Hungary's import dependence on the Soviet Union has decreased over time with respect to automobiles, parts for motor vehicles (which are distinct from parts for road motor vehicles), packaged medicine, blast-furnace coke, and general purpose telecommunication units.

Hence, Hungary has demonstrated a noticeable reluctance to exchange its manufactured goods for Soviet manufactured goods. This reluctance has remained strong because Hungary has not yet been able to implement the market-oriented alternative to its current separable notion of foreign trade—fuels and raw materials from the Soviet Union, advanced technology and otherwise unavailable fuels and raw materials from developed capitalist countries (ECAP + OCAP in Table 8-2), and the mutual exchange of machinery and equipment and industrial consumer goods with other East European countries.

Finally, let us define "balanced import sourcing" to mean that the trade intensity coefficients of a particular commodity imported from the USSR, RCMEA, and ROW are equal to or exceed 0.5. In

Table 8-4. Distribution of Hungary's Top Exports in Value Terms
to the USSR, RCMEA, and ROW

(Percentage of Total Export Value of Each Commodity)[a]

1986 Export Rank	1976			1981			1986		
	USSR	RCMEA	ROW	USSR	RCMEA	ROW	USSR	RCMEA	ROW
1	69.9	26.4	3.7	66.3	25.3	8.4	71.0	26.3	2.7
2	50.6	37.5	11.9	53.1	32.1	14.8	59.5	33.6	6.9
3	2.8	14.1	83.1	6.4	27.4	66.2	4.6	1.8	93.6
4	2.9	91.4	5.7	75.4	17.0	7.6	56.7	31.7	11.6
5	73.2	20.4	6.4	64.6	23.1	12.3	60.4	28.9	10.7
6	8.6	12.9	78.5	7.2	9.6	83.2	17.6	10.1	72.3
7	29.3	15.6	55.1	48.6	7.2	44.2	39.0	1.1	59.9
8	48.1	43.5	8.4	27.8	48.5	23.1	24.3	40.3	35.4
9	20.0	3.3	76.7	60.0	5.0	35.0	40.1	4.4	55.5
10	64.5	21.7	13.8	63.8	15.4	20.8	56.1	12.4	31.5
11	2.3	10.7	87.0	2.1	6.2	91.7	0.4	4.2	95.4
12	-	-	-	3.8	20.4	75.8	1.7	6.9	91.4
13	33.9	25.2	40.9	57.7	15.9	26.4	54.9	14.3	30.8
14	63.5	9.3	27.2	56.6	12.6	30.8	56.3	11.6	32.1
15	55.2	38.5	6.3	57.7	34.7	7.6	66.2	29.2	4.6
16	56.3	31.2	12.5	59.5	24.3	16.2	67.6	12.2	20.2
17	0.9	15.9	83.2	2.3	6.7	91.0	7.6	7.3	85.1
18	0.3	63.7	36.0	0.0	40.2	59.8	5.7	23.7	70.6
19	41.8	48.1	10.1	47.9	44.2	7.9	68.8	28.5	2.7
20	39.6	45.9	14.5	56.4	37.6	6.0	68.8	27.0	4.2
21	34.2	26.0	39.8	42.7	24.8	32.5	48.9	11.8	39.3
22	25.4	16.6	58.0	29.7	14.3	56.0	31.9	21.2	46.9
23	64.3	15.4	20.3	61.7	8.1	30.2	55.4	11.9	32.7
24	0.0	27.9	72.1	0.0	50.1	49.9	0.0	39.9	60.1
25	16.6	18.7	64.7	19.7	11.1	69.2	22.9	13.5	63.4

a. The forint value of total Hungarian exports is distributed as follows:

	USSR	RCMEA	ROW
1976	30.2	26.3	43.5
1981	33.4	21.0	45.6
1986	33.9	21.2	44.9

Source: KSE (1976, 10-12, 163-242; 1981, 10-11, 179-255; 1986, 9-11, 159-219).

Table 8-5. Distribution of Hungary's Top Exports in Quantity Terms
To the USSR, RCMEA, and ROW

(Percentage of Total Export Quantity of Each Commodity)[a]

1986 Export Rank	1976			1981			1986		
	USSR	RCMEA	ROW	USSR	RCMEA	ROW	USSR	RCMEA	ROW
1	74.1	22.3	3.6	74.1	22.1	3.8	71.8	26.5	1.7
2	55.8	28.5	15.7	44.4	28.2	27.4	62.4	29.8	7.8
3	-	-	-	-	-	-	-	-	-
4	2.8	91.1	6.1	68.1	24.3	7.6	60.7	33.3	6.0
5	-	-	-	-	-	-	-	-	-
6	11.0	15.0	74.0	10.4	12.8	76.8	19.1	13.9	67.0
7	35.3	25.2	39.5	54.6	10.7	34.7	56.1	1.3	42.6
8	52.3	45.4	2.3	33.0	60.1	6.9	27.7	39.0	33.0
9	26.5	4.1	69.4	62.0	8.6	29.4	55.7	3.1	41.2
10	66.9	16.8	83.7	64.8	13.7	21.5	69.3	13.3	17.4
11	-	-	-	-	-	-	-	-	-
12	-	-	-	2.7	24.0	73.3	1.1	8.4	90.5
13	35.6	11.2	53.2	62.8	13.1	24.1	58.8	15.4	25.8
14	69.9	9.0	21.1	67.6	13.1	19.3	74.0	11.1	14.9
15	54.1	39.5	6.4	61.3	33.1	5.6	67.4	29.4	3.2
16	57.6	33.0	9.4	59.4	22.7	17.9	69.3	10.1	20.6
17	4.5	11.6	83.9	1.1	5.8	93.1	2.4	4.2	93.4
18	0.4	79.3	25.3	0.0	51.3	48.7	8.4	29.4	62.2
19	-	-	-	-	-	-	-	-	-
20	-	-	-	-	-	-	-	-	-
21	39.5	29.5	31.0	51.3	28.0	20.7	57.1	16.9	26.0
22	27.1	11.8	61.1	37.3	14.7	48.0	40.8	20.4	38.8
23	62.3	13.5	24.2	64.9	9.7	25.4	53.5	12.4	34.1
24	0.0	33.2	66.8	0.0	54.8	45.2	0.0	44.0	56.0
25	27.1	23.9	49.0	33.9	18.4	47.7	39.8	21.2	39.0

a. The commodities for which no percentages appear did not have quantity measures associated with them because of their heterogeneous nature.

Source: KSE (1976, 10-12, 163-242; 1981, 179-255; 1986, 9-11, 159-219).

1976, packaged medicine and rolled steel exhibited balanced import sourcing; in 1981, the same was true for black coal and anthracite, rolled steel, and blast-furnace coke; and in 1986, only black coal and anthracite reflected balanced import sourcing (Table 8-7). Hungary thus appears to have limited opportunities to switch its imports among markets.

This observation is consistent with the difficulty Hungary has had in restricting $-imports. The primary reason is that few substitutes exist for Hungarian $-imports. This can be seen from Table 8-2, where we define essential $-imports as $-imports from categories 3, 4, 5, and 7 (fuels, ores, minerals, metals, chemicals, and nonfood raw materials). During 1974-1986, essential $-imports constituted 51.7 percent of all imports from European capitalist countries (ECAP), 50.9 percent of all imports from other capitalist countries (OCAP), and 67.5 percent of all imports from developing countries (DEV). Fuels and raw materials are considered "essential" because they are factor inputs needed to prevent production bottlenecks from occurring in Hungary. Also, CMEA markets offer terms for *increased* deliveries of these fuels and raw materials that are inferior to the terms offered by ECAP, OCAP, and DEV.

Furthermore, most of the remaining $-imports are machinery and equipment, which are technologically superior to the corresponding CMEA counterparts. We find from Table 8-2 that during 1974-1986, 32.8 percent of all of Hungary's imports from ECAP and 34.4 percent of all of Hungary's imports from OCAP came from category 1 (machinery and equipment).

Now that we understand the asymmetric pattern of East European-Soviet trade and the negative consequences of separability, let us return to East Europe's response to declining Soviet terms of trade. Given that most East European countries accumulated large net TR-debt to the Soviet Union during the 1970s and early 1980s, each East European country, beginning in 1987, has faced the following alternatives (Köves 1988, 8-10):

1. become a net lender to the Soviet Union by continuing the rapid growth, in volume terms, of exports to the Soviet Union even after that country's net debt to the Soviet Union has been paid;

Table 8-6. Hungary's Top Imports: Rank and Share of
Total Hungarian Imports
(In Descending Order of 1986 Rank)

Description	Quantity Measure	1986 Rank	1981 Rank	1976 Rank	Percentage of Total Hungarian Exports		
		(In Value Terms)			1986 Import Share	1981 Import Share	1976 Import Share
Crude Oil & Pet. Prod.	Tons	1	1	1	11.27	9.60	8.45
Natural Gas	1,000 Cu. Mtr.	2	2	31	3.82	2.61	0.62
Basic & Press-Matter Plastic Materials	Tons	3	6	5	1.89	1.37	1.79
Automobiles	Number	4	4	8	1.89	1.41	1.63
Parts for Road Motor Vehicles	Tons	5	7	9	1.59	1.33	1.54
Metallurgical & Remelted Aluminum	Tons	6	9	11	1.43	1.23	1.28
Fodder for Animals from Vegetable Oil Ind.	Tons	7	3	2	1.34	2.19	2.16
Unroasted Coffee	Tons	8	11	10	1.33	1.19	1.41
Trucks	Tons	9	13	12	1.19	0.96	1.27
Chemical Fibers	Tons	10	8	7	1.11	1.25	1.63
Parts for Motor Vehicles	Tons	11	16	18	1.07	0.88	0.87
Raw Cotton	Tons	12	5	6	1.03	1.40	1.76
Black Coal & Anthracite	Tons	13	17	26	1.03	0.86	0.69
Auxiliary Chemicals for General Industrial Use	Tons	14	14	29	0.97	0.90	0.67
Packaged Medicine	-	15	28	60	0.89	0.64	0.33
Pharm. Raw Matls.	Tons	16	23	32	0.89	0.68	0.60
Rolled Steel	Tons	17	12	4	0.88	1.18	2.08
Paper	Tons	18	15	15	0.83	0.90	1.07
Chemical Protectives for Plants	Tons	19	18	13	0.77	0.84	1.23
Machine-Shaved Plates Processed with Resin	Cu. Meters	20	21	16	0.70	0.71	1.04
Blast-Furnace Coke	Tons	21	10	17	0.64	1.21	0.92
Leather & Artificial Leather Footwear	1,000 pairs	22	*	*	0.62	0.20	0.17
Hot-Rolled Semi-Finished Steel Products	Tons	23	24	28	0.61	0.68	0.68
Finished Cotton & Cotton-Type Textiles	Tons	24	41	*	0.59	0.41	0.22
General Purpose Mechanical Telecom Units	-	25	31	54	0.58	0.50	0.36
Total					38.96	35.13	34.47

* Rank lower than 75.

Source: KSE (1976, 98-162; 1981, 113-78; 1986, 107-58).

Table 8-7. Distribution of Hungary's Top Imports in Value Terms
to the USSR, RCMEA, and ROW
(Percentage of Total Import Value of Each Commodity)[a]

1986 Import Rank	1976			1981			1986		
	USSR	RCMEA	ROW	USSR	RCMEA	ROW	USSR	RCMEA	ROW
1	73.9	1.8	24.3	75.0	0.4	24.6	90.3	3.8	5.9
2	81.4	18.6	0.0	94.3	5.7	0.0	98.5	1.5	0.0
3	7.9	10.0	82.1	7.8	5.2	87.0	23.6	7.6	68.8
4	46.0	52.5	1.5	31.8	67.2	1.0	27.1	64.4	8.5
5	32.1	51.7	16.2	27.3	51.7	21.0	30.2	54.3	15.5
6	79.6	20.3	0.1	98.2	1.6	0.2	96.9	2.9	0.2
7	0.0	0.0	100.0	0.0	0.0	100.0	0.0	0.0	100.0
8	0.0	1.5	98.5	0.0	0.1	99.9	0.0	0.2	99.8
9	29.5	70.5	0.0	29.2	70.5	0.3	29.5	70.3	0.2
10	4.8	8.9	86.3	5.2	9.5	85.3	5.7	9.2	85.1
11	4.2	29.3	66.5	3.7	18.8	77.5	1.2	21.3	77.5
12	27.9	0.0	72.1	51.2	0.0	48.8	36.5	0.0	63.5
13	25.6	74.3	0.1	29.9	49.3	20.8	38.7	36.6	24.7
14	2.7	7.1	90.2	0.5	6.2	93.3	0.4	7.1	92.5
15	19.6	38.6	41.8	13.6	35.3	51.1	6.0	35.8	58.2
16	3.1	3.0	93.9	1.6	2.0	96.4	1.6	1.6	96.8
17	67.3	14.4	18.3	59.6	12.9	27.5	65.3	10.0	24.7
18	44.7	9.8	45.5	43.2	7.9	48.9	46.1	6.7	47.2
19	1.4	10.7	87.9	3.7	11.4	84.9	0.1	6.9	93.0
20	92.8	5.6	1.6	82.7	3.0	14.3	93.3	2.7	4.0
21	57.8	39.8	2.4	24.6	10.4	65.0	15.0	26.8	58.2
22	0.0	86.7	13.3	0.0	65.8	34.2	0.0	28.3	71.7
23	79.9	20.0	0.1	96.3	2.8	0.9	85.9	8.5	5.6
24	12.1	2.3	16.4	2.3	4.3	93.4	0.7	22.6	76.7
25	5.9	12.4	81.7	6.4	12.4	81.7	3.3	19.1	77.6

a. The forint value of total Hungarian imports is distributed as follows:

	USSR	RCMEA	ROW
1976	27.5	24.1	48.4
1981	28.6	19.3	52.1
1986	30.9	20.3	48.8

Source: KSE (1976, 10-12, 98-162; 1981, 10-11, 113-78; 1986, 9-11, 107-58).

Table 8-8. Distribution of Hungary's Top Imports in Quantity Terms
to the USSR, RCMEA, and ROW
(Percentage of Total Import Quantity of Each Commodity)[a]

1986 Import Rank	1976			1981			1986		
	USSR	RCMEA	ROW	USSR	RCMEA	ROW	USSR	RCMEA	ROW
1	-	-	-	-	-	-	-	-	-
2	97.0	3.0	0.0	95.0	5.0	0.0	98.7	1.3	0.0
3	21.2	16.4	62.4	22.2	8.8	69.0	51.7	10.9	37.4
4	41.3	58.3	0.4	28.0	71.7	0.3	24.7	71.7	3.6
5	27.3	63.1	9.6	44.5	48.9	6.6	35.6	59.2	5.2
6	80.3	19.7	0.0	98.0	2.0	0.0	97.0	3.0	0.0
7	0.0	0.0	100.0	0.0	0.0	100.0	0.0	0.0	100.0
8	0.0	1.3	98.7	0.0	0.5	99.5	0.0	0.4	99.6
9	29.0	71.0	0.0	23.2	76.7	0.1	20.0	80.0	0.0
10	18.9	19.3	61.8	20.2	18.0	61.8	20.2	23.2	56.6
11	7.9	34.2	57.9	3.6	29.4	67.0	0.6	27.2	72.2
12	42.7	0.0	57.3	66.1	0.0	33.9	52.5	0.0	47.5
13	27.8	72.2	0.0	39.5	52.0	8.5	53.5	33.9	12.6
14	5.9	22.8	71.3	1.4	30.2	68.4	0.6	33.5	65.4
15	-	-	-	-	-	-	-	-	-
16	-	-	-	-	-	-	-	-	-
17	77.1	15.7	7.2	79.7	14.5	5.8	85.8	10.7	3.5
18	72.3	10.2	17.5	75.0	8.1	16.9	76.3	8.0	15.7
19	6.5	35.1	58.4	21.6	36.4	42.0	0.1	43.2	56.7
20	92.8	6.1	1.1	89.9	3.5	6.6	95.0	3.0	2.0
21	61.4	37.5	1.1	46.1	8.3	45.6	16.4	21.6	62.0
22	0.0	83.4	16.6	0.0	74.3	25.7	0.0	34.5	65.5
23	78.7	21.3	0.0	96.2	3.0	0.8	87.1	9.3	3.6
24	35.0	21.4	43.6	12.6	10.2	77.2	4.6	34.0	61.4
25	-	-	-	-	-	-	-	-	-

a. The commodities for which no percentages appear did not have quantity
measures associated with them because of their heterogeneous nature.

Source: KSE (1976, 98-162; 1981, 113-78; 1986, 107-58).

2. reach a zero TR-debt with the Soviet Union, then allow future growth, in volume terms, of exports to the Soviet Union to equal future growth, in volume terms, of imports from the Soviet Union, thereby maintaining the zero-debt position while expanding bilateral trade; and

3. reach a zero TR-debt with the Soviet Union, then let the volume of exports to the Soviet Union decline in accordance with the decline in Soviet terms of trade.

East European countries have tended to select the third alternative primarily because they do not want to extend trade credit to the Soviet Union at a 2-percent interest rate—the current rate applied to intra-CMEA trade imbalances—or to exchange additional shipments of their manufactured goods for additional shipments of available Soviet manufactured goods. Thus far, the Soviet Union has been unwilling to exchange fuels, raw materials, or desirable manufactured goods, such as passenger cars, to offset its deterioration in terms of trade.

The GDR provides a clear example of such East European behavior, partly because it already reached zero TR-debt vis-à-vis the Soviet Union.[25] The GDR's machinery exports to the Soviet Union during 1986-1988 have declined in real terms and have been much lower than the mutually agreed upon levels found in the Soviet-GDR trade agreement for 1986-1990. The original annual export levels were based on the assumption of stable prices for Soviet energy exports during 1986-1990. However, the collapse of the world market price of oil in late 1984 and its continued decline in 1985, along with the subsequent application of the CMEA Price Clause, invalidated this assumption. The GDR has not met its original export commitments because it would have meant either extending trade credit to the Soviet Union at a 2-percent rate or receiving types of "unwanted" Soviet machinery.

Other East European countries are still in debt to the Soviet Union, so their response is not as transparent. Nonetheless, the large cutbacks in the quantity of Czech and Hungarian exports to the Soviet Union during 1987-1988 coincide with their improved

25. This example is based on the analysis of Jan Vanous, as expressed in *PlanEcon Report* IV, 37-38: 22-33, September 30, 1988.

terms of trade with the Soviet Union.[26] Bulgaria also has benefited from improved terms of trade, but it has accumulated large bilateral trade surpluses since early 1985 in response to the Soviet request that Bulgaria's large TR-debt be repaid.[27] Poland is another country with an enormous TR-debt to the Soviet Union, but its current economic crisis has prevented the Soviet Union from putting pressure on Poland for rapid repayment.

V. CONCLUSION: MORE TRADE WITH THE WEST

The institutional disadvantages of intra-CMEA trade, public criticism of the CMEA by the leaders of almost all CMEA countries, and the CMEA's growing problems all contribute to the feeling that CMEA reform is forthcoming. This section begins with two different views of CMEA reform, then summarizes the earlier analysis to conclude that more trade with the West is on the horizon under either of these two types of CMEA reform. Finally, the paper ends with a few brief observations on the link between CMEA reform and Soviet perestroika.

Let us consider two views of CMEA reform—one Soviet and the other Hungarian. It is not surprising that the Soviets and the Hungarians have different views about CMEA reform because: (1) the Soviet Union now is less interested in obtaining East European allegiance via trade subsidies and more interested in obtaining high-quality manufactured goods, and (2) the Soviet Union and Hungary differ with respect to pattern of trade and willingness to trust market outcomes.

My interpretation of the Soviet viewpoint about the CMEA's future is that the CMEA should be altered so that:

1. the Soviet Union will be able to export its manufactured goods more easily to East Europe;
2. Soviet and East European firms will have more direct contact with each other; and

26. *PlanEcon Reports* IV, 35: 2, September 9, 1988; IV, 42-43: 2, November 11, 1988.
27. *PlanEcon Report* IV, 22-23: 7, June 3, 1988.

3. technological transfer and joint ventures can be organized in a less bureaucratic manner.

This is a far cry from the Hungarian perspective. Hungarians want intra-CMEA trade to be:

1. transacted in some type of convertible currency;
2. freed from the constraints of bilateral balancing and contingency lists; and
3. negotiated between enterprises rather than between government representatives.

Essentially, Hungarians want all East European and Soviet enterprises to encounter the same conditions in intra-CMEA trade as in trade with western enterprises. It should be clear to all CMEA countries that they need to eliminate the separability that characterizes their foreign trade to reduce bureaucratic interference in enterprise decisionmaking.

From an East European point of view, the Soviet version of CMEA reform is too cautious and does not recognize the macroeconomic failure that characterizes much of East Europe. Moreover, East Europe is coming to the more general conclusion that the separability of its foreign trade is one of the major causes of its macroeconomic failure. Consequently, if a Soviet-inspired CMEA reform is introduced, East Europe will begin to redirect its trade away from the CMEA toward ROW. This has occurred since 1986, partly in response to the decline in Soviet terms of trade with East Europe.

If a Hungarian-inspired CMEA reform is introduced, then the CMEA will be characterized by much more competition among East European exporters, especially within the Soviet market; relative intra-CMEA FTPs that are roughly equal to relative world-market prices (WMPs); an absence of Soviet implicit trade subsidization of East Europe (although the Soviet Union could provide other forms of economic aid to secure East European allegiance); and transactions conducted in a convertible currency. In this case also, East Europe will begin to redirect its trade away from the CMEA toward ROW for two reasons. First, East Europe's dependence on the Soviet Union has been higher than economic criteria alone could justify. Soviet political preferences are now changing, and the adoption of a Hungarian-inspired CMEA reform would imply the end to trade subsidization.[28] Thus, it is likely that Soviet-East European trade would move to a lower, more natural level. Second, the exchange of outdated manufactured goods among East European countries was based on a reluctance to endure the short-run transition costs of becoming competitive on world markets. The introduction of a Hungarian version of CMEA reform would be a strong signal that such reluctance has been overcome, and the production of these outdated goods would gradually be phased out. Therefore, trade among East European countries may well decline to some extent, at least in the medium term.

As a concluding statement, I wish to present brief observations about the linkage between CMEA reform and Soviet perestroika. Three factors suggest that CMEA reform and Soviet perestroika may reinforce each other:

1. Gorbachev realizes that the Soviet Union must be technologically and organizationally transformed to achieve the productivity levels and quality standards of advanced western countries.
2. The CMEA's current structure is a major obstacle to the technological and organizational transformation of the Soviet Union.
3. The logic behind the current structure of the CMEA has been weakened by changing long-term Soviet preferences. In particular, the Soviet Union seems to be willing to abandon its reliance on taut central planning, to integrate itself into the world economy, and to place a lower value on East European allegiance.

However, there is one major stumbling block to the side-by-side implementation of CMEA reform and Soviet perestroika: the Soviet Union is implementing CMEA reform too slowly to be of significant help to East Europe during the next five years. Three

---

28. If the Soviet Union still wishes to obtain nonmarket benefits from East Europe, it could purchase them via lump-sum payments.

explanations for the Soviet Union's caution may be put forward. First, the Soviet Union is wealthy in fuels, minerals, ores, and precious metals that are easily saleable on world markets. In addition, it has an insignificant amount of $-debt. Consequently, the Soviet Union is not under great pressure to introduce a comprehensive CMEA reform immediately. Second, Soviet perestroika, at this point, seems to be much too inward-looking to be a solution to East European problems. The Soviet Union is reluctant to trust market forces or to introduce competitive pressure into its own economy. Hence, Soviet-inspired rather than Hungarian-inspired CMEA reform is more likely to be implemented. Third, the Soviet Union is facing substantial domestic opposition to its internal restructuring. Until this conflict is resolved, CMEA reform is impossible.

East Europe, then, is in the midst of macroeconomic crisis and does not have the time to wait for a slow and gradual CMEA reform. In the best case, East Europe will simply redirect some of its trade to the West and hope to survive. In the worst case, domestic upheavals will occur throughout East Europe, endangering not only CMEA reform, but Soviet perestroika as well.

REFERENCES

Alton, Thad P., Krzysztof Badach, Elizabeth M. Bass, Joseph T. Bombelles, Gregor Lazarcik, and George J. Staller. 1988. "Economic Growth in Eastern Europe, 1970 and 1975-1987." Occasional Paper No. 100. New York: L.W. International Financial Research.

Chapman, Janet G. 1988. "Gorbachev's Wage Reform." *Soviet Economy* 4, 4.

Gács, János. 1987. "Import Substitution and Investments in Hungary in the Period of Restrictions (1979-1986)." Revised version of a paper presented at the Tenth U.S.-Hungarian Economics Roundtable, Budapest.

Gorbachev, Mikhail S. 1987. *Perestroika: New Thinking for Our Country and the World.* New York: Harper & Row.

Hewett, Ed A. 1988. *Reforming the Soviet Economy: Equality versus Efficiency.* Washington, DC: The Brookings Institution.

Inotai, András, ed. 1986a. *The Hungarian Enterprise in the Context of Intra-CMEA Relations.* Budapest: Hungarian Scientific Council for World Economy.

——. 1986b. "Intra-CMEA Relations of Some Hungarian Chemical Enterprises." In Inotai (1986a), pp. 55-60.

Kornai, János. 1980. *Economics of Shortage.* Amsterdam: North-Holland.

——. 1986. "The Hungarian Reform Process: Visions, Hopes, and Reality." *Journal of Economic Literature* XXIV: 1687-1737, December.

Kornai, János, and Agnes Matits. 1984. "Softness of the Budget Constraint—An Analysis Relying on Data of Firms." *Acta Oeconomica* 36, 3-4: 223-49.

——. 1987. *A Vállalotok Nyereségének Bürokratikus Ujraelosztása (The Bureaucratic Redistribution of Enterprise Profit).* Budapest: Közgazdasági és Jogi Könyvkiadó.

Köves, András. 1988. "A New Situation in Hungarian-Soviet Trade: What is to be Done?" A paper presented at the conference "The Challenge of Simultaneous Economic Relations with East and West." Bellagio, Italy, February 29-March 5.

KSE (annual volumes). *Külkereskedelmi Statisztikai Évkönyv (Hungarian Foreign-Trade Statistical Yearbook).* Budapest: Központi Statisztikai Hivatal.

Marrese, Michael. 1980. "The Hungarian Economy: Prospects for the 1980s." In *Economic Reforms in Eastern Europe and Prospects for the 1980s.* Eds. Economics Directorate NATO. Oxford: Pergamon Press, pp. 183-201.

———. 1981a. "The Evolution of Wage Regulation in Hungary." *In Hungary: A Decade of Economic Reform.* Eds. Paul Hare, Hugo Radice, and Nigel Swain. London: George Allen & Unwin, Ltd., pp. 54-80.

———. 1981b. "The Bureaucratic Response to Economic Fluctuation: An Econometric Investigation of Hungarian Investment Policy." *Journal of Policy Modeling* 3, 2: 221-43.

———. 1982. "Is Unemployment the Only Answer to Labour Shortage in Hungary?" In *Employment Policies in the USSR and Eastern Europe.* Ed. Jan Adam. London: Macmillan, pp. 96-119.

———. 1983. "Agricultural Policy and Performance in Hungary." *Journal of Comparative Economics* 7, 3: 329-45.

———. 1986a. "Hungarian Agriculture: Moving in the Right Direction." In *East European Economies: Slow Growth in the 1980s.* Vol. 3 of the Joint Economic Committee of the U.S. Congress. Washington, DC: Government Printing Office, pp. 322-40, March.

———. 1986b. "CMEA: Effective But Cumbersome Political Economy." *International Organization* 40, 2: 287-327.

———. 1988a. "The Separability of Hungarian Foreign Trade with Respect to the Soviet Union, the Rest of the CMEA, and the West." *Comparative Economic Studies.*

———. 1988b. "Hungarian Foreign Trade: Failure to Reform." A revised version of a paper presented at the conference "The Challenge of Simultaneous Economic Relations with East and West." Bellagio, Italy, February 29-March 5.

Marrese, Michael, and Jan Vanous. 1983. *Soviet Subsidization of Trade with Eastern Europe: A Soviet Perspective.* Berkeley, CA: Institute of International Studies, University of California.

———. 1988. "The Content and Controversy of Soviet Trade Relations with Eastern Europe, 1970-84." In *Economic Adjustment and Reform in Eastern Europe and the Soviet Union: Essays in Honor of Franklyn D. Holzman.* Eds. Josef C. Brada, Ed A. Hewett, and Thomas A. Wolf. Durham, NC: Duke University Press.

O sovershenstvovanii. 1986. "O sovershenstvovanii organizatisii zarabotnoy platy i vvedenii novykh tarifnykh stavok i dolzhnostnykh okladov rabotnikov proizvodstvennykh otrasley narodnogo khozyaystva" (On the Improvement of the Organization of Wages and the Introduction of New Wage Rates and Salaries of Workers in the Material Branches of the Economy). *Sobranie postanovlenii pravitel'stv SSSR,* otdel pervyi 34: 603-62, September 17.

Oblath, Gábor. 1988. "Internal Regulation of Foreign Trade with Respect to Socialist Trading Partners: A Comparison of the Finnish and the Hungarian System." A paper presented at the conference "The Challenge of Simultaneous Economic Relations with East and West." Bellagio, Italy, February 29-March 5.

Oblath, Gábor, and Péter Pete. 1983. "The Development, Mechanism, and Institutional System of Fino-Soviet Economic Relations." Manuscript.

Osnovnyye napravleniya. 1986. "Osnovnyye napravleniya ekono-micheskogo i sotsial'nogo razvitiya SSSR na 1986-1990 godi i na period do 2000 goda" (Basic Guidelines for the Economic and Social Development of the USSR for 1986-1990 and for the Period Ending in 2000). Moscow: Izgatel'stvo polititicheskoi literaturi.

Osnovnyye polozheniya. 1987. "Osnovnyye polozheniya korennoy perestroyki upravleniya ekonomiki" (Basic Theses for the Radical Restructuring of the Management of the Economy). *Pravda,* June 27.

Pártos, Gyula. 1986. "The Hungarian Light Manufacturers' Link with the CMEA Region." In Inotai (1986a), pp. 79-86.

Petrakov, Nikolay Ya. 1987. "Prospects for Change in the Systems of Price Formation, Finance and Credit in the USSR." *Soviet Economy* 3, 2: 135-44.

PlanEcon Report (various issues). Ed. Jan Vanous. Washington, DC: PlanEcon, Inc.

Rácz, Margit. 1986a. "A Summary Analysis." In Inotai (1986a), pp. 9-41.

———. 1986b. "On the Intra-CMEA Relations of Some Hungarian Manufacturers of Electronics-Intensive Products." In Inotai (1986a), pp. 69-78.

SE (annual volumes). *Statisztikai Évkönyv (Hungarian Statistical Yearbook).* Budapest: Központ; Statisztikai Évkönyv.

Török, Adám. 1986. "Intra-CMEA Relations of the Hungarian Engineering Enterprises." In Inotai (1986a), pp. 61-68.

The USSR in Figures for 1986. 1987. Moscow: Finansy i statistika.

Zaslavskaya, Tat'yana I. 1984. "The Novosibirsk Report." *Survey,* No. 28: 88-108, Spring.

CHAPTER 9

The CMEA's Dilemma:
A Soviet Perspective[1]

ALEXEI KVASOV

Dr. Marrese's thought-provoking paper provides a useful opportunity for a discussion of several topical issues. At the same time, I have several disagreements with both the analysis and the conclusions.

The point of departure for the analysis is the notion that the needs of the Soviet Union clash sharply with the needs of East European countries because of the differences in attitudes toward the role of market mechanisms in the restructuring of the economies of the respective countries. Let us begin by examining the divergence of attitudes toward market mechanisms. First, this must be true to some extent, but the degree of reluctance of the Soviet Union to rely greatly on market mechanisms is, in my view, greatly exaggerated. Second, the notion that other East European countries besides the Soviet Union are quite ready to introduce market signals is also overstated. The source of this somewhat mistaken view lies in great part in the attempt to explain all the economies of East Europe in terms of the Hungarian economy, which is not very representative due to several factors.

First, the Hungarian economy is rather small, even by East European standards. Second, its economy traditionally has been export oriented, with five major exporting complexes: agriculture, buses and automotive parts, pharmaceutical materials and medicine, aluminum, and raw steel, although the last industry has declined considerably in recent years. These five sectors represented about 29.5 percent of all Hungarian exports in 1986. All

---

1. This paper was written in response to Michael Marrese's conference paper, which appears in this volume in a revised form as Chapter 8.

of these industries are competitive in international markets, even in the case of agricultural exports, because of the highly developed canning and food processing facilities. Therefore, the potential for exports to the West exists in the Hungarian case, contrary to what we see in many other socialist European countries. In this context, the large hard-currency indebtedness makes it even more logical for Hungary to seek more export to the West.

The third factor is the pace of the Hungarian reform, which was the most successful and impressive among the socialist countries of Europe. Also very profound and impressive was the preparatory work of Hungarian economists, sociologists, and other proponents of the reform in that country. Here we, together with Dr. Marrese, share the same respect and appreciation for the work of such people as János Kornai, among others. But the rather dynamic reform we see in Hungary is not the case with the other East European countries. I think that today the Soviet concepts of the reform are more far-reaching than in many other CMEA countries. In terms of theoretical development and legislation in place, I would put the Soviet Union's efforts right behind Hungary's.

The major argument for less intra-CMEA trade put forward by Dr. Marrese, described as "conceptual contradictions of the reform" in the Soviet Union on one hand, and in remaining East European countries on the other, appears to be invalid.

To return to the major issue of East versus West export trade-offs, one might challenge the very theoretical ability of such a trade-off. For instance, an increase in trade with the West in competitive goods might appear as a result of joint ventures or other forms of economic cooperation among East European countries, which would be reflected in increased intra-CMEA trade.

There are also some other factors that inhibit intra-CMEA trade, according to Dr. Marrese. Among these is an eagerness of many East European countries to export machinery and equipment and industrial consumer goods to the West. In addition, CMEA states have heavy dollar debt burdens, so they cannot extend large trade loans to the Soviet Union.

To begin with the second factor, intra-CMEA trade is not conducted in hard currency, so the lack of U.S. dollars can hardly be a direct impediment of trade transactions between CMEA countries. As to the first proposition, every CMEA state now desires more trade with the West, but, with few exceptions, the quality standards are too low to make their products competitive in the western markets. Therefore, the Soviet Union's willingness to buy machinery from East European countries saves many enterprises in the region from bankruptcy. In general, these lower-quality goods still satisfy relatively unsophisticated individual and industrial consumers in CMEA countries, but the quality of goods from CMEA partners has been criticized recently, in some instances in the Soviet press, making the quality issue a major problem in intra-CMEA trade.

It should again be emphasized that more trade with the West is desirable for every CMEA country, including the Soviet Union, but how it can happen remains to be seen. The prospects for a decrease in intra-CMEA trade should also be addressed in more detail.

RECENT TRENDS IN CMEA TRADE

The case study of Hungarian foreign trade does not provide sufficient information on how intra-CMEA trade developed in the last two decades. It is exactly the macro approach that produces serious reservations on possibilities of any significant reorientation of CMEA countries' trade with each other in the near future.

Some calculations based on United Nations unified statistical data show clearly a large and very fast increase in intra-CMEA trade in the 1980s (Table 9-1). The increase in the shares of intra-CMEA trade took place after a large decrease in the 1970s. In the 1970s alone, the share of internal CMEA (only European) exports fell by almost 10 percentage points, and imports by more than 11 percentage points. The most visible reasons for that were the following:

1. the spirit of détente, which materialized due to granting most-favored nation status to several countries;
2. large imports from the West by a number of East European countries as a consequence of huge hard-currency borrowing from western banks in the 1970s, especially by Poland, Hungary, and Romania; and

3. a great increase in the share of non-CMEA-oriented trade of
    the Soviet Union due to the rise of oil and gas prices and other
    raw materials, which are the main sources of Soviet hard-
    currency gains.   While this development inflated the value
    terms of Soviet exports to the West, it also gave the Soviet Union
    greater purchasing power in the western markets.

The data presented in Table 9-1 also clearly show that the
degree of the dependence of East European countries on trade with
the Soviet Union was considerably larger than noted.   In fact, the
share of intra-CMEA trade of East European countries was higher
in 1981 than the share of the Soviet Union's trade with these
partners by 14 percentage points in exports and 18 percentage
points in imports.   The situation changed during the decade, but
the differences still remained in 1986 to the amount of more than
7 percentage points on both sides of the trade balance.   In general,
with all other things being equal, this leads us to a conclusion that
challenges that drawn by Dr. Marrese.

To some extent, the roots of CMEA dependence could be
attributed to several decades of commercial transactions between
the Soviet Union and its East European allies at artificially
disadvantageous terms of trade for the former, a fact correctly stated
in Dr. Marrese's paper.   The subsidies hidden in much lower-
than-international prices for exported Soviet oil and gas—and also
paid in the form of more expensive than necessary imports of East
European industrial and consumer goods to the Soviet Union—
were justified at that time by political reasons, as their byproduct
resulted in a disservice to the economies of some CMEA countries.
Such a pattern of trade did not stimulate development of energy-
saving technologies, effective use of raw materials, and more
productive use of resources at large.   At the same time, low
standards of quality required on manufacturing exports to the Soviet
market, which had to be maintained to balance energy imports,
inhibited improvements in the competitiveness of East European
goods.

Will such hidden subsidies (or their elimination, more
precisely) play a major role in the development of intra-CMEA
trade in the future?   Hardly a large one.   In fact, prices on energy
exports from the Soviet Union to the CMEA countries came much

closer to the world price (a lower one) in the 1980s, yet there was still an increase in internal CMEA trade. That is not to say that structural problems caused by the trade subsidies will be easily and quickly solved, but it is clear that terms of trade do not explain the full dynamics of intra-CMEA commerce.

At this point, it is logical to look at some external factors that theoretically might work as a counterbalance to expanding intra-CMEA trade, and to explore the possibilities of a repeat of the 1970s in East-West trading patterns.

EXTERNAL FACTORS

One of the final conclusions Dr. Marrese draws in his paper predicts that increased trade with the West seems more likely to occur than increased intra-CMEA trade. Despite my differences with portions of Dr. Marrese's arguments, I agree with his conclusion and find it to be a very desirable goal.

Let us examine some economic trends that should be of great concern to the CMEA. Summarizing the statistical findings of Table 9-2, one might easily come to the conclusion that the CMEA, if the present trend continues, will face what amounts to economic isolation from the rest of the major industrial and trading states of the world. It should be viewed as a rather uncomfortable symptom not only by the socialist countries, which have to see it first of all as a consequence of inefficiency of their overly centralized and "market-ignoring" economic mechanisms. This should be a sub-ject of mutual concern to the West.

The transition to an interdependent world economic system is inevitable, and it might cause some pain and create considerable disturbances in many states. It appears that the transitional period will be peaceful if there is cooperation among all segments of the global economic community. Presently, the CMEA countries have not become involved to the extent that their constituent economies need to be involved.

In this context, the following question is of interest: Are there any indications from the West of a return to the era of détente in terms of East-West trade? First, the increase in economic contacts in the 1970s was undoubtedly the result of well-known developments in foreign policy.   The speed with which many channels were opened for cooperation with the East can be also explained by wide support in the West for the idea of inter-dependence between commerce and peace. But a decade later, in the conservative 1980s, this idea was labeled by many as a "mere echo of the liberal optimism of Jeremy Benthan and Richard Cobden," and as "Utopia."[2] Thus, now on the threshold of the 1990s, when the Cold War is said to be over, there is an unmistakable sense of change in international politics; as a result, some of the possibilities for bilateral trade may reopen. However, with continuing COCOM regulations, and the Jackson-Vanik and Stevenson amendments in place, one can hardly anticipate the same feeling of warmth that existed in the early 1970s.

Second, after a rather long time, some western banks began extending new commercial credits to the Soviet Union in the late 1980s, which will be reflected in a growth of Soviet imports from the West by $2-3 billion a year. A return to the 1970s in this area of financial credits is unlikely because of serious debt problems in almost every East European country except the Soviet Union.

Third, depressed oil and gas prices and falling demand on many raw materials will also negatively affect the Soviet Union's purchasing power in hard-currency markets in the foreseeable future.

In my opinion, the overall effect of a new rapprochement in East-West relations might result in a considerable increase in trade volume due to the Soviet Union's imports, and, to a lesser extent, to other CMEA countries' trade. But the level of "externally propelled" CMEA trade with the West in real terms will be less significant than in the 1970s.

THE CMEA'S NEW CONCEPTS OF COOPERATION AND FOREIGN TRADE

Most of the failures and difficulties in the process of establishing international economic contacts and cooperation by East European countries, particularly in developing intra-CMEA integration, are

2. See, for example, Zielonka (1988).

Table 9-1. Shares of Intra-CMEA Trade of East European Countries, 1970-1986[a] *(In Percentages)*

	1970		1980		1986	
	Exp.	Imp.	Exp.	Imp.	Exp.	Imp.
East Europe[b]						
Share of EE + USSR	63.9	63.5	56.4	54.8	60.6	59.8
USSR						
Share of EE	52.8	56.5	42.1	42.9	53.1	52.7
East Europe & USSR						
Share of EE + USSR	59.3	60.8	49.4	49.5	56.7	57.3

a. Data for 1986 is for the end of the third quarter.
b. Without USSR.

Source: United Nations (1988, 5.103-104).

Table 9-2. Shares of CMEA[a] Trade with the West, 1975-1986[b]

Share of Total CMEA Trade	1975	1986	Change (in %)
North America[c]			
Exports	2.4	1.1	-54
Imports	0.6	0.6	0
Japan			
Exports	3.9	1.9	-51
Imports	2.1	1.6	-24
West Europe[d]			
Exports	5.5	3.2	-42
Imports	3.8	3.5	-8

a. All East Europe, including Soviet Union.
b. At the end of the third quarter.
c. USA and Canada.
d. West Germany, France, Great Britain, Italy, Belgium, Netherlands, Luxembourg, Sweden, Switzerland, Denmark, Finland, Austria, Norway, and Ireland.

Source: United Nations (1988, 5.100, 5.105, 5.106).

deeply rooted in the ineffectiveness of the economic and management systems of socialist countries.

The list of shortcomings related to foreign trade and stemming
from internally generated dysfunctions might be rather long, but
it is generally agreed that it should include the following:

1. anti-import, autarkic economic strategies of East European
   countries based on Stalinist economic philosophy. This kind of
   policy led to the creation of parallel, duplicate economic structures within the CMEA, which was a clear disincentive to
   establishing trade and other forms of cooperation;
2. lack of an effective coordination mechanism on the CMEA
   level, mainly due to the bureaucratic nature of planning mechanisms in all participating countries;
3. the unimpressive (if any) role of individual enterprises in
   external economic relations, and the predominance of the
   administrative-bureaucratic model of "state-to-state" interaction;
   and
4. neglect of and resistance to the full-scale introduction of market
   and money instruments, which resulted in a lack of a reliable
   system of convertibility of national currencies, barriers to flows
   of investments, unrealistic price formation, and other problems.

Deep restructuring of the economic cooperation system within
the CMEA has been under way for two or three years, and the most
important benchmark of this process was the 44th Session of the
CMEA in Prague in the summer of 1988.

The major guidelines for restructuring worked out in collective
discussions in general could be summarized as:

1. the shift from inter-industry to intra-industry cooperation,
   which means a qualitatively new stage of economic integration;
2. the stress on the direct relationship between producers and
   consumers within the CMEA;
3. the creation of a genuine common market;
4. a change in the system of price formation and the currency
   mechanism, and an extensive use of contract prices;

5. introduction of a common currency; and
6. the creation of joint ventures.

The basis for all these changes is perestroika in the Soviet Union and the acceleration of reforms in the East European economies. In many respects, the faith of the new model of CMEA cooperation depends on the success of these reforms. Every new step in that direction will result in the considerable growth of intra-CMEA exchange of goods and services.

At the same time, another important feature of the new concept of the socialist international division of labor[3] is determination of the CMEA members to increase their export potential for trade with the West. One of the landmarks in this field was the recently signed declaration establishing official relations between the CMEA and the European Economic Community.

The restructuring of the system of external economic relations in the Soviet Union and East Europe is paving the way for more East-West trade for the following reasons:

1. A new Soviet regulation on joint ventures has already brought into existence, as of the beginning of December 1988, 143 Soviet-foreign joint venture agreements, the majority of which are with western corporations, involving total capital of about US$1 billion; another 300 ventures are now under consideration.

2. As a result of the decentralization of decisionmaking in foreign trade with the Soviet Union, roughly half of the Soviet Union's international trade in 1988 was conducted through individual enterprises rather than state trading bodies.

The process of introducing the new economic mechanisms in Soviet foreign trade brings about a deeper understanding of the remaining obstacles, as well as the following new problems:

1. The decentralization and creation of new "subjects" in the sphere of international economic contacts of the Soviet Union was not accompanied by a corresponding elimination of old

3. See Shiryaevs (1988a, 1988b) for a discussion of this topic.

"command" structures. In many cases, the bureaucratic system of management of foreign trade transactions was duplicated, and, as a result, a new, multi-staged process of decisionmaking has emerged.

2. The system of incentives for individual enterprises to export still needs more attention. The same is true of trading firms, which are still not fully reconverted into self-financing institutions.

3. A new set of regulatory tools has to be introduced to match the organization of Soviet foreign trade, including the system of tariffs, customs controls, trade statistics, and currency regulations. In the absence of such a system of universal controls, some individual decisions made by unsophisticated exporters might cause considerable damage to the Soviet Union's economic interests. Such an example was given in the Soviet press:

> One Italian company earlier this year offered the Soviet trading firm "Exportkhleb" 30,000 tons of Soviet yeast. It was previously acquired from an Austrian company, which might have bought it in Yugoslavia. In their turn, Yugoslavs received this yeast as a barter for equipment shipped to a yeast-processing factory in Odessa. One could hardly guess the initial super-low price of the yeast, or the super-high price of the equipment. Either way, the losses were very high, since in the end, even being transferred several times from firm to firm, the yeast was offered at a very good price.[4]

Nevertheless, changes occurring in this field are impressive by all standards. What is equally important, newly introduced legislation and regulations became, unlike long-standing tradition, more flexible, more realistic, and more receptive to successive amendments required by the changing situations. A few items on the current agenda for further restructuring of Soviet foreign trade include the following:[5]

1. Beginning in 1989, the current system of case-by-case licensing for international trade will be replaced by an open general

4. *Pravda*, August 16, 1988.

5. See, for example, a report on a press conference of the Deputy Chairman of the State Foreign Economic Commission of the USSR in the *International Herald Tribune*, October 15, 1988.

license for most transactions. In a process of gradually introducing a more liberal trade policy, individual enterprises will
be freed to make decisions on trade, investment, and financing
without prior state approval.

2. From 1991, a rationalized customs tariff structure will be fully
   operational, which will place the Soviet Union on equal footing
   with other industrialized trading nations.
3. For export promotion purposes, the ruble will be traded at a
   new, more realistic official rate by the end of 1990.
4. Other steps will be taken to make the ruble convertible; a full
   convertibility is to be attained by 1995.
5. New measures will be introduced to increase the attractiveness
   of joint ventures and other forms of foreign investment,
   including free trading zones.

Corresponding measures taken in other countries of East Europe
will integrate CMEA trade and currency systems with the
international framework sometime in the late 1990s. During this
period, we are likely to witness a gradual but steady increase in
East-West trade and economic cooperation accompanied by possibly
even faster growth of intra-CMEA trade turnover.

REFERENCES

Shiryaevs, Un. 1988a. *Voprosy ekonomiki,* No. 1: 97-106.
———. 1988b. *Kommunist,* No. 6: 87-96.
United Nations. 1988. U.N. Commission for Europe. *European Economic Survey, 1986-87.* Part II.
Zielonka, Jan. 1988. "East-West Trade: Is There a Way Out of the Circle?" *The Washington Quarterly:* 131-33, Winter.

Socialist Economic Integration: Achievements and Prospects

JOSEF C. BRADA

I. THE CMEA IN ECONOMIC PERSPECTIVE

The CMEA and Its Achievements

The functioning of the CMEA can be viewed as that of an international regime or a club.[1] It can be viewed as a regime in the sense that it has regularized and routinized interstate economic relations among its members, creating modes of economic intercourse that are, for its members, more convenient, less time consuming, less costly, and therefore more beneficial than they would be in its absence. The CMEA can also be viewed as a club because the benefits that it provides its members take the form of a public good and because the costs of providing these goods is borne by the members in a relatively clearly defined way. The benefits that the CMEA provides its members are the economic benefits of CMEA's customs-union-like structure, the creation of rules for price setting in intra-CMEA trade, the clearing of trade payments, and the coordination of economic plans. These benefits are public goods in the sense that any CMEA member's benefits from these arrangements need not reduce the availability of these benefits to other members.

---

1. For a survey of international regimes, see Krasner (1983). For an examination of the functioning of the CMEA as a club or regime, see Brada (1988).

The theory of clubs assumes that agents, in this case the member countries of CMEA, pursue their own self-interest.   However, a group of such agents may discover in certain situations that the existing environment supplies an insufficient quantity of a public good.   The agents have an incentive, then, to band together to supply themselves with a greater quantity of the public good.   If the club is effective, all members will attain higher levels of welfare despite the fact that they have to contribute resources to the club and may have their freedom of action restricted by its existence.   As with all schemes to provide public, or collective, goods, clubs are susceptible to difficulties arising from the "free rider" problem, which reflects the incentives that members have for shirking either by undercontributing to the operation of the club or by overusing or abusing the public good that it provides.   Therefore, the creation of the CMEA and its operation cannot be explained solely by structural factors such as the distribution of power among its members or by their ideological cohesion.   Rather, CMEA must be viewed as a regime that balances those elements of member self-interest that promote adhesion to its practices against those elements of self-interest that incite members to shirk.

In the case of the CMEA, the public good desired by the member countries was an international regime for promoting trade and economic integration among members.   The need for a unique, socialist, trade regime existed not only because the West excluded the Soviet bloc from the world trading system in the early postwar period.   The international trade and payments system adopted by the rest of the world also did not meet the need of the planned economies.   The stress on currency convertibility of the Bretton Woods system was inconsistent with the conception of central planning held then by all, and today by most, CMEA members.   The emphasis of the General Agreement on Tariffs and Trade (GATT) on the systematic reduction of tariff barriers was simply irrelevant to nations whose foreign trade was conducted through state monopolies.   Moreover, the GATT's insistence on nondiscriminatory treatment of trade partners was both at odds with the notion of socialist integration and solidarity and in any case was not observed by the industrialized West in its trade policies vis-à-vis the planned economies.

In creating the CMEA, its members sought an alternative international regime that would facilitate decisionmaking about, and yield the best possible execution of, intra-CMEA trade and development. The desire for such an organization was based not only on the failure of the existing international trade and payments system to provide mechanisms appropriate to the needs of the planned economies. Perhaps more important was the fact that planned economies require an international regime to mediate trade among them more than do market economies. Among the latter, trade takes place between private agents at market determined prices. States need to interact with each other only to set the rules for such transactions, to enforce contracts, and to promote the functioning of markets. Among planned economies, international trade is a state monopoly. Thus, markets cannot function, because each transaction confronts a monopolist with a monopsonist. As a result, in trade among the planned economies there is less information, transactions are much costlier to negotiate, and states must interact with each other directly as parties to each transaction rather than merely as creators and guarantors of the rules of the game. The CMEA pricing rule, by basing prices on world market prices, eliminates the need for CMEA members to interact as intensively as they would if they had to negotiate prices independently of such a rule.

Similar differences between planned and market economies exist over structural policies. In market economies, private agents seek out investment opportunities on the basis of expected markets at home and abroad and the anticipated behavior of competitors. Governments are free to influence the general level of economic activity and to engage in structural policies, but the consequences of these policies are left to the market to sort out. Among planned economies, both macroeconomic and structural development are the responsibility of the state. Thus, the macroeconomic and structural policies of one planned economy are seen not as an environmental factor to which firms in other countries must respond, but rather as a factor influencing the ability of other CMEA members to manage and develop their economies in the way they desire. Therefore, the CMEA's efforts to develop schemes for plan coordination and industrial specialization are based not only on economic factors such as economies of scale and benefits of specialization, but also on the desire to reduce inter-member transaction costs in the settling of structural policy.

Consequently, in comparison to market economies, among planned economies there is less information on the conditions of, and a greater level of state-to-state interaction over, trade and integration. This difference results in a greater need for a regime in planned economy states to mediate these interactions and to produce substitutes for market-generated information. Such a regime could not have as its objective the elimination of bargaining and negotiation among its members. Rather, the objective of the CMEA, or the public good that is provided, must be the creation of an environment within which the future behavior of member states would be stable and predictable. In such an environment, a network of mutual obligations and expectations regarding future behavior could be established, thus routinizing interactions among states, lowering transaction costs, and creating substitutes for market-generated information.

The most visible and most successful aspect of CMEA integration was the expansion of intra-CMEA trade. Trade theories ascribe two sets of benefits to increased trade among members of preferential trading schemes. The first are static effects, which derive from the international specialization that results from increased trade and the subsequent increase in the efficiency of resource utilization. It is generally assumed that such static effects are proportional to the increase in intra-group trade over the level that would exist without integration. If this criterion is accepted for the CMEA, then it is evident that the CMEA's ability to increase inter-member trade is, given the physical characteristics of its members and their level of development, as effective as western integration schemes such as the EC and EFTA (Brada and Mendez 1985).

There is also a second set of benefits that accrue to members of a regional integration scheme, the so-called dynamic effects. These accrue from the stimulus of greater inter-member exchanges on innovation and technological progress, economies of scale, managerial skills, and the level of investment. While there is no evidence that the CMEA was able to increase the volume of investment of member countries, it was able to accelerate the other above-mentioned dynamic elements to a level comparable to that achieved by western integration schemes.[2]

CMEA integration was much less successful in promoting less traditional means of exploiting differences in factor endowments and technology among its members. The transfer of technology through the exchange and sale of technology has been limited and generally unsatisfactory. Until 1971, the exchange of technology among members of the CMEA was free, an arrangement that clearly did not encourage those countries that had useful technology to make any effort to assure its successful transfer to countries that desired it. The institution of a system of payments for technology in 1971 did little to improve the situation for several reasons. The first of these is that unlike commodities, technological advance is unique and difficult to price. For example, the price of coal or a machine can be determined with fair accuracy because many transactions in each of these (or roughly comparable) commodities take place many times on the world market. On the other hand, the formula for a new drug or a new way of producing a product may be sold only a few times, if at all, and there is thus no way of judging its price by referring to the market. In addition, the costs and benefits of a particular technology are very uncertain. Firms do, of course, know what their research outlays are, but these are virtually impossible to apportion among successful innovations and, more important, among successful and unsuccessful ones. Moreover, many improvements in production processes are the result of an accumulation of many minor improvements made by engineers and production workers on the shop floor. The wages of these individuals do not figure in research and development expenditures, and so the seller's evaluation of the cost of this sort of technological improvement is, to some extent, arbitrary.

Buyers of technology also face considerable uncertainty regarding the value of the technology they purchase. This is due in part to the fact that some forms of technology are not protected by patents and licenses. As a result, it may be that if the seller were to reveal sufficient detail about the technology to the buyer to permit the latter to evaluate its value, sufficient knowledge would be

2. Nevertheless, these dynamic elements represent much smaller gains than are commonly supposed. See Brada and Mendez (1988).

imparted to the buyer to enable him to implement the technology without further assistance from the seller. Clearly, buyers in such cases will not reveal fully the details of their technology. In other cases, the buyer faces uncertainty regarding the future stream of benefits that will result from a purchase of technology because that particular technology could be supplanted by a rival technology that might be developed at some time in the future.

In market economies, these barriers to technology transfer are overcome by multinational corporations (MNCs). MNCs internalize the failures in the market for technology that prevent the sale of their technology to foreigners by establishing affiliates in foreign countries. These affiliates then make use of the parent's technology without the need for costly and uncertain efforts to determine a price for such technology. There are no mechanisms for setting up affiliates of the enterprises of one country in the other member countries within the CMEA, and this must serve as a severe constraint on the flows of technology among CMEA members.[3]

The CMEA also lacks a mechanism for transferring other productive resources from one country to another. Labor movements are infrequent and are associated largely with construction work implemented in connection with the development of natural resources in the Soviet Union. The lack of a mechanism to transfer capital from one country to another is also evident. Joint investments have been carried out, but generally they have proven unpopular, particularly in the East European countries that have been the principal creditors to such projects.

The CMEA has attempted to create substitutes for the free flow of technology and factors of production that are required to maximize the benefits of economic integration. It has done so largely by trying to foster scientific-technical cooperation and specialization. Cooperation in science and technology, however, is limited in its ability to transfer technology among cooperating countries because it can only transfer certain kinds of technology or knowledge. Firm-specific advantages in knowledge regarding technology, business techniques, and organization likely remain outside the

---

3. Joint ventures such as Haldex are the exception that demonstrate the problem at hand.

scope of such agreements, although the evidence on the behavior of MNCs suggests that such knowledge predominates in technology transfer among market economies.

Specialization also has its shortcomings. In specialization agreements, CMEA members divide up the production of certain products or product lines among member countries. Data on the share of products produced under production specialization agreements show that their share in intra-CMEA trade in manufactures is increasing, but the effectiveness of specialization in capturing the technological advantages of individual countries is limited. First, in many cases specialization agreements often cover products that would be traded even in the absence of such agreements. This is particularly true in the case of the more developed CMEA countries. For example, Czechoslovakia has over 200 bilateral and multilateral specialization agreements in general engineering. However, over 90 percent of specialized exports of this sector are covered by eight agreements. All of these eight agreements cover very traditional products of the engineering sector, products that Czechoslovakia would be exporting even in the absence of specialization agreements. Second, it is not clear that specialization in various products is not parceled out more on the basis of political criteria and the need to give every member a piece of the action rather than on the ability of individual countries to master the technology required. Often, certain countries fail to meet the needs of the other CMEA members in the products that are the object of specialization agreements.

Finally, the CMEA financial system in practice provides only an accounting function. The smaller CMEA member countries tend to maintain balanced trade with each other, and only the Soviet Union has run large bilateral surpluses and deficits. The transferable ruble is neither a reserve asset nor a viable medium of exchange. Indeed, because it is overvalued relative to western currencies, for many CMEA countries it serves as a poor unit of account that distorts the perception of their geographic distribution of trade.

The members of the CMEA did not, of course, set out to design a system that was dysfunctional. Rather, they sought a system that would best serve their needs, given the constraints under which it had to function. The most important constraint was, and is, the domestic economic mechanisms in some, if not all, of the CMEA countries.

II. REFORMING THE CMEA

To the extent that the CMEA fails to evolve so as to provide a desirable trading regime for all its members, it risks becoming irrelevant to their foreign trade behavior. A number of members, especially Hungary, Poland, and the Soviet Union, are seeking to reform their foreign trade systems by moving to a more decentralized market-based mechanism that would eventually lead to the convertibility of their currencies. Other CMEA members, such as Romania and the German Democratic Republic, prefer to see a continuation and strengthening of the existing CMEA system of trade and payments. These disagreements and the need for unanimity on major CMEA decisions have frozen CMEA in its old mold and channeled members' foreign trade reforms into the area of East-West trade.

In this section, I develop a proposal for reforming the CMEA mechanism that would meet the realistic needs of its reform-oriented members for a more market-oriented basis for their trade, while at the same time moving their currencies toward convertibility. The proposal is also consistent with the distorted price structures and excess demand for consumer goods that exist within member countries as well as with the rather asymmetric manufactures-for-fuels and raw materials nature of Soviet trade with other CMEA members. Finally, the proposed reform does not require the participation of all members; rather, only those countries that wish to trade under the new regime need do so—all others can continue to conduct their CMEA trade under existing arrangements.

The preconditions for a radical reform of the CMEA mechanism are the dismantling of the state's monopoly over foreign trade and the devolution of trading rights to individual enterprises. At the same time, reforming countries must attempt to equilibrate their consumer-goods markets, particularly the markets for manufactured goods, and to have prices for such goods more accurately reflect the costs of production. At this time, and in the near future, even the most reformed CMEA economy displays tremendous distortions in prices and the pattern of production. The consumption of agricultural products is heavily subsidized, with retail prices well below the prices paid to agricultural producers. Fuels and raw materials are priced substantially below the cost of obtaining them domestically or through imports, and capital goods are also underpriced domestically. Worse yet, the pattern of subsidization and the extent of both macro- and microeconomic distortions varies widely from one CMEA member to another. Nor can such a pattern of distortions be eliminated by domestic reforms alone, because domestic prices must reflect trading opportunities as well as domestic resources and demands, particularly for the smaller CMEA members.

Because of these distortions in each CMEA member's economy, it would be impossible to attempt to engage in a reform of the CMEA trading mechanism that covered all commodities, even if all CMEA members would be willing to attempt such a reform. A more feasible, yet far-reaching, reform would be to marketize trade in some commodities, while maintaining the existing CMEA system for trade in other commodities.

Fuels, raw materials, and agricultural products would constitute the bulk of the goods that would continue to be traded on the basis of the traditional system of long-term, state-to-state agreements. In the case of fuels and raw materials, it is unlikely that the importing countries would be willing to yield decisions over such strategic inputs to enterprise-to-enterprise contacts. Moreover, to make the importation of such commodities profitable to firms would require either massive subsidization of importers, with its attendant inefficiencies, or an increase in the domestic prices of fuels and raw materials and the consequent inflation of all prices. In the case of agricultural products, both the desire to maintain adequate supplies for domestic consumption and the subsidization of the consumption of food argue against dismantling the existing system of state-to-state trade. Because producer prices are higher than consumer prices in all CMEA agricultural sectors, few firms would be willing to import food purchased at the wholesale prices of another CMEA member if it were to be sold at the retail prices of the importing country. On the other hand, no CMEA country would be willing to export many agricultural products if foreign enterprises were to purchase them at retail prices, because sales at these prices are highly subsidized. Thus, both within each CMEA country and in CMEA trade, fuels, raw materials, and agricultural products would be produced, bought, sold, and traded by traditional means, mainly at fixed prices. For these "fixed-price" goods, the existing arrangements are simply too costly to dismantle.

Consumer manufactures and capital goods would make up the so-called "free-price" goods. These goods would be traded on an enterprise-to-enterprise basis at prices that would be negotiated between the buyer and seller. Consumer goods could thus be imported either by retail establishments for sale to the general public or by producing enterprises for sale to their own workers. In this way, the effort to develop a functioning internal market and to stimulate competition on national markets that are often monopolized or oligopolized would be materially aided by the foreign trade sector.[4]

Prerequisites for such enterprise-to-enterprise trade on a large scale, rather than on the very limited scale now being attempted with the CMEA, are the creation of internal markets for these goods and the development of a monetary regime that would permit enterprise-to-enterprise transactions in national currencies to take place. The development of domestic markets is perhaps the most daunting barrier, because it is commonly believed that there is significant excess demand for consumer goods in all the CMEA countries. Nevertheless, it should be borne in mind that a large part of this excess demand makes itself felt on the markets for foodstuffs, housing, services, and certain consumer durables, such as automobiles. At the same time, there are many consumer manufactures, such as clothing, footwear, and some consumer durables, that, given the assortment and quality of their production within the CMEA, are in adequate if not excess supply. Thus, with foodstuffs a fixed-price good and housing and services not traded, the creation of a genuine domestic market for consumer manufactures may be quite feasible. For those consumer manufactures that are in short supply, such as automobiles, tariffs can be erected to limit the volume of imports. In the case of capital goods, the current austerity

4. Moreover, the competition from socialist enterprises in other CMEA countries would be a "fairer" and more equal competition than that provided by imports of western goods, where the preferences of the buyers would be overwhelmingly for the western good.

measures and investment cutbacks in most CMEA countries would appear to have created a situation where the supply of machinery and equipment, especially of the less sophisticated and more standardized variety, may also exceed available demand.

The monetary regime required to implement such a scheme is quite simple. Enterprises in each CMEA country participating in this scheme would be permitted to buy and sell free-price goods in any other CMEA country participating in the scheme. The foreign exchange—that is, the domestic currency of other CMEA countries—earned through the export of free-price goods could be converted into domestic currency by the national bank of the exporter's country. Similarly, enterprises seeking to import free-price goods can do so either by offering to pay in the importing country's currency or by purchasing the exporter's currency from the importer's national bank. Thus, each country's national bank would hold reserves of the currency of each of the other participating countries and would fix a rate at which it would buy and sell its currency against that of the others. If one country found itself with an undesirable surplus or deficit in a particular currency, it could eliminate it either through a currency swap with another central bank, or it could change the exchange rate.[5]

The CMEA could also develop new institutions or modify existing ones to make the reformed trading system function more smoothly. One problem will be that the prices of consumer manufactures and capital goods may evolve quite differently in the short run. Thus, depending on whether a country is a net exporter of consumer manufactures or of capital goods, it may experience an improvement or deterioration of its terms of trade. A fund to provide compensation for losers might be organized along the lines of the European Community's Common Agricultural Policy. All CMEA members would contribute to the fund, while those suffering the largest terms of trade losses would be compensated. Such a measure should, of course, be seen as a transitional one, to be phased out over an agreed-upon period of time. Another useful role for a CMEA institution would be to create an auction where

5. Note that although the exchange rate between the currencies of countries A and B would be set independently by their two central banks, transactions would only be made at the more favorable rate, thus creating a single exchange rate between A and B.

members' central banks could sell and purchase the currencies of other members according to their reserve needs. Since such currencies would now be freely convertible into free-price goods, the commodity inconvertibility that plagues the transferable ruble would be avoided.

The proposal that I have put forward here has, to my mind, a number of desirable features. First, it is feasible in that it can be adopted under the CMEA's "interested countries" principle, thus avoiding the need to have reform of CMEA trade tied to the pace of its least reform-minded members. Moreover, the domestic reforms required to achieve this limited form of convertibility are modest. From such undemanding measures a great deal of good can result. Domestic production and intra-CMEA trade in free-price goods will be rationalized, creating greater efficiency, competition, and the allocation of production according to the principle of comparative advantage. Consumers will also benefit, not only from a wider choice among goods but also because the surpluses of one country will be available to reduce the shortages in another. By making each of the currencies of CMEA members at least partially convertible into goods, this proposal would do much to eliminate the problems of bilateralism, commodity inconvertibility, and the issues of hard goods versus soft goods that currently plague the CMEA. Finally, the effort to establish convertibility within the CMEA would entail much less dislocation and much less pressure on the economies of these countries than would an effort to first achieve convertibility against such hard currencies as the dollar and the yen. Indeed, intra-CMEA convertibility should be seen as a modest but effective step toward achieving the convertibility of the CMEA currencies against western currencies.

REFERENCES

Brada, Josef C. 1988. "Interpreting the Soviet Subsidization of Eastern Europe." *International Organization* 42, 4, Autumn.

Brada, Josef C., and José A. Mendez. 1985. "Economic Integration Among Developed, Developing and Centrally Planned Economies: A Comparative Analysis." *Review of Economics and Statistics* LXVII, 4, November.

——. 1988. "An Estimate of the Dynamic Effects of Integration." *Review of Economics and Statistics* LXX, 1, February.

Krasner, Stephen D., ed. 1983. *International Regimes.* Ithaca and London: Cornell University Press.

_____

CHAPTER 11

New Trends in World Economic Development and East-West Relations

ALEXANDER VOLKOV

As we approach the 1990s, we are at the beginning of a long and largely unexplored road toward the adjustment of economic relations between East and West. This road presents itself largely because of the profound conceptual turn toward new political thinking in the Soviet Union's foreign policy, especially due to a new concept of the relationship between class and universal human principles in the modern world. These developments require a new look at East-West economic relations in light of the changes that have taken shape in the world economy in recent decades.

THE ECONOMY AND POLICIES OF THE TRANSITIONAL PERIOD

The outstanding feature of the mid-1970s to mid-1980s was the beginning of intensive structural changes in most of the industrially developed countries' (IDCs) economies, particularly those in the United States. The essential element in these changes is the parallel development of science-intensive branches and the radical refitting of the so-called "smokestack industries." The interval during which old economic proportions are being broken down and new ones are being formed is effectively a transitional period from one economic structure to another.

The transitional period of the economy cannot be evaluated on the basis of traditional concepts of external growth factors. At a time when interbranch ties are being restructured, the dynamic behavior of all economic indices, such as the external payments balance and inflation, is "abnormal" in a certain sense: the need to mobilize substantial financial resources within a relatively short period of time and to funnel them into developing certain branches inevitably produces disproportions and disequilibria. The deficit in the U.S. trade balance is one of the most telling examples of such a disequilibrium.

From 1980 to 1987, the U.S. foreign trade deficit increased 6.2 times and reached a level of $159.2 billion. Viewed from within a traditional framework, perhaps those who regard this trend as a fundamental danger to the U.S. economy are right: a rising dollar created the foreign trade deficit that affects the exchange rate, which in turn helps to lower the competitiveness of the country's goods and ultimately may lead to a high rate of inflation.

Interpreting the U.S. foreign trade deficit as a phenomenon of a transitional period leads to a different conclusion. About one-third of the worsening in the U.S. foreign trade balance in the 1980s was caused by the stream of machinery and equipment imports. Importing capital goods is advantageous to U.S. corporations for at least two reasons. The currency exchange rate relationships among IDCs in the 1980s led to a situation in which imported basic capital goods became less expensive than their U.S.-produced counterparts. As a result, it was more efficient for them to acquire a finished new machine than to spend time and money developing and producing one themselves. For instance, from 1981 to 1987, the index of imported prices for machine-building production and transportation increased 15.3 percent, while wholesale prices for these trade groups on the domestic market rose by 16.3 percent. According to present estimates, the import of products from abroad in 1986 held down the growth rate of U.S. domestic prices by a total of 5.5 percent (*Statistical Abstract* 1988). All this permits us to draw the conclusion that, in the course of structural reorganization, foreign trade enables U.S. corporations to reduce the volume of the accumulation fund, which is essential for its existence.

The necessity of mobilizing substantial financial resources to carry out economic transformations during a transitional period is one of the principal reasons for the origin and growth of U.S. foreign indebtedness. The transformation of the United States into the world's largest importer of capital attracted the attention of economists, entrepreneurs, and journalists. Articles appeared one after another in the U.S. press with disturbing headlines about the "sale" of the United States, and there were serious discussions about what to do if foreign investors suddenly decided to acquire such corporations as General Motors. There were corresponding calls for protecting the United States from the encroachments of foreigners by placing reliable barriers to the penetration of foreign capital into the country's economy.

However, emotions aside, it must be recognized that the United States during the 1980s gained more from the flow of foreign capital than it suffered. From our viewpoint, the foreign financial credits that poured into the U.S. economy provided an invaluable service to the Republican Party; with their help, the Reagan administration managed to achieve simultaneously three hardly compatible goals: maintaining military expenditures at a high level, carrying out a structural reorganization of the country, and avoiding lowering the living standards of the U.S. population.

During the 1980s, direct foreign investments increasingly contributed to the technological reequipping of enterprises in the traditional sector—the so-called Rust Belt—of the U.S. economy. Japanese entrepreneurs alone have invested more than $5 billion in redeveloping the U.S. Northeast. This money went to build new factories and to acquire and open formerly shut-down enterprises from their U.S. owners. The high proportion of the local component (about 70 percent) in these factories' products attests to the fact that foreign capital investments are creating important additional demand in certain parts of the United States. Foreign capital exerts a powerful multiplier effect on the U.S. economy on the macroeconomic level as well.[1]

Thus, one can conclude that new trends in world economic development (the intensified flood of goods and capital into the United States) have on the whole contributed to solving tasks during this transitional period in the U.S. economy. The abnormal dynamic in the indices of foreign trade and the balance of

1. According to our calculations (omitted here for reasons of space), the absolute multiplier effect of all forms of foreign capital on aggregrate demand in the U.S. economy is approximately 8.

payments should, in our view, be regarded as payment for the rapid pace and relative social and political painlessness of structural reorganization.

Therefore, in our opinion, the dynamism of foreign trade indices, regarded as dangerous when viewed from traditional standpoints, should not be considered disturbing. Naturally, this does not mean that the increased foreign trade deficit and foreign debt represents a blessing for the U.S. economy. Over a certain period of time, the U.S. economy will gain from the flood of goods and capital from abroad. The question is how effectively it is utilizing import resources and whether its structural reorganization will succeed in bearing fruit before debts have to be paid. Yet there can be little doubt that so far the positive effects on the U.S. economy from the flood of goods and capital from abroad exceed the potential consequences.

The isolation of transitional periods in the course of economic development makes it possible to advance several theoretical joints concerning the foreign economic ties of any country. First, if the importance of foreign trade in solving domestic economic tasks is acknowledged, it ceases to be considered only as a pump for extorting money from other countries. Estimates of its effectiveness should not be based on whether a country sold goods and services abroad worth $10 billion more than it acquired; the main criterion, in our view, should be the contribution made by foreign trade to the modernization of industry, even if this results in a deficit in the trade balance.

Second, the very phrasing of the question—what should the trade balance be?—is incorrect. The appropriate amount of external stimulus or restraint depends on the condition of a particular country's business cycle. An external deficit helps fend off inflationary pressures, while a surplus can provide stimulus needed to escape a recession.

Third, a flow of foreign capital to a country signifies, on the most general level: (1) the appearance of an extra factor of economic growth, and (2) not so much an increase in its dependence on financial resources from foreign capital as an intensified interdependence between creditor and debtor.

This has a direct bearing on prospects for East-West economic relations. During the 1980s, the Soviet economy entered into a

transitional period, just as the U.S. economy did. The basic parameters, goals, and directions of structural change in the Soviet
economy are generally similar to those in the U.S. But at the
same time, there are significant differences in the changing
economic contours of the two countries. A basic peculiarity of the
late 1980s is that foreign economic factors have played a minimal
role in the implementation of the economic restructuring of the
Soviet Union. This result is all the more dismaying, in that a very
major reform of foreign economic ties was carried out during the
mid-1980s with the goal of improving their effectiveness.

In our opinion, the primary reason for the failure of the foreign
economic factor contributing to the reforms lies in a lack of
understanding of the transitional nature of the present stage in the
country's development. It is especially important to understand that
the political sphere, along with the economic sphere, plays a
central role in the transitional period. The question of integrating the Soviet Union into the world economy and expanding
East-West economic ties is a political, not economic, question.
Reforms in the economic area in the Soviet Union have, strange as
it seems, far outstripped the level of political concepts about the
normal course of developing the country's foreign economic sphere.
It is still believed that the trade balance with western countries
must be positive, that borrowing on the world credit market should
not exceed "acceptable" proportions.

Political views have become more fluid and more subject to
change during the transitional period. It is likely, therefore, that
the role of East-West economic relations in the Soviet Union's
national economic development will undergo a political reevaluation, which will most likely occur in stages. We believe there
will be two principal stages in this process.

During the first stage, judging from world experience
(primarily that of the United States), the Soviet Union will
recognize that there is a need for an "abnormal" dynamic in the
country's foreign trade indices during the transitional period in
order to achieve a faster and more effective restructuring of the
Soviet economy. To realize these changes in practice will also
require a revision of western positions with respect to integrating
the Soviet Union into the world economy. One of the most
frequently encountered arguments against activating this process is

that cooperation with the West will give the Soviet Union one-sided advantages. Although it would be impossible to repudiate this notion completely, it is essential to take into account the fact that such a development would not occur in all areas. Western countries would gain from broader cooperation in some spheres. Besides, in our view, it is better to sacrifice a small advantage to gain a greater one. To be sure, during the initial stage of cooperation the Soviet Union could gain more from improved East-West economic relations than its western partners. If western countries recognize the "lawfulness" of the Soviet Union's receiving one-sided advantages for a certain time, many obstacles to developing inter-systemic relations will be removed.

The second and more complicated stage presupposes a political evaluation of the possible internal consequences of expanded East-West economic cooperation. For example, a serious commitment to attracting foreign capital to the Soviet Union presupposes the use of forms other than simply direct foreign investments. Foreign capital functioning in the country takes four forms: (1) direct investments, (2) portfolio investments, (3) official assets, and (4) bank deposits. Only in combination can they exert maximum effect on the economy of the receiving country. Emphasis on attracting only one form of foreign capital is like trying to drive a car that is not equipped with all its wheels: the motor will run, but the car will not go very far. On the other hand, the attraction of foreign portfolio investments to the Soviet Union will require a radical reform of the economic mechanism, including the creation of a securities market.

Moreover, it is essential to note that a massive influx of foreign capital into the Soviet Union, even in the form of direct investments, could have profound political consequences on Soviet society. As is well known, major western corporations establish rewards and incentives for employees of their foreign enterprises with the goal of increasing production efficiency, and these rewards and incentives are not in line with pay scales in those countries. The ground is thus prepared for substantial social differentiation within a society. The need arises to form political organizations reflecting the interests of these social groups.

So far, it is clear only that both East and West have entered a transitional phase in their development. In our view, an expansion in their economic cooperation is most likely at this point, although it will require serious political rethinking on both sides. For a fuller examination of prospects for East-West economic relations, we must also take into account trends in the development of leading world economic centers, including West Europe, the United States, and Japan.

A NEW STAGE IN EUROPEAN INTEGRATION

In the early 1980s, the idea of forming a unified internal market emerged as one of the first priorities in the European Economic Community (EC). In the Unified Europe Act, signed in February 1986, a goal was set to create by 1992 an expanse within the limits of which free movement of workforce, services, and capital would be guaranteed. Apart from purely internal reasons, an important role in the acceptance of this decision was played by foreign economic factors. According to data from a recent study conducted by the *Wall Street Journal* and the English company Bus-Allen and Hamilton, Inc., a fragmented market is the main obstacle to the growth of the competitiveness of West European goods in comparison to those made in the United States and Japan. This factor's contribution to the increase in production costs of each product is on average 10 percent.[2] At the same time, in our opinion, the elimination of this burden would not effect a dramatic or fundamental change in international economic relations, at least not in mid-range terms, for the following reasons:

1. The achievement of the EC's goal is an important, though not definitive, factor in world economic development. The results of economic reforms in the United States and the dynamics of development in Japan's "second economy" will be of equal significance.
2. The unified internal market of the EC has from the very start been an international formation. Strange as it may seem, U.S. multinational corporations are one of the most active supporters of its creation. According to data from the International Bank

2. *Wall Street Journal,* March 1987.

for Reconstruction and Development, companies from fifteen countries, including twelve from Europe, took part in the production of Ford Escorts, which took place in factories in Great Britain and West Germany (World Bank 1987, 39). By forming a wide net of suppliers in different countries for the production of one model, U.S. companies are making "global car-building" possible, which incorporates hundreds of facilities all over Europe and tens of thousands of workers into one mechanism. Thus, the material precursors of a unified internal market are being established. In addition, U.S. companies interested in limiting production expenses are making the liberalization of the flow of products, capital, and the workforce in West Europe possible in a number of ways.

3. The formation of a unified internal market in West Europe will most likely not bring anything cardinally new to the already established trends in world trade. In the 1970s, growth of the share of machine production in the general volume of U.S. imports and exports was already being observed: from 1970 to 1986, it grew from 42 percent to 46.2 percent and from 28 percent to 43.7 percent, respectively (*Statistical Abstract* 1988). This trend has been common in world economic development since World War II. At the same time, as historical experience shows, in periods of major structural change, this trend intensifies. It is completely possible that by the time economic changes in Europe begin, and adequate structures for the unified internal market economy form, U.S. industry will already possess modernized equipment, and it will be the "old world's" turn to catch up. Thus, despite the possible growth of the share of machines and equipment in the volume of foreign trade turnover of individual West European countries, this will not cause a serious change on the level of world trade structure indicators.

The above analysis suggests that a unified internal market in West Europe has already been formed. However, despite the fact that the target dates for each phase have been strictly set, the probability of achieving the EC's goal on time is decreasing due to several serious obstacles, the foremost of which is tax barriers. The standardization of taxes (on corporations, for example) is an extremely complicated question, because it demands a radical restructuring of national tax systems. Inasmuch as this affects the most important areas—budgetary, social, and political—in national policy, not all the member nations are attempting to put the decision on taxes into practice. After all, identical tax rates for all governments would mean a decline in revenues for some countries and an increased fiscal burden for others already fraught with social unrest. On the whole, many European countries perceive the standardization of tax systems as a threat to national sovereignty. Under a general lack of regulation of the economies of the IDCs, the loss of fiscal methods of regulation is looked upon as a loss of the right to self-determination of economic policy.

A no less serious obstacle to the creation of a unified internal market lies in the area of technology, specifically in national norms and standards in industrial production and manufactured goods. Differences in the standardization of individual components, sanitary and technical norms, or packing demands create added complications in introducing new products into new national markets, which significantly limits production efficiency. For example, to sell its products in Europe, the Phillips Company had to issue twenty-nine types of sockets, produce fifteen types of irons, and make twelve cord modifications. The attempt to use norms and standards for protectionist ends, as well as to bring them into conformity with particular national norms and standards, makes overcoming technical barriers all the more difficult. As a rule, reworking standards takes several years and, in some cases, almost a decade.

Steps in this direction began in 1985, when the European Union approved a new approach to standardization policy by establishing basic guidelines for products. If a model conformed to national standards satisfied these basic demands, then it was accepted and sold in all EC countries. However, despite conformity and unification of national standards, there is still a long way to go.

The third obstacle lies in the national contracts market. Considering that in the early 1980s 15 percent of the gross domestic production of the EC countries went for national contracts, the liberalization in the current system of national contracts could become an important factor in the formation of an internal market. However, at this time, there are many exceptions that enable state organizations to select contractors from a number of national firms, which is evident in international trade data from several European countries. In the early 1980s, all contracts announced for bidding in Italy were awarded to Italian companies; in West Germany, France, and the United Kingdom, similar indicators were, respectively, 99.7 percent, 99.1 percent, and 98.3 percent.

On the basis of the above observations, we can draw the following conclusions:

1. The establishment of a unified internal market in West Europe by the beginning of the 1990s is highly doubtful. It is more likely that the EC will still be in a transformation period then, and it will include characteristics of both the old and new systems.
2. Even if such a market is created in the allotted period of time, it is unlikely that it will have significant influence on the already noted trends in the structure of the world economy. Generally, it will consist of growth in the share of manufactured goods, primarily machines and equipment and assembled goods. Also, it is likely that the situation will stabilize by the mid-1990s. As far as changes in the geographic distribution of the flow of goods are concerned, isolation of Europe from the United States and Japan is possible.
3. The achievement of a qualitatively new level in European integration is an important step toward creating a unified and interdependent world.

From the point of view of East-West relations, these trends may be interpreted as follows:

1. The creation of a unified internal market in Europe will make the establishment of closer trade and economic ties between the EC and the socialist countries possible (on the alliance/bloc level).
2. The formation of a first-ever unified intercountry internal market raises the question of economic security in East-West relations. Traditionally, this has meant economic security of individual countries or groups of countries. In perspective, the

question must pertain not to the guarantee of security for blocs of countries with differing socioeconomic systems, but to the guarantee of security for all countries of the world community. The actions of individual countries and blocs will determine the achievement of this goal on the global level.

3. The formation of a unified internal market in West Europe is one of the factors guaranteeing the Soviet Union a variety of options in selecting trade and economic partners. This means that while previously only the United States was considered "equal" as a potential economic partner, now the "new world" has some serious competition. Such a turn of events makes increased development of the Soviet Union's ties with both the United States and West Europe possible. Periodically, under the bipolar system of East-West relations, disagreements could persist for decades; now, the number of competitors intent on their share is making it difficult to drag one's feet in establishing ties between the two socioeconomic systems.

THE ROLE OF THE U.S. IN THE WORLD ECONOMY

The U.S. role in the world economy is one of the most important factors determining the course of East-West relations in the coming decades. In connection with this, we must note the recent appearance of assertions as to the decline of the U.S. role in the world economy. Two pieces of evidence are usually presented in support of this hypothesis: one concerns the decline in the U.S. share of the world's total economic output, trade, and industry, while the other concerns the United States as the world's largest debtor nation. In our view, which goes against traditional conceptions of world economy, the evidence is insufficient for the following reasons:

1. The notorious reduction of the U.S. share of world trade and production in the past ten years has not exceeded 4 percent, while over the same period the volume of world trade has increased by 244 percent. Under such conditions, the relative decline of the U.S. share in world economic indicators means a deepening of the international division of labor and

increasing economic interdependence of the United States and
other nations.

2. The above-mentioned trend shows that rating the position of a
   nation in the world must be done not with quantitative but
   with qualitative indicators. From this point of view, the United
   States may be likened to a gigantic holding company that,
   while owning a small amount of the total stock, has the ability
   to control an amount of capital ten times greater than its
   owned stock indicates.

3. Current economic policy indicates that the IDCs have a
   significantly greater interest in securing the U.S. economy
   from crisis than any other group of countries in the world. A
   collapse in the United States, more than in any other country,
   would mean worldwide failure of the global financial system
   and a breakdown in international trade.

4. The United States possesses significant reserves, including
   leadership in the main trends in the technological revolution,
   the increased role of multinational corporations, currency and
   financial mechanisms, and the huge draw of its trade market
   and capital.

Currently, for the U.S. economy, as for any IDC, renewal is no
longer possible without foreign capital. Its constant flow is becoming one of the necessary conditions for U.S. economic growth.
To an increasing extent, the capitalist world is becoming the arena
for the accumulation of capital in the United States. In connection
with this, it may be suggested that the U.S. position in the world
economy is not weakening, but in many ways is even being
strengthened. For example, to achieve a new stage in the technological revolution, the developed capitalist countries must
mobilize resources and their distribution in relation to their goals.
Under such conditions, the United States to a certain degree can
play the role of such a distributor, and the U.S. economy can
provide a huge market for West Europe and Japan. Consequently, a
situation could emerge in which successful development of the
entire capitalist world could come to depend even more on the state
of the U.S. economy. The United States is becoming a nucleus of
world capitalist development. Foreign capital in the U.S. economy
not only mixes with U.S. financial resources, but also finds a use

adequate for its level of maturity elsewhere. From this point of view, the flow of foreign capital into the United States has more meaning for the world financial system as a whole. Upon entering the United States and including itself in the reinvestment process of a more highly developed capitalist country, foreign capital matures faster than it would in any other country.

It is interesting to note that other capitalist nations are unhappy with the prospect of rapid outflow of capital from the United States, particularly after the completion of the restructuring in the U.S. economy. In the first case, there is the problem of the no less effective use of capital in other countries. The majority of financial resources functioning in the U.S. economy is loaned capital. For its use, it is necessary to have the corresponding profitable production capital. Currently, there is not one country or region that can compete with the United States at this level. In the second case, the United States, having reached a new techno-economic base with the help of other countries, can now begin its counteroffensive on these countries.

In addition, we must not forget that even though at first glance the massive flow of foreign capital may seem to be an uncontrolled process, in reality it was planned in the most serious way. In the early 1980s, the U.S. government had already concluded that foreign investment did not pose a threat to, but rather offered a chance to strengthen, the economic structure and improve the economy. Therefore, the Reagan administration took special measures aimed at attracting foreign investment. The repeal of the 30-percent tax on foreign profits from investment in U.S. securities in one year produced a tripling of the amount of foreign stock in this form.

Considering the specific aims of the U.S. economy, and also the country's long-term economic development strategy, we can draw two primary conclusions:

1. The traditional division of countries into debtors and creditors by purely quantitative data can no longer be a viable criterion for determining a country's position in the world economy. In addition, the ability to use excess capital abroad is proof not so much of weakness as of strength.

2. It is unlikely that in so short a period of history a country that does not occupy a dominant position in the world economy could, at the right moment, mobilize a large enough amount of capital to take over that position. In this connection, we must note that capital in other countries often becomes "excess" only upon the appearance of a relatively more favorable condition for investment in the United States.

Thus, both central arguments regarding the decline of the U.S. role in the world economy are open to questions. In addition, there is not one serious candidate in the world right now capable of taking on the role of leader of the capitalist world. Aside from purely economic reasons for such a situation, we must take into account military and political factors. Also, few nations, if any, are ready to take upon themselves the burden of expense that goes along with occupying the leadership position.

At the same time, the above does not go against the coordination of the economic policy of the IDCs, but, on the contrary, assumes its necessity. Today, the position of leader consists not in carrying out policy that is advantageous to itself with no regard for the interests of one's partner, but in working out and putting into practice a multilateral policy aimed at the achievement of common goals. The level of interaction among the economies of the industrially developed countries is so high that virtually any decision made at the national level affects the interests of others almost to the same extent. Under such conditions, the position of the leader in opposition to other states can have only a negative effect. On the other hand, a closer relationship in financial and trade policy holds significant development potential.

In our opinion, the preservation of the U.S. leadership position in the world arena in the foreseeable future will have three main consequences:

1. Without the participation of the United States, at least until the late 1990s, serious developments in East-West relations will not be possible. Today, the acceleration or deceleration of this process depends directly on the U.S. position. Political factors, not economic, determine the position of the United States,

which means that a rethinking of the U.S. attitude toward economic ties with the East is necessary.

2. On the other hand, as to the formation of a unified internal market in Europe and the increase of Japan's role in the world economy, the possibility of maneuvering for the leadership in the determination of East-West relations is to a large extent limited. Hence, by the mid-1990s, the United States will no longer be so able to determine unilaterally the IDCs' policy in relation to the East.

3. The current system of leadership necessitates a reworking of important economic decisions (under the direction of the United States) in the narrow circle of IDCs. However, the consequences of these decisions have effects not only on the national economies of the western states, but also on the economies of the socialist countries. It follows that until the East takes part in decisionmaking affecting its own interests, relations between the two social systems will be neither stable nor mutually beneficial.

THE INTEGRATION OF JAPAN INTO THE WORLD ECONOMY

The appearance of Japan among the most active participants in international economic relations is one of the most interesting and significant trends in world economic development in the past several decades. The high competitiveness of Japanese products, together with the advantageous situation on the hard-currency market, has meant that for the first half of the 1980s, Japan's trade surplus has increased twenty-six times, reaching $56 billion. This has been one of the main factors in Japan's becoming the world's largest creditor nation. By 1986, the amount of export capital from Japan had reached $130 billion, compared with $11 billion in 1980 (*Midland Bank Review* 1987, 18). Such rapid growth in capital exports prompted a number of predictions for Japan's position in the world economy in the last decade of this century. Their common denominator is that Japan will most likely become a world banker responsible for financing major problems of the world economy. Several experts see the formation of a specific new global division of labor between the United States and Japan: the

United States will take the lead in solving military and political questions, and Japan will be left to support economic stability.

The potential effects of these trends on East-West relations depend mainly on how well-founded the above concepts are. Western experts no longer doubt that in the next decade Tokyo will become, along with London and New York, the third pillar of the world financial system (*Midland Bank Review* 1987, 22). At the same time, the rapid rate of development of this process gives rise to serious doubts. First, in the early 1990s, a decline is expected in the growth of one of the main factors in the outflow of capital, the active trade balance (current account). In the 1980s, its growth was explained mainly by the abnormally high share of imports in the cyclical rise between 1983 and 1988 in the United States. Such a position cannot last forever, and other markets of such capacity do not yet exist. The advantages of low production costs in the manufacturing industry are already being perceptibly undermined by competitors from the newly industrializing countries. Note, for example, the success of South Korea in ship-building and car production. The yen's rise also weakens the competitiveness of Japanese products. According to current estimates, by the early 1990s, the yen will be valued to the dollar around 130, which is 20 percent lower than it was in mid-1986.

Second, a reduction in Japan's trade surplus according to current operations is expected, which in principle could compensate for the disadvantageous trends in foreign trade. From 1986 through 1991, its assets should fall from $85 billion to $60 billion, by a total 29 percent (*Midland Bank Review* 1987, 20). The main reason for this reduction is the sharp change in the structure of Japan's export capital, which is expected on the eve of the 1990s. The share of portfolio investments, having attained a high percentage, will decrease at a time when the main support will be made on direct investment of capital, the real return from which will begin to appear five years after the investment. In the short term, this will cause a relative decline in Japan's role as a world creditor. However, the evolution of the Japanese economy will occur beyond its borders. In the United States alone, Japanese entrepreneurs intend to produce 1.7 million cars a year by the late 1980s.

Japan's participation in the world economy, as a money-lender rather than an artisan, gives Tokyo more hopeful long-run prospects.   On the other hand, the growth of foreign industry inevitably will cause Japan the problem of saturated markets, which will force it to look for new trade partners.

Third, Tokyo faces the need for serious financial reforms in the near future. The basic elements of the financial system to a great degree are oriented toward the domestic rather than the international market.   Laws currently in effect limit the flow of foreign capital into the Japanese economy.   In 1986, there were only sixty non-Japanese companies registered on the Tokyo stock market.   The relatively closed nature of the Japanese domestic market for the influx of foreign capital hinders the transformation of the nation into one of the world's main financial centers.   The modification of the domestic credit market can slow the rate of export of capital from Japan in the 1990s.

The changes expected in the development of Japan's external economic ties coincide with general trends in world trade development: the increase of Japanese companies' participation in the international division of labor will make possible the growth in the share of manufactured products in the wholesale indicators of its external trade.   In addition, the intensification of the export of capital in the form of direct investments can reduce Japanese imports of raw materials.

It is quite probable that the growing interest of Japanese entrepreneurs in the establishment of facilities abroad may indicate the beginning of yet another interesting stage for the world capitalist economy. In the last few decades, many economists have worriedly noted the appearance of a new trend in export capital, which Japanese economist I. Kashibagi calls "the money game."[3] According to the "money game," financial resources migrate from country to country in search of the most advantageous place for speculation. Among them is a large share of Japanese capital. As long as the world economy is developing for the most part at a stable rate, the negative effect from the "economic casino" is not so apparent. However, in the event of a crisis, a chain reaction of bankruptcy due to speculation can cause a crash of the existing financial system. In connection with this, the trend toward the reduction of the share of loaned capital and the corresponding

3. The 1986 Per Jacobsson lecture.

growth in the share of direct investments in the overall export of Japanese financial resources can be seen as one of the directions of the transfer of "speculative" capital into real capital.   Overall, this would make the stabilization of the world financial system possible, though at the same time it would give rise to new problems in other areas, such as the search for new markets, the accommodation of standards of other countries, and the range of growth in another country.

The analysis of the prospects of Japanese participation in the world economy allows us to come to three more general observations:

1. For Japan, the search for new markets for its products will be particularly urgent, seemingly much more so than for any other nation.   However, current development trends in U.S. and West European markets do not favor an increase in the sale of Japanese goods.

2. The main form of export capital from Japan in the late 1980s and early 1990s will be direct investments.   It is particularly important that a change in their system toward an increase in the share of investment in the manufacturing industry is likely, especially at a time when capital investment in the service and operations industry will necessarily experience a relative decline.

3. Further activization of Japan's external economic strength is highly probable on the regional level.   On this basis, the formation of new economic and financial centers is possible, as is the increase in the capacity of regional markets.

CONCLUSION

From the foregoing interpretation and analysis, we can draw four main conclusions:

1. The development of trade and financial relations of the IDCs in the end of the 20th century provides essential empirical material for rethinking the traditional concepts of international relations.

2. A more serious phenomenon in the international flow of capital will most likely be the further growth in the rate of direct foreign investment. The development of this process not only among individual groups of countries, but on a global level as well (including among differing socioeconomic systems), will demand significant political efforts from all participants in these relations. If these efforts are to be successful, extensive recognition of the need for such a development of events is necessary.

3. To assure effective East-West cooperation, special working groups need to be created. These groups would consist of representatives from all interested sides and would deal with both theoretical and practical questions of ties between systems. (We have in mind here something analogous to the Vienna or Helsinki accords on disarmament).

4. The main goal of East-West cooperation must not be unilateral or bilateral advantages, but the guarantee of stability in world economic development in the interest of the entire population of our planet.

REFERENCES

Midland Bank Review. 1987. London: Midland Bank Ltd., Summer.

Statistical Abstract. 1988. Department of Commerce, Bureau of the Census. Washington, DC: Government Printing Office.

World Bank. 1987. *World Development Report.* Washington, DC: World Bank.

The Soviet Union and the GATT, IMF, and World Bank

Catherine Sokil

In August 1986, the Soviet Union formally applied for permission to participate in the eighth round, the so-called Uruguay Round, of international trade negotiations under the GATT (General Agreement on Tariffs and Trade). Moscow's letter of application to the GATT, dated August 15, apparently said it wanted to "'gather information and experience' without committing itself to applying for either observer status or full membership" (Kaser 1986). The request was summarily rejected, but the issue of Soviet involvement in international economic organizations, including the GATT, International Monetary Fund (IMF), and World Bank, is expected by many observers to resurface in the not-too-distant future. In attempting to reform its foreign trade sector as well as activities on global credit markets, the Soviet Union under Gorbachev has admitted severe shortcomings in its current pattern of foreign trade and has signaled its desire and intention to become a more active player in the world economy. The issues of GATT, IMF, and World Bank membership raise the question of whether increased Soviet involvement in the world economy will proceed along bilateral lines, or whether it can occur within the multilateral framework. This paper examines the prospects for the multilateral approach.

For related research, see "Issues of Soviet Participation in the GATT, IMF, and World Bank," by this author, in Stubbs (forthcoming).

The postwar international economic order was based on the concept of free trade and the establishment of three complementary institutions to facilitate free trade. The International Monetary Fund was designed to address balance-of-payments difficulties of member countries. Its sister institution, the International Bank for Reconstruction and Development (IBRD), or World Bank, was to provide long-term loans to member countries in need. Its first loans went to France for postwar reconstruction; today, developing countries whose per capita GNP is below a specific threshold are eligible for development loans. Finally, the GATT promoted the expansion of free trade by multilateral negotiation of the lowering of tariffs. The GATT was all that remained of the idea of the International Trade Organization (ITO), an institution whose functions would have been much more comprehensive had it been established.

At the outset, the Soviet Union was a participant in the discussions leading to the formation of these institutions. The decision not to become a member at that time reflected Stalin's perception that the costs of membership—political as well as economic—outweighed the benefits. Forty years later, under the leadership of Mikhail Gorbachev, the perception of the costs and benefits of joining the postwar, free-market-based arrangements has changed.

AN OVERVIEW OF SOVIET NONPARTICIPATION
IN THE INTERNATIONAL ORDER

Initially, the Soviet Union participated in the discussions leading up to the establishment of the Bretton Woods institutions until the first Board of Governors' meeting of the IMF in March 1946. The Soviet Union attended the Bretton Woods conference and signed the Articles of Agreement in 1946, but failed to ratify the accord, thereby keeping itself out of the IMF and the World Bank. The Soviet Union was then not invited to attend the Geneva tariff conference in late 1947, which set up the GATT (Brabant 1988a).

Although Moscow has never officially explained why it did not follow through with membership in these institutions, western analysts have attributed Stalin's apparent change of attitude to several factors.[1] To begin with, the Soviets mistrusted the proposed system, because their request for a large recovery loan and reparations from the defeated Axis countries was denied. In their opinion, the United States would clearly dominate these institutions and use them to its advantage in promoting its hegemonic power. The Soviet Union would at best have second-class status in these organizations (particularly in the GATT, because its founders were mostly western industrial nations) and might be bound by western economic policy prescriptions (Marer 1986). Moreover, by participating, the Soviet Union would have to share economic information it might not want to divulge (on gold reserves, for example), and would make itself vulnerable to a perceived pending worldwide economic depression. A Soviet economist, discussing in 1978 why most centrally planned economies (CPEs) had not participated in the IMF, added that Article VIII of the IMF charter, obligating members not to limit their foreign exchange payments and transfers on current account, was "totally unacceptable to the socialist countries with their state monopoly of foreign trade and monetary operations and other economic administrative principles which [contrast] to capitalist [ones]" (Marer 1986).

Stalin countered by establishing international socialist trade and financial institutions. Guided by his desire to create two world markets, the Council for Mutual Economic Assistance (CMEA) was established in 1949. Stalin's successors completed the task by creating the International Bank for Economic Cooperation (IBEC), the socialist version of the IMF, in 1964, and the International Investment Bank (IIB), their equivalent of the World Bank, in 1971.[2]

Since the inception of the Bretton Woods institutions, Moscow has been critical of the existing international economic order. Within the United Nations Conference on Trade and Development (UNCTAD) forum, in particular, the Soviet Union has shown a recurrent interest in establishing a new international economic order. In 1964, it went so far as to submit a draft resolution that seemed to call for the establishment of a new ITO (Brabant 1988b). It comes as no surprise that Soviet preferences for this new order

1. See Brabant (1988a) for details.
2. See Sobell (1986) for details.

appear to center on greater stability of interest rates, exchange rates, and commodity prices (especially oil), increased technology flows, and reduced protectionism against raw materials and fuels.

Today, however, most Soviet allies have some relationship with at least one of these institutions. The status of some socialist economies in the GATT, IMF, and World Bank is presented in Table 12-1.

WHY THE RECENT SOVIET INTEREST?

The Soviet application for participation in the GATT is seen by western observers as a reaction to its long-time economic isolation; currently, the Soviet Union and East Germany are the only industrialized CPEs with no affiliation with the GATT or IMF/World Bank (membership in the IMF and World Bank go hand-in-hand). Moreover, economic isolation is fundamentally incompatible with Gorbachev's foreign policy and with the "openness" in Soviet society that the General Secretary seeks. Furthermore, the Soviet application appears to be related to perceived trade and debt prospects in the context of drastic reductions in its terms of trade as oil prices declined in 1986.

Declining revenues from oil, the Soviet Union's primary export, magnify Soviet concerns over their traditional pattern of trade. The Soviet Union is dependent on raw materials and energy exports to finance imports of manufactures. Oil constituted 34.3 percent of nonsocialist and 33.1 percent of socialist exports in 1987; machinery constituted 27 percent of nonsocialist and 49.9 percent of socialist imports in 1987.[3]

Soviet spokespersons have expressed the desire to change this trade pattern for the Soviet Union to become a world-class exporter of manufactures. Joint ventures with western firms are an intimate part of this strategy. Membership in the GATT, which gives a country most-favored nation (MFN) treatment vis-à-vis all its members, would aid the Soviet Union in changing its pattern of trade to favor manufactured products. GATT membership could provide a boost to joint ventures with the Soviet Union directly, by

3. *PlanEcon Report*, August 5, 1988.

Table 12-1. Date of GATT Observer Status, GATT Full Membership, and IMF/World Bank Membership of Selected Nonmarket Economies

Status	GATT Observer	GATT Full	IMF, IBRD
Soviet Bloc:			
Czechoslovakia	-	Founder	-
Romania	1957	1971	1972
Hungary	1966	1973	1982
Poland	1965	1967	1986
Bulgaria	1967	-	-
Vietnam	-	-	1976
Non-Soviet Bloc:			
Yugoslavia	1950	1966	Founder
PRC	1982	1989-90?	1980

Sources: GATT - Brabant (1988a); IMF and World Bank - Sobell (1986); Marer (1988).

lowering tariffs, but more likely indirectly, by promoting confidence in the Soviets' entry into the world economic system.

Given traditional Soviet foreign trade patterns, recent reductions in its terms of trade, and the need to borrow in the West to finance Gorbachev's program of perestroika, membership in the IMF and the World Bank would also be helpful. Membership in the IMF would facilitate financial dealings on western markets. It is, arguably, less crucial than GATT membership, because the Soviets have been able to borrow on western capital markets with relative ease without membership in the IMF. Some examples are found in the recent Soviet bond issue for 110 million Swiss francs and the loans from West German, Italian, and Japanese banks. Nonetheless, contact with the IMF and World Bank has been initiated.

Of the three institutions, membership in the World Bank is probably the least important to the Soviets, as they would likely not be eligible for loans, based on their per capita income. Being above the threshold still has its benefits, however, because Soviet enterprises would be able to bid on World Bank development contracts for projects in less-developed countries. With time, this privilege might conceivably grow in importance for the Soviets. Of course, the other, more qualitative benefits of membership in the World Bank are substantial.

The Soviets apparently believe that the experiences of the other nonmarket economies (NMEs) in these three institutions have been generally favorable. In particular, the application to the GATT by the People's Republic of China during the current Uruguay Round may have sparked greater interest by the Soviet Union. The resolution of China's application, especially in light of the 1989 political turmoil, will also provide valuable insights into how the institutions might handle the membership application of a large CPE.

The experience of other NMEs in these organizations raises another strategic issue for current members, namely: how might other Soviet-bloc members of the GATT, IMF, and World Bank be affected by Soviet membership? The East European countries presumably established relations with these institutions in part out of a desire to divert more of their trade to the West. Soviet bloc members' closeness to the IMF and World Bank generally has varied inversely with their closeness to the Soviet Union (Assetto 1988). At the same time, East European countries were considered reliable borrowers in the 1970s in part because of the Soviet "umbrella"; how would this umbrella be affected by increased Soviet indebtedness to the West, which may be a natural byproduct of its greater involvement in the international economy, at least in the short run? Given current trends toward more autonomy on the part of several East European countries, the answer would appear to be that each country would increasingly be treated independently by the international community.

ISSUES OF MEMBERSHIP IN THE GATT

Economic relations between East and West have been and will continue to be intertwined with politics, human rights, and military considerations. A brief look at noneconomic considerations traditionally surrounding East-West trade suggests that these also need to be rethought and renegotiated.

Export Controls and Human Rights Compliance

U.S. experience to date with the linkage of economic sanctions to political and social issues—in the cases of the Carter grain embargo and the Reagan gas pipeline equipment embargo, for example—has at best been mixed, largely because our allies have shown an unwillingness to abide by restrictions on which they have not been consulted. The lesson learned is that carrots and sticks alike would be much more effective with multilateral participation. For example, U.S. export control policies toward the Soviet Union have always been more stringent than those of our allies, and as a result they have put U.S. firms at a competitive disadvantage. A 1987 study by the Panel on the Impact of National Security Controls on International Technology Transfer "conservatively" estimated that the quantifiable cost alone of U.S. export controls in 1985 exceeded $9 billion and involved a $17 billion loss in U.S. GNP (Holzman 1989). Through the multilateral economic framework, a closer collaboration with our allies on technology embargoes and other strategic interests might contribute to western goals of expanding trade without aiding Soviet military capabilities.

Currently, under the Jackson-Vanik Amendment, the U.S. conditions bilateral MFN status and access to Export-Import (EXIM) Bank financing at concessionary rates for communist countries to one dimension of the human rights issue: Jewish emigration policies. Under Jackson-Vanik, the United States currently does not extend MFN status to the Soviet Union. If it achieved membership in the GATT, the Soviet Union presumably would be granted MFN status by all members, including the United States. So, it is unlikely that the United States would approve membership without conditions linked to human rights.

Can human rights issues be successfully linked to economics? Perhaps, but they can be linked more successfully via the multilateral framework. For the United States, economic sanctions are more stringent than those of our allies. Establishing, with other GATT members, the preconditions of Soviet membership in an international economic institution might constitute an effective multilateral effort to sanction true social reform in the Soviet Union. Among the problems for the United States, however, is

West Europe's generally less sympathetic regard for linkage of economic and political matters.

This linkage, it can be argued, is counterproductive or even unreasonable, given that the issue of emigration has no tangible impact on the purpose or performance of these international economic organizations themselves. Countries that do not share the linkage viewpoint might also argue that the conditions of Jackson-Vanik discriminate against communist countries, and thus there are serious asymmetries in the requirements imposed on different countries.[4]

Currently, the Bush administration is considering temporarily waiving the Jackson-Vanik Amendment in response to recent political liberalization in the Soviet Union, which has involved the freeing of a number of political prisoners and an increase in levels of Jewish emigration. President Bush has challenged the Soviet Union to take further steps toward openness and democratization that would be rewarded by the West, and he has promised to work with the U.S. Congress on a waiver of Jackson-Vanik, paving the way for MFN status, should the Soviet Union "codify its emigration laws in accord with international standards and implement its new laws faithfully."[5] Jewish groups responded favorably to the Bush challenge. Indeed, the American Jewish Congress was disappointed that the President did not waive Jackson-Vanik immediately, to encourage the Soviet Union to continue the high levels of emigration of the first part of 1989.[6]

Another approach seeks to enhance the linkage between economic and political matters. One proposal links GATT membership more comprehensively to human rights issues. Accordingly, Soviet membership would be conditioned on its acceptance of "worker rights" issues in the admission process. "Worker rights" could be interpreted so as to test not only the freeing of markets, particularly labor markets, in the Soviet Union, but also to challenge human rights violations in general. An amendment to this effect, the Pease Amendment (named for

4. I thank Eric Stubbs for bringing this point to my attention, and for other insightful comments on an earlier draft.

5. *The Washington Post,* May 13, 1989.

6. In April, 4,557 Jews were allowed exit permits, and 14,018 arrived in Israel or the west during January-April 1989 (Ottaway 1989).

its author, Rep. Don Pease [D-Ohio]), was approved by the House of Representatives in the 99th Congress. It remains to be seen whether it could become U.S. law, and whether it would be accepted by other GATT members (Majak, in Chapman 1987). More recently, in June 1989, Rep. Pease introduced HR 2307, which would authorize the President to grant MFN status to imports from the cooperative sector in communist countries, provided these co-ops recognized standards of workers' rights.

ECONOMIC REQUIREMENTS FOR ACCESSION TO THE GATT

Reciprocity

Soviet accession to the GATT, a trading "club," would require resolution of several critical economic issues of membership, including nondiscrimination, reciprocity, and transparency. Any concession granted to one member of the GATT must be extended to all others as well by the most-favored nation provision. Transparency refers to the agreement to provide accurate information about one's economy. Given price structures that do not accurately reflect cost conditions or supply and demand in the nonmarket economies, special provisions have to be made for their accession.

Unlike the GATT, the ITO Charter contained specific provisions for the incorporation of nonmarket economies—so-called state-trading countries—into its framework. Instead, the GATT's provisions covering monopolies operating in market economies have been used as criteria for the accession of nonmarket economies. As the only document formally proposing to integrate into one multilateral economic institution countries of differing economic systems, the proposal for the ITO may provide some insights into how to deal with the possible accession of the Soviet Union (Brabant 1988a).

The draft proposal tolerated the Soviet Union's state monopoly of foreign trade and payments, offering technical arrangements to help reconcile that monopoly with the goals of trade expansion based on reciprocity. The technical arrangements would be based primarily on purchase arrangements—that is, the nonmarket economy's commitment to purchase at least some minimum negotiated value of goods from the other members in exchange for tariff reductions by the market economies.[7]

In practice, in the accessions of NMEs other than the Soviet Union, the GATT appears to have taken a country-by-country approach to resolution of the reciprocity issue (Kennedy 1988). However, these country-specific approaches fall into two broad categories. In the first, the new member essentially admits to centralized control of imports and is admitted under a purchase arrangement. This was the arrangement for Poland, which pledged to increase imports from GATT members by 7 percent per year. Romania's import commitment was tied to that for all imports as specified in its five-year plan (Kennedy 1988). In the second broad category, the country is admitted "as a market economy," or on the presumption that its economic reforms have sufficiently decentralized and marketized import decisionmaking, so that tariff concessions are meaningful. This premise was the basis for both Yugoslavia's and Hungary's accessions.

It appears to at least one knowledgeable observer[8] that the Soviet Union would likely reapply under the latter provision, that is, on the grounds that it has sufficiently reformed its system of economic decisionmaking to make tariffs meaningful. However, the Soviet Union's position as a world superpower makes it less likely that it can "squeak by" on the presumption of being (at least on the road to) a market-based economy.

It might be suggested that Soviet participation in the GATT be tied initially to some form of import commitment. The Soviet Union might pledge to expand its purchases from other GATT members by some negotiated percentage per year. This growth rate of imports might even be based on the historical growth rate of foreign trade for the United States, a country with whom the Soviet Union's size and openness might appropriately be compared. However, provisions would have to be made to preclude this increased trade from accruing overwhelmingly to the other NME members of the GATT in order to preclude political polarization of the institution.

---

7. Brabant (1988a) gives further details on pp. 14-15.
8. Hewett (1988) gathers this from interview material.

In the longer term, substantial market-type economic reforms might be required for full membership in the GATT. What systemic economic reforms would constitute a necessary precondition of the Soviet Union's accession? The necessary reforms that would "marketize" the process of international trade would include reforms of the pricing and exchange rate systems as well as decentralization of foreign trade decisionmaking.

REFORMS IN THE PRICING AND EXCHANGE RATE SYSTEMS

Prices in CPEs typically are determined by central authorities to serve functions of accounting and administrative control rather than market allocation. Producer prices are set based on average branch cost of production plus a mark-up, which assures a profit for some ("below-average cost") enterprises, while less profitable ("above-average cost") enterprises will likely continue to produce with government subsidies. Thus, prices do not provide an important market function—that of guiding which enterprises ought to be operating, and which ought to be producing which goods, based upon how productive and efficient they are.

Consumer prices are entirely separated from producer prices by an elaborate system of turnover taxes and subsidies. The authorities make some attempt to set prices to clear at least some consumer goods markets, and so they "make up the difference" either by taxing or subsidizing the good at the retail level. At the same time, many goods are subsidized for social policy reasons (to make them affordable to all), with the result that, under shortage conditions, goods are rationed by queues and administrative means (such as coupons) rather than by prices.

The CPE pricing and subsidy system makes it difficult to discern the true costs of production, which in turn makes issues such as the determination of dumping on international markets highly controversial. A crucial long-run economic issue for the Soviet Union will be this separation of the domestic price system from world market prices, a basic incompatibility between market and nonmarket economies. So long as the Soviet domestic pricing system remains entirely divorced from the rest of the world, the benefits of import competition cannot be assumed, and the ruble cannot be made convertible.

Ruble Convertibility

The issue of convertibility is exceedingly complex. First, a suitable definition of the type of convertibility that would be appropriate for membership in international organizations needs to be spelled out. What form of convertibility is required by GATT membership? Is this form also sufficient for membership in the IMF and World Bank? What economic reforms are necessary to achieve these forms of ruble convertibility?

Types of convertibility may be defined based upon what may be converted, and by whom. Financial convertibility allows one to buy financial assets denominated in, say, rubles, and then to convert these assets back into another currency. Commodity convertibility allows one to buy goods for rubles. Domestic convertibility allows these transactions to be performed by domestic residents or organizations, whereas external convertibility gives the right to make these transactions to foreigners. Convertibility is also distinguished by whether items in the current account versus the capital account of the balance of payments are affected (Marer 1988).

In addition, a distinction must be made in CPEs among three separate currencies that coexist in the economy but are not freely convertible into each other: money (cash and savings) in the household economy, which can generally buy domestic consumer goods freely, but only if they are available; bank balances of enterprises that are controlled by the centralized banking system and that are not convertible into goods unless planned; and foreign currency, including the transferable ruble used in intra-CMEA transactions. As with enterprise balances, foreign exchange cannot be used without authorization.

The issue of convertibility is complex, because in the traditional CPE the currency is not even domestically convertible. Money plays a passive role in the domestic economy, as the financial plan is a mirror image of the material, or real, plan. This is another way of saying that financial flows occur only if they are accounted for in the real plan.   An individual or an enterprise may not necessarily be allowed to make a transaction, even if it possesses the requisite funds, if the transaction is not a part of the real plan.

Domestic convertibility does, however, appear to be a goal of the current phase of economic reform in the Soviet Union. Under the system of *khozraschet,* or "economic accountability," enterprises are to be responsible for their own finances—for profits and losses— and thus presumably would have the freedom to use their financial resources as they see fit. This, of course, is contingent upon the development of a wholesale trade network, another goal of perestroika, which would allow horizontal trading relationships among enterprises to substitute for vertical, hierarchical directives from above. Of course, the reform documents place a limit on the scope of "free trade" among state enterprises by continuing to demand the fulfillment of state orders *(goszakazy)*. Although enterprises are not to receive obligatory annual plans, they are to receive "nonbinding *control figures*" with each five-year plan, covering major economic indicators such as value of output, total profits, and foreign exchange receipts. In addition to the control figures, the enterprise will have to take into account various *normatives,* or coefficients linking the formation of enterprise (wage, bonus, and other) accounts to final results (probably sales according to contract). Given that all of these announced reforms are still only in the initial stages of implementation, it is unlikely that even domestic convertibility of the ruble by Soviet enterprises will be easy to achieve.

Whereas some western economists contend that inconvertibility is endemic to the centrally planned economic system, proposals for commodity and/or financial convertibility have been made to achieve limited ruble convertibility within the CPE framework. Indeed, establishment of an efficient, limited market for foreign currency is conceivable should enterprises be allowed to bid for scarce foreign exchange. However, in order to function efficiently, such an auction market must be based on economic considerations of profitability, a condition that itself would require substantial independence—financial autonomy and responsibility—on the part of Soviet enterprises, of the type envisioned in the new Law on State Enterprises, but which is far from full implementation. Accompanying reform of the price system is also necessary.

Recent Soviet economic reforms entail an "interim solution" to the pricing and exchange rate problem, involving special exchange rates for each of about 2,000 product groups that compensate for the irrationalities of the unreformed domestic pricing system. For example, the exchange rate ("coefficient") applied to machinery and equipment is devalued (say, to $0.50-1 per ruble) compared to the official tourist exchange rate (which is currently approximately $1.70-1.72 per ruble), while that applied to raw materials is revalued (say, to $2 per ruble) (Hewett 1988). These differing valuations compensate for the relative overpricing of machinery and underpricing of raw materials under the domestic pricing system. They essentially replicate the former cost-based pricing system without resolving its shortcomings, including the insulation of the domestic economy from world market prices.

The Soviets themselves have announced ruble convertibility as a goal, although the concrete form of convertibility and the steps intended to bring it about are rather vague. The June 1987 Plenum of the Communist Party of the Soviet Union (CPSU) called for a progression toward convertibility of the ruble, first in CMEA trade and then on the world market.

GATT rules require governments to control trade only indirectly, through tariffs, rather than through quantitative restrictions (Marer 1988). Tariff reductions must be effective in promoting trade, which cannot occur if domestic producers—leaving out the general population, which is even more unlikely, even in the future—are not free to choose between domestic and foreign suppliers. GATT membership, then, would presumably require at least some limited form of external commodity convertibility. Foreign firms should be reasonably free to buy Soviet goods, and Soviet firms should have some authority to export and import goods. The decisions of both should be affected by relative prices rather than by administrative edict. Commodity convertibility would require not only the abolition of compulsory plan directives (modeled, for example, on the Hungarian New Economic Mechanism), but also correcting the arbitrariness of domestic pricing and the government monopoly over foreign trade that characterizes traditional CPEs (Holzman 1974).

GATT-based negotiation of tariff structures would require but could also aid in the Soviet Union's reform of its wholesale pricing system. Indeed, the long-anticipated price reform has become the most controversial of all the economic reform documents and decrees in the Soviet Union. Price reform is now not expected before the early 1990s. If and when achieved, a price reform ideally would allow more Soviet prices to be linked to world market prices, smoothing the transition to commodity convertibility of the ruble.

Reforms in the Foreign Trade Decisionmaking System

Perhaps not coincidentally, the Soviets timed recent foreign trade reforms to coincide with their letter to the GATT.[9]   The Central Committee and the Council of Ministers approved reforms in August 1986, to be effective January 1987. These reforms involved organizational changes in the foreign trade bureaucracy, which as yet have had an uncertain to ambiguous effect on the market orientation of Soviet trade. The August 1986 reforms also strengthen the rights and responsibilities of industrial enterprises in foreign exchange management, including access to international credit markets.[10]

The foreign trade reforms, on paper, appear to be on track; however, their actual implementation is proceeding rather slowly. For admission into international economic organizations, their full implementation and verification are needed to confirm that microeconomic decisionmaking units in the economy have the authority to make foreign trade decisions, and that they make these decisions based upon financial and economic considerations. But verification may be difficult: how is the decentralization of decisionmaking visibly evidenced?

Additional Issues of Membership in the IMF and World Bank

Given the functional complementarities of the three institutions, the issues of membership in the GATT, IMF, and World Bank

---

9. Many have commented on the timing of the reorganization relative to the request to the GATT—see, for example, Brabant (1988a).
10. For details on these measures, see Gardner and Popov, this volume.

differ. Structurally, as well, the GATT differs considerably from the IMF and World Bank, so that should the Soviet Union join the GATT, a host of issues would still have to be resolved if Moscow applied to the IMF and World Bank.[11]

Voting Status

The World Bank and IMF do not allow any form of "observer" or "associate" status, as does the GATT. Whereas the GATT is formally based on the "one country—one vote" principle, voting power in the IMF and the World Bank is weighted by a country's paid-in quota, which in turn is based on the relative importance of its currency in international transactions and is negotiated upon admission.[12] For example, in the IMF, in both the Board of Governors (responsible for admission of new members, determination of quotas, and a few other issues) and the Executive Board (responsible for everything else), a system of weighted voting is used, in which each member has a basic allotment of votes plus additional votes in proportion to the size of its quota (Marer 1988).

In the postwar negotiations leading to establishment of the IMF, it became clear that the Soviet Union would have been the third (after the United States and the United Kingdom) in ranking by voting power, with over 12 percent of the total votes. Under an early draft of the charter, only 10 percent would be required for veto power of major decisions. In the charter finally accepted, a 20-percent share was required. This share has been reduced to 15 percent as of 1978. As Table 12-2 shows, the current U.S. voting share in the IMF is well ahead of any other country, at approximately 19 percent.

Membership by the Soviet Union would dilute the weighted share of the United States. However, whether it would do so to the

11. This statement is not meant to imply that GATT membership would necessarily precede membership in the IMF and World Bank. However, with most other Soviet bloc countries, the order of accession has involved the trade organization (the GATT) first and the financial and development organizations (IMF, World Bank) second.

12. Marer (1988) provides many more details on decisionmaking arrangements in each of the three organizations.

Table 12-2. Major Voting Powers in the IMF
April 30, 1988

Country	Percentage of Total
United States	19.14
United Kingdom	6.63
Federal Republic of Germany	5.78
France	4.81
Japan	4.53
Saudi Arabia	3.44

Source: IMF Annual Report 1988.

point of eliminating U.S. veto power (that is, down from its current 19-percent share to below 15 percent, the cut-off for veto power, which could also be renegotiated) would depend in part on the Soviet quota, which would be negotiated upon admission.[13] It would, of course, also depend upon other countries' weights. At issue is whether the U.S. will continue to hold a monopoly on veto power in the IMF and World Bank, given its declining share of world GNP.   Most notably, the slowly declining share of the United States has been accompanied by an increased share on the part of Japan. Whether Japan's current 4.5 percent voting share in the IMF will be doubled to reflect its true share of world GNP will be an issue to watch for in the 1989 review of IMF quotas.[14] A revision in Japan's quota, along with admission of the Soviet Union, could conceivably challenge U.S. veto power.

In practice, however, formal votes are rarely taken in the IMF and World Bank; in most cases, decisions are arrived at by consensus (Marer 1988). Therefore, it is particularly important that membership, should it be granted, be accompanied by improved cooperation by the Soviet Union on all diplomatic fronts, so

---

13. This negotiation process upon admission would itself provide interesting and valuable information on the size and structure of the Soviet economy, which could be enlightening to the Soviets themselves as well as the West.

14. *Business Week*, October 3, 1988.

as not to inhibit the smooth decisionmaking processes of the IMF and World Bank. In the issue of membership, the Soviet Union's prospects for being a cooperative partner may be more important than the precise size of its quota.

Inconvertibility Revisited

Inconvertibility poses two operational problems, particularly to IMF membership. First, by the IMF charter, each member must pledge to move toward convertibility. Second, if a member country's currency is inconvertible, its financial contribution to the Fund is less "usable" (Marer 1986). Thus, inconvertibility arguably presents greater formal obstacles to IMF and World Bank membership than to membership in the GATT. But the form of convertibility required by IMF/World Bank membership might actually be easier to institute. While GATT membership would appear to require at least a limited form of commodity convertibility, and thus would necessitate substantial accompanying economic reforms, the relevant concept of convertibility for IMF membership is external financial convertibility for current account transactions, which might not necessitate as fundamental a dismantling of the central planning framework. However, the IMF code may be interpreted to also require domestic financial convertibility (Marer 1988), which would require substantial loosening of the reins of central planning.

Would the Soviet Union make good on a pledge to work toward convertibility? As a prerequisite, they could be asked to take a first step in that direction by resolving a fundamental issue of convertibility by joint venture partners: namely, how to enable joint venture companies to convert their ruble earnings into convertible currency. This would constitute a form of external financial convertibility that would be limited to joint venture partners. An expanded form of commodity convertibility would be required in order to submit domestic firms to competition from foreign firms—a requirement that could also conceivably be required by the International Monetary Fund and the World Bank for membership.

Access to Lending and Conditionality

If the Soviet Union wanted to borrow significantly from the IMF, it would be obligated to follow the IMF's procedures and suggested economic policies. A major tool of the Fund is conditionality, a "tool to encourage the borrowing countries to implement policies that will reestablish their creditworthiness" (Marer 1988). Because excess demand is often an important cause of balance-of-payments difficulties, IMF-prescribed adjustment programs frequently rely on restraining bank-, budget-, or foreign-financed spending as well as currency devaluations (1988).

Conditionality raises a host of issues, including the acceptability to the Soviet Union of IMF demand-management prescriptions should it at some time face balance-of-payments difficulties. Indeed, the effectiveness of demand-management policies in an economic system that is not demand-driven is unclear. The experiences of Hungary and Poland in this regard have been rather mixed. At the same time, these countries also provide good examples of the potential close cooperation between a reforming CPE and the IMF and World Bank. Indeed, particularly in the Hungarian case, the IMF and World Bank have provided valuable support—not only financial—for the reform process. Would the Soviet Union be as willing to consider IMF advice?

To reduce domestic absorption, IMF programs typically rely on restrictive money, credit, and exchange rate policies. However, these policies do not operate in CPEs in the same way as in market economies. Due to the soft budget constraint of enterprises and the forced savings of the population, tight money and credit tends not to constrain expenditures (Wolf 1985a). Tighter credit does not lead to its more efficient use, even if domestic relative price structures are at all reflective of relative scarcities, as credit tends to be rationed by political and bureaucratic rather than economic means. Importers and exporters are insulated from the external sector, and thus exchange rate devaluations tend to be ineffective. Administrative intervention is more likely to be effective in restraining domestic demand (Marer 1988), but such intervention, ironically, is fundamentally incompatible with the free-market orientation of the IMF and World Bank.

It is highly significant that the IMF and World Bank have made considerable efforts to better understand the functioning and performance of CPEs.[15] This work has helped to tailor adjustment programs for the smaller, more open economies of East European member countries, but conceivably could also be applied to conditions of membership, and of borrowing, by the Soviets.

Aside from these purely economic considerations, there is a political dimension to membership: adjustment programs of the Fund impose no contractual obligations on the borrowing country, only on the Fund (Marer 1988). Therefore, again, it is crucial that Soviet membership in these organizations be based on reliability, trust, and assurances of cooperation, not only in international economic affairs, but in global issues overall.

Information Requirements

"The large amount of statistical data and information that the Fund and the Bank collect, standardize, and make available is a public good" (Marer 1988).[16] Increased "openness" of information on the Soviet economy would be required by membership in any of these institutions, and particularly for the IMF. Although Soviet economic statistics are notoriously unreliable, they do appear to be improving, if slowly.

Greater provision of information is compatible with—and arguably a requirement of—economic reform in the Soviet Union, and likely would improve the availability of credit to the Soviet Union from private sources as well. Given the much greater information available on Soviet finances today versus immediately after the war (partly because of Soviet borrowing in the West), is this still a major issue?[17] If the Soviets are increasingly willing to submit to arms treaties, missile silo inspections, and the like, need any economic statistic remain top secret? (Hewett 1978).

---

15. The work of Thomas Wolf at the IMF is particularly important.

16. A good example is the very complete World Bank-commissioned expert study of issues of measuring and converting into U.S. dollars CPE national product accounts (Marer 1985).

17. See Marer (1986) for more.

CONCLUSION

Perestroika is broadly compatible with greater participation in international organizations, as it involves greater openness as well as a greater role for market principles in the Soviet economy. It seems likely that the issue of increased Soviet participation in the world economy is not likely to go away if perestroika continues. The international community stands to benefit from increased Soviet openness and participation.

Within existing economic institutions, the world has a framework within which to pursue greater international cooperation at a time when the international trade and finance arena appears to be becoming increasingly "compartmentalized" (witness the EC in 1992 and the U.S.-Canada Free Trade Agreement). Soviet membership could be used to counter claims that the GATT, in particular, has become obsolete, given the volume of trade by members outside the GATT framework. Within the GATT, IMF, and World Bank, resolution of the issues of international trade and finance among market and nonmarket economies might proceed within a multilateral framework that would promote greater cooperation among all countries. At the same time, these institutions need not necessarily compromise on their basic principles of free trade to accommodate the Soviet Union. A careful elaboration of the prerequisites to Soviet involvement in these institutions, preferably agreed upon by all members, would be of mutual benefit.

REFERENCES

Assetto, Valerie J. 1988. *The Soviet Bloc in the IMF and the IBRD.* Boulder, CO: Westview Press.

Brabant, Jozef M. van. 1988a. "Integration Reform: New Horizons for the CMEA and East-West Economic Relations." Paper delivered at the Geonomics Institute for International Economic Advancement conference in Middlebury, Vermont, October.

———. 1988b. "Planned Economies in the GATT Framework: The Soviet Case." *Soviet Economy* 4, 1: 3-35.

Chapman, Margaret. 1987. *Forum on U.S.-Soviet Trade Relations.* Washington, DC: American Committee on U.S.-Soviet Relations.

Diebold, William. 1988. "The USSR and the World Trading System." Paper prepared for the Council on Foreign Relations Study Group on the Soviet Union in the International Economy, January 25.

Gardner, Stephen H. 1988. "Restructuring the Soviet Foreign Trade System." *Columbia Journal of World Business* 23, 2, Summer.

Hewett, Ed A. 1978. "Most-Favored Nation Treatment in Trade Under Central Planning." *Slavic Review.*

———. 1988. "The Foreign Economic Factor in Perestroika." *The Harriman Institute Forum,* August.

Holzman, Franklyn D. 1974. *Foreign Trade Under Central Planning.* Cambridge, MA: Harvard University Press.

———. 1989. "Reforms in the USSR: Implications for U.S. Policy." *American Economic Review* 79, 2.

Kaser, Michael. 1986. "Why Moscow is Turning to Marketing." *The Financial Times,* August 28, p. 10

Kennedy, Kevin C. 1987. "The Accession of the Soviet Union to GATT." *Journal of World Trade Law:* 23-39, April.

Marer, Paul. 1985. *Dollar GNPs of the USSR & Eastern Europe.* Baltimore: The Johns Hopkins University Press.

———. 1986. "Growing Soviet International Economic Isolation." *PlanEcon Report,* No. 31: 1-11, July 31.

———. 1988. "Centrally Planned Economies in the IMF, the World Bank, and the GATT." In *Economic Adjustment and Reform in Eastern Europe and the Soviet Union.* Eds. Josef C. Brada, Ed. A Hewett, and Thomas A. Wolf. Durham, NC: Duke University Press.

Ottaway, David. 1989. "Jewish Groups Hail Bush Stance on Soviet Trade Waiver." *Washington Post*, May 13, p. 1.

Sobell, Vladimir. 1986. "The USSR and the Western Economic Order: Time for Cooperation?" *Radio Free Europe Research Report*, No. 128: 1-7, September 15.

Sokil, Catherine M. 1989. "Soviet Participation in the GATT, IMF, and World Bank." *Global Economic Policy* 1, 1: 79-89, Spring.

———. Forthcoming. "Issues of Soviet Participation in the GATT, IMF, and World Bank." In *Soviet Foreign Economic Policy and International Security*. Ed. Eric Stubbs. New York: M.E. Sharpe.

Stubbs, Eric. Forthcoming. *Soviet Foreign Economic Policy and International Security*. New York: M.E. Sharpe.

Wolf, Thomas A. 1985a. "Economic Stabilization in Planned Economies: Toward an Analytical Framework." *IMF Staff Papers* 32, 1, March.

———. 1985b. "Exchange Rate Systems and Adjustment in Planned Economies." *IMF Staff Papers* 32, 2, June.

_____

CHAPTER 13

Perestroika and International Security

IGOR MALASHENKO

Reforms in the Soviet Union have received unprecedented attention in the West. Possibly for the first time since the 1950s, when the word "sputnik" became widely used throughout the world, two Russian words—perestroika and glasnost—have become part of the West's political lexicon and do not need translation. Nor should they be translated, for when one changes "perestroika" to "restructuring" and "glasnost" to "openness," the specific meaning of these words is lost, as is the passion with which these words are pronounced in the Soviet Union today. Perestroika is the search for answers to those numerous problems accumulating in Soviet society for decades. Today that society is undergoing a process of fundamental change, and a qualitatively different society is emerging before our eyes. This process attracts attention from the West not only because of the interest stemming from social, economic, political, and spiritual changes on a vast scale, but also because of their inevitable influence on international security as a whole.

The profound changes in the political course of the new Soviet leadership were evident first of all in the foreign and military policy of the Soviet Union. The first premise of new thinking arises from the need to bring our ideas into accordance with the realities of the modern era. The realization of new political thinking presupposes a profound and consistent deideologization of approaches to international problems, that is, the rejection of both *a priori* ideological frameworks and outmoded military-political stereotypes. The main points of reference must become national interest—the objective needs of society—satisfied by developing the socioeconomic and political system chosen by that society.

Of course, in the world arena there is a multitude of countries, each guided by its own national interests. Traditionally, these interests were weighed through a balance of power (primarily military power). In practice, only the interests of several of the most powerful states were served. If the mechanism broke down, war served as a method of correcting the imbalance. However, under present conditions, war could lead to the total destruction of the system rather than balancing it. Moreover, in this interdependent world, attempts by even the most powerful states to employ military power on a limited scale to satisfy their egotistical interests have boomeranged. These facts lie at the basis of a definite devaluation of military power and the emergence of other, nonmilitary, factors to ensure security.

It is imperative to develop new approaches to security—both national and international—by relying on nonmilitary guarantees. It is not yet clear what form the new mechanism of the balance of interests will assume. It is obvious that the United Nations will be called upon to play a leading role in this plan, because it possesses a great capacity for strengthening peace and stability (as the role of the United Nations in regulating a number of regional conflicts testifies), but it certainly has not realized this potential to its the fullest. The effectiveness of the United Nations— and the viability of any international system—depends to a great extent on the policies of the major powers. A first step toward creating a new mechanism for a balance of interests and a comprehensive system of international security, entails, paradoxically, that each member of the international community strive to achieve its own national interests.

After all, the goal of a modern society does not necessarily conflict with the interests of its partners, as each is interested in peace and development. The task we all face is to free our concepts about national interests and the methods to secure them from outdated stereotypes, ideological overlays, and opportunistic interpretations. The nature of the present debate shows that this is an urgent task for American as well as Soviet society.

The question of our country's national interests was not a subject of discussion for a long time. The Revolution in Russia was viewed by those who were present at its beginnings as part of a world revolution, and the creation of the Soviet Union as the prologue to a world republic of soviets. Western discussions on the subject of "national interests" were perceived as a ruse of the ruling bourgeoisie to pass off its own interests as the interests of the entire society. Of course, such substitution does in fact occur. However, real common interests also exist in every normal society, otherwise centrifugal forces would simply tear it apart. In our country, on the other hand, the idea that national interests were identical to the interests of the state was widespread. This attitude was not conducive to profound discussion of these problems; if the view is widely held that the state is destined to wither away, it would be pointless to focus on the question of its interests.

In reality, however, everything became considerably more complex. Expectations of a world revolution were replaced by the task of building socialism in one country, and the prospect of the withering away of the state gave way to its hypertrophic growth under conditions of Stalinism. As a result, in our country, the state and the bureaucracy acting in the state's name subordinated the entire society to the state, instead of always acting in accordance with the interests of society. The task of ensuring state security was brought to the fore, while the question of how state security correlates with national security (the latter refers to the security of the entire society) was not addressed.

These two concepts are not identical. Naturally, from the viewpoint of the entire society, guaranteeing state security—its sovereignty and territorial integrity—is a vital national interest. However, state security is not an end in itself. It must in turn guarantee the security of the entire society. By concentrating only on questions of state security—primarily on meeting external threats—we greatly underestimated the economic and sociopolitical problems that had grown in our society. Thus, our national security failed to grow during the pre-perestroika period, despite the fact that during the 1970s and 1980s our ability to ward off external threats increased to an unparalleled height. Only a healthy, dynamic, society, confident in itself, can ensure its own security and the security of the state. Therefore, perestroika is the most important factor in strengthening national security.

This broader approach to the problem of national security presupposes a reevaluation of traditional ways. Traditionally, a military threat from without was viewed as the chief threat to national security. The most reliable guarantee of national security was seen as the achievement, and then preservation, of military-strategic parity, that is, rough equality in nuclear arsenals with the United States. The postwar arms race, however, could only promise equal destruction to both sides, despite the emphasis on parity in recent years. Furthermore, the arms race has escalated to such a degree that even parity ceases to serve as a factor deterring nuclear catastrophe.

It is worth mentioning that the term parity appeared in the writings of American specialists in the mid-1950s, when it first became theoretically possible for the Soviet Union to deal a retaliatory blow, even in the case of a massive nuclear strike by the United States. Former U.S. Secretary of Defense Robert McNamara now states, for example, that parity existed in October 1962, during the Caribbean crisis, despite the fact that the United States had a seventeen-to-one superiority in the number of warheads. In his words, neither he nor President Kennedy considered a nuclear attack on the Soviet Union, because they understood the inevitability of catastrophic consequences for the United States itself (McNamara 1986).

Until the early 1970s, the term parity was understood as the ability of both the United States and the Soviet Union to inflict unacceptable damage on the other, regardless of who dealt the first blow. Accordingly, once parity was achieved, the mutual accumulation of nuclear arsenals became senseless. Since the beginning of the 1970s, parity has been interpreted in the United States as equality of nuclear arsenals, according to basic quantitative and qualitative indices or according to battle potential. This new concept of parity has had the effect of stimulating the arms race. Instead of establishing the mutual vulnerability of both countries in the face of the nuclear threat, parity has been transformed into a complicated mathematical formula, intelligible only to the *cognoscenti.* Even the rules devised for counting weapons within the SALT process have played in parity equations. These rules, which are of a strictly technical, auxiliary nature, have become the criteria for evaluating the military-strategic balance. In this process, we have lost sight of the fact that even the most limited nuclear war is absolutely unacceptable to both societies in view of its political, social, and moral consequences.

The "mirror" interpretation of parity has gradually come to seem self-evident. As a result, the complex problem of national security, mired in the definitions of parity, has been reduced to military-technical calculations. A paradoxical situation has arisen: despite the enormous reserves of strategic power we have created, many people think the military threat has grown steadily—"by 100 warheads," or "by a new bomber." Accordingly, the opponent's new arms system can be neutralized only by an analogous system, "our own 100 warheads," and so forth. In fact, it is not necessary to strive to achieve "mirror" parity to maintain the military-strategic balance, to make it impossible for either side to resort to nuclear weapons while seeking political goals. Experts on the Committee of Soviet Scientists for the Defense of Peace and Against the Nuclear Threat have shown in one of their research papers that the military-strategic balance possesses great dynamic range, and that differences in the nuclear arsenals are largely nullified as a result (Sagdeev and Kokoshin 1987).

The "mirror" concept of parity is under critical review by the Soviet leadership, which at the same time emphasizes the need to maintain the military-strategic balance that prevents war from breaking out. But it is not necessary to participate in the arms race on the basis of parity. It is interesting to look at the experience of those powers that have restricted themselves to the minimum potential for containment. Why, for instance, has socialist China limited itself to an extremely small number of nuclear weapons? Despite all of its problems of internal development, this great power clearly could have mobilized the resources to create a far greater nuclear capacity. Clearly, it is not so much the size of a nuclear arsenal, or scenarios for its use, but the likelihood of a nuclear war as such that plays a restraining role.

The reexamination of traditional military-political stereotypes in light of the Soviet Union's national interests is revealed in concrete steps taken by the Soviet Union. For example, the Soviet leadership has stated that it will not duplicate the Strategic Defense

Initiative (SDI) program, nor develop a symmetrical response to it. If the Soviet Union tried to copy SDI, it would mean that the "mirror" interpretation of parity and the old concept of a new weapon being neutralized by the same weapon were correct. It seems that those SDI supporters in the United States who had hoped to draw the Soviet Union into a new race in new arms systems are gravely disappointed by the Soviet position.

The "double zero" option for medium-range and short-range missiles also does not fit the definition of "mirror" parity—after all, the Soviet Union is eliminating far more weapons than the United States. Because Washington proposed this solution, many U.S. policymakers apparently were certain that Moscow, guided by the usual stereotypes, would not agree. However, new political thinking made it possible to solve the INF problem in a way that met the national interests of both the Soviet Union and the United States—and to find a balance of interests for both countries.

This rethinking of the concept of parity is not limited to the nuclear sphere. As Soviet leaders point out, the idea that the military might of the Soviet Union must equal that of any possible coalition of opponents does not stand up to examination. In the first place, such an approach ignores the fact that security can and must be guaranteed by political and not military-technical means. Second, it is well known that the Soviet Union's GNP is several times smaller than that of those countries that could theoretically form a coalition against it, and a full-scale arms race therefore becomes a very heavy burden on the Soviet economy and a direct threat to its security.

For Soviet society, the arms race becomes not only a waste of material and human resources, but an obstacle on the path toward a thorough economic restructuring. It is precisely in the military sector that the laws of the administrative-command system operate in the clearest possible form, and it is this system that has pushed the Soviet economy to the brink of crisis (typically, where there are elements of such a system in the American economy, they are in the military sector). Therefore, the preservation of a large sector of the military economy, including the rules under which it functions, has a negative effect on perestroika in general.

The concept of a reasonable or sufficient defense, advanced by the Soviet leadership and actively being worked out by Soviet specialists, is aimed at breaking out of the vicious circle of the arms race (Shurkin et al. 1987). The goal is to have adequate armed forces to meet strictly defensive tasks. Both bilateral (or multilateral) agreements and unilateral actions can serve as a means toward this end.

Genuinely deep cuts in armed forces and armaments, with a simultaneous strengthening of strategic stability—given that a simple reduction in military capacities would still not eliminate the threat of aggression—are possible on a reciprocal basis. Moreover, agreements on disarmament are important simply as political methods for strengthening security; they lead to a strengthening of trust, without which genuine security is impossible. An atmosphere of trust facilitates the achievement of new agreements, strengthening mutual security in turn. A feedback loop is created between increased mutual trust and enhanced security. In the course of an arms race, we confront the opposite situation, where increased distrust and diminished security are interrelated.

During recent decades, attempts by the United States and the Soviet Union to ensure their security through unilateral growth in military power were shown to be counterproductive. However, security may be strengthened through unilateral actions, if they are based on an awareness of mutual dependence. For example, the present structure of NATO and Warsaw Pact forces actually encourages both sides to resort to large-scale offensive operations in the initial period of a war. The fear of a sudden attack leads to the accumulation of military capacities. In this situation, if one of the sides adopts measures strengthening its capacity for defensive actions while reducing its offensive possibilities, its own as well as mutual security could be strengthened. Such steps—for example, creating a forward boundary of strategic defense and withdrawing behind it those forces designated for a counterattack aimed at restoring the status quo ante—make a country better prepared to repel a sudden attack, because the threat of losing its battle-ready units is not so great. At the same time, there is increased security for the other side, which receives material guarantees that its opponent does not contemplate aggression. As Soviet researchers have noted, the experience of World War II, in particular the Battle of Kursk, during which the Soviet army stopped the Nazi attack and started a major counteroffensive, is instructive in this regard (Kokoshin and Larionov 1987).

Substantial unilateral reductions of the Soviet military forces were declared by General Secretary Gorbachev at the United Nations in December 1988. Naturally, unilateral steps to lessen military confrontation are restricted to definite military-strategic limits. Deeper changes are possible on the basis of mutual efforts, a striving by each side to strengthen its own security by means of strengthening mutual security. However, initial steps by one side can act as a catalyst, stimulating the partner to act similarly, thereby making it possible for the initiator of this process to take new steps. This process would also be based on the mechanism of positive feedback, established through the channel of military-political cooperation between the parties, and not necessarily through formal negotiations.

There is the apprehension, however, that unilateral actions aimed at lowering the level of confrontation may weaken national security. But why should the Soviet Union have to obtain the West's agreement in negotiations each time it takes actions in this sphere, as long as those actions correspond to its national interests? The tasks of perestroika require the lightening of the economic burden of the arms race by making use of the resources saved from a military build-up.

The elimination or, at the very least, the reduction of military-political competition in the Third World would serve the national interests of the Soviet Union and the United States. The idea of working out a code for superpower conduct has long been popular in the United States. But why work out such a code jointly, provoking universal suspicion of attempts to establish a Soviet-American condominium? Would it not be more effective to be guided consistently by one's own national interests? It is apparent that the Soviet Union, for example, could quite painlessly exclude itself from the struggle for spheres of influence (largely foisted upon us, incidentally, by the United States) in regions having no real importance to our national security. It would not suffer, even in the event that the American leadership did not display the same realism and did not take analogous steps. How Americans spend their national resources is a matter for Americans to decide.

We are now certain that our national resources must be used primarily to improve the living standards of the Soviet people.

Unfortunately, since the mid-1970s, we have lagged far behind the United States in GNP growth rates, and in recent years in labor productivity as well. According to some calculations by Soviet economists, the Soviet standard of living is somewhere between 50th and 60th place among the world's countries,[1] certainly not reflecting the potential of our society. Life expectancy in the Soviet Union has fallen over the past two decades, an unprecedented phenomenon in the history of modern industrial societies. Alas, the list could be continued. However, it is already clear that our national resources must be directed primarily toward solving the tasks of domestic development.

Some saving of resources may be obtained by reducing the burden of foreign political obligations. Of course, the Soviet Union is a gigantic continental power, and we cannot be indifferent to what happens on our borders. However, it is important to separate inevitable geopolitical considerations from ideological factors, as was, for example, the case with Afghanistan. The effort to help a neighbor that had seemingly embarked on the road to socialist development, along with an understandable effort to reinforce the security of our southern borders, has led to great material and human losses, while Washington has spent far less supporting the Afghan armed opposition.

It was precisely ideological concepts that were largely responsible for the significant expansion of the Soviet Union's foreign political obligations during the rule of Leonid Brezhnev. This period of stagnation within the country was accompanied by heightened activity in the world arena. The activity was aimed at embracing an ever larger number of areas and drawing more countries into the orbit of Soviet foreign policy. The future of socialism and national security became tied up with the fate of regimes to which a socialist orientation was often arbitrarily ascribed.

In practice, however, the Soviet Union became tied to a struggle for a sphere of influence that was alien to the foreign policy credo of socialism. Stagnation within the country thereby worsened,

1. *Moskovskiye novosti,* August 21, 1988.

both because a substantial share of our national resources was diverted toward these goals and because illusory foreign policy "successes" interfered with a realistic appraisal of the problems that had accumulated within society. To the extent that crisis tendencies grew within Soviet society, the Soviet Union lost its role as a model for socioeconomic development for developing countries.

Military-political competition with the United States in the Third World evidently impressed the Brezhnev leadership, which was accustomed to seeing itself as standing at the helm of a superpower fully the equal of the United States, just as parity eventually became a symbol of equal status with the United States in the world arena. At one time, the slogan "to catch up with and overtake America" was popular in the Soviet Union, but the talk about the possibility of achieving parity with the United States over a broad range of living-standards indices gradually disappeared. In 1989, our newspapers and magazines again posed the question: Why not try to equal the United States in furnishing hospitals with the latest equipment, in the number of personal computers, or modern conveniences? Unfortunately, considering the real state of the Soviet economy, it is unrealistic to consider this a practical possibility. But now there is at least a greater realization that the principal measure for ensuring our national interests is the level of socioeconomic development, not the parameters of military might.

Today, economic aspects play an increasingly important role for both national and international security. Previously, we tended to judge a state's economic security by the degree of its independence from the outside world, which in our own country was often translated into a demand for economic autarky. A similar philosophy guided those socialist countries that tried to create a full-scale industrial complex, producing everything from matches to airplanes, regardless of the size of their own economies. In practice, this emphasis led to overstraining their economies and resources. In accordance with the Soviet concept of economic security, we also tried to help developing countries by equipping large, heavy-industry plants, the construction of which was not always based on the real needs of their economic development.

Previously, the costs of isolated development had been absorbed by the Soviet economy, but today the situation has changed radically. The domination in our economy of an administrative-bureaucratic system that rejects the achievements of scientific-technical progress has led to a situation in which a large part of our industrial production does not meet world standards, to which it had never been compared. The overwhelming majority of our economic ills developed only in isolation from the world economic system. We have paid dearly for rejecting the convertibility of our national currency, as well as for the policy of nonparticipation in many international economic and financial organizations. Our national security certainly did not gain from the self-imposed isolation, because it led to a slowdown in socioeconomic development and a decline in aggregate national power.

The concept of self-sufficiency as economic security does not correspond to the realities of a mutually interdependent world. Today, genuine security is determined by how much a particular country is really included in the world economy, by how much it depends on others, and, in turn, by how much its partners depend on it. Only mutual economic dependence among states can serve as a guarantee of security. Clearly, one cannot speak of security with respect to a developing debtor-nation with a single-crop economy. By contrast, if a country is fully incorporated into a complex and diversified system of economic relations, it will strengthen its security and become an element of support for the system as a whole.

It is, however, apparent that the rebirth of the Soviet economy in the course of perestroika and its inclusion into the system of world economic ties will be a difficult and lengthy process. The strategic task—to contain the widening gap separating us from the most developed countries, and then to reduce it—must not obscure the more immediate prospect, the task of increasing integration with CMEA member countries. It can hardly be considered normal that to this day there is no real convertibility of the currencies of socialist states. The move toward a qualitatively higher level of cooperation within the CMEA framework suits the national interests of all parties concerned, both from the viewpoint of their own economic development and from the vantage point of ensuring greater sociopolitical stability. Both national and international security can only gain.

The system of world economic interdependence also significantly limits the scale of military force capable of creating a threat to the modern international economic system. The fact that extensive trade among European countries at the beginning of the century did not prevent World War I is sometimes offered as proof to the contrary. Today, however, international trade is merely the bottom floor of an incomparably more complicated system of economic interdependence, which for all practical purposes excludes the use of military force among the countries of West Europe. Economic interdependence has acquired a truly comprehensive character. It was hardly a coincidence that the famous crash on the New York Stock Exchange of October 19, 1987, followed the American Navy's shelling of Iranian oil platforms in the Persian Gulf.

Under the conditions of an interdependent world, many members of the international community feel a definite uncertainty and even suspicion concerning the intentions of those states that seek to isolate themselves. Despite the painfulness of the process, emergence from a state of isolation can improve not only national security (primarily by stimulating a country's economic development), but international security as well, by strengthening mutually profitable ties and mutual trust along with them.

The problem of trust cannot be solved solely by expanding trade and economic cooperation. Trust—the essential condition for security—arises among those societies that have a good understanding of each other's values, even if they do not share them. However, despite the enormous spiritual potential of human civilization, the idea of a mutually interdependent and integral world is having special difficulty receiving acceptance in both the East and the West. From our viewpoint, a series of U.S. administrations has misused political rhetoric on humanitarian issues and bears a large share of responsibility for this.

For a long time, we did not recognize that a state's approach to humanitarian problems can also serve as a serious indication of its intentions in the foreign political sphere. Such a denial contradicted our own concept of the interrelatedness of domestic and foreign policy. For decades, the existence in our society of problems visible to everyone was dogmatically rejected, thus provoking doubts about the basic values of the socialist structure. Indeed, it is hard to reconcile declarations about the priority of social needs with inadequate levels of appropriations for health care, education, and housing construction. The many years of concealing real human problems and the tragic pages in our history did not help to improve the "dehumanized" image of Soviet society in the West.

Thanks to perestroika and glasnost, there is greater trust and understanding of Soviet society in the world today. Although still far from solving many problems, we are clearly demonstrating that we do not intend to treat our ailments by driving them inward, but intend to look for solutions through an open and honest discussion of even the most painful problems. This approach will end the confrontational situation that has arisen in the past when the West brought up the question of human rights. When a society is confident that the state of affairs in the humanitarian sphere corresponds to its own aspirations, it loses a heightened sensitivity toward the subject.

Many real complications are related to the fact that different societies have dissimilar hierarchies of humanitarian values, and the West often does not want to take this reality into account. Therefore, questions raised by the West often fail to correspond to the important problems confronting Soviet society. To overcome disagreements in the humanitarian field, we and our partners must rely on those general human values lying at the basis of modern civilization, which requires they be freed from the rhetoric.

A foreign policy philosophy that categorized the world on the basis of ideology led inevitably to an overly simplified, black-and-white picture of international relations, where participants were firmly divided into "us" and "them." Such a view of the world was widespread in both East and West during the Cold War. Every gain by the United States was considered a loss by the Soviet Union, and vice versa. From the viewpoint of the principal participants in the confrontation, the old adage, "who is not with us is against us" expressed the essence of political wisdom. Such logic required every country to take sides in this global struggle. Many countries were thereby deprived of a real choice in international affairs.

An exceedingly simplistic view of the world weakened our security. Exaggerated threats to our security (both real and imaginary) assumed the aspect of a global siege. The feeling stayed with us both during both times of real crises and conflicts and more quiet periods, and was directly related to an ideological approach to the external world. Concepts of the Soviet Union as a besieged fortress are largely rooted in the theory and practice of Stalinism, because they were used to strengthen a regime of personal power. These tenacious concepts resulted in the creation of a counterweight (primarily military) aggregate power equal to any possible coalition of opponents, overstraining national resources and leading to political tension with the West.

With perestroika, we have concluded that our approach to the external world needs radical revision. Having recognized that the command-bureaucratic system caused grave harm to our internal development, we asked ourselves whether it had a negative influence on our foreign policy as well. As Gorbachev has noted, even the most important decisions in this area were sometimes made without a thorough, collective discussion and analysis (Gorbachev 1988). Superficially, it seemed that the leaders who made decisions in foreign policy enjoyed complete freedom. In reality, however, they often turned out to be captive to their own prejudices and could not conceive of alternative solutions to the problems. For society as a whole, this approach led to great losses, because no attention was given to the relative costs of various courses of action.

Only the sustained democratization of society can serve as a reliable antidote to the domination of the command-administrative system in the foreign policy sphere. In most countries, the problems of security and foreign policy are the focus of political discussions, in which the leadership tries to defend official policies in the face of criticism from all directions. This state of affairs did not arise by chance. Although the press and public opinion may sometimes irritate policymakers, such discussions make it possible to work out alternative approaches and to avoid many mistakes and omissions.

Soviet society today is faced with a very paradoxical situation. Although Soviet Foreign Minister Eduard Shevardnadze expresses new ideas and calls for the open discussion of foreign policy questions in the press, his invitation, originating from above, has been met with little response from the press until now (Shevardnadze 1988). Interesting articles on questions of foreign policy are the exception rather than the rule. To a large extent, this results from the lack of a tradition for such discussions.

Society must, however, possess a certain amount of reliable information to hold such discussions. In our country, in the sphere of national security, every department's natural inclination to keep bureaucratic secrets is combined with the traditionally closed nature of all information, however distantly related to national security. Only society itself can define the national interests and balance the interests of various departments to arrive at the common interest. At present, however, Americans often know more about our armed forces than does the Soviet public. Naturally, glasnost in the military sphere is one factor strengthening international security, and one can only welcome the fact that an American Secretary of Defense was able to sit at the controls of a super-secret Soviet bomber. However, glasnost should not exist solely to be exported. Today, Soviet experts and representatives of the public are for more access to information on military and foreign policy questions. An increase in glasnost in this sphere and serious discussions within society itself leading to decisions made with open eyes will strengthen national security. An important breakthrough in this sphere was the publication in early 1989 of Warsaw Pact data on the military balance in Europe.

The processes of democratization in Soviet society are also related to the tasks of democratization in international relations, acknowledging the tremendous diversity in the world arena. Such recognition constitutes an important factor strengthening both international security and the security of every member of the international community. Freedom of choice must become the inalienable right of countries and peoples, the right to choose one's own path of development without looking apprehensively at even the most powerful states. Many states—the United States and the Soviet Union included—find it hard to admit this right. Each carries the weight of traditions and ideological prejudices, and there is thus a great temptation to consider one's choice not only the correct one, but to foist it upon others as well.

Such a policy is clearly unproductive today, because diversity is a fact in the contemporary world. To acknowledge the universality of the principle of freedom of choice means to bring one's concepts into line with contemporary realities. If we continue as previously to view the confrontation between the Soviet Union and the United States as the only axis of international relations and to restrict other countries to that choice, then sooner or later Soviet-American competition will lose any meaning from the viewpoint of the real processes of international development, and the denial of freedom of choice to others will become a dangerous anachronism.

Our country had to defend the choices it made through difficult historical times. We are not indifferent to the fate of people who choose the path of constructing a new society, and we have always tried to help them realize that choice. Today, however, it is more important than ever before to determine what real choice a particular society is making. At the end of the 1970s, the Soviet leadership was evidently convinced that Afghanistan had unequivocally made a socialist choice that had to be supported. In practice, however, it turns out that Afghan society does not accept socialist transformations and is striving to make a choice reflecting the special characteristics of its history and peoples. New political thinking made it possible to evaluate reality soberly and objectively. Today, thanks to the Geneva Accords, the Afghan people have the opportunity to fully realize their right to a choice.

The realization in practice of the principles of the new political thinking thereby contributed to strengthening both national and international security. The beginning of the Afghan settlement provoked a chain reaction. Prospects have taken shape for the political solution of lingering regional conflicts in the Persian Gulf, in South Africa, and in Southeast Asia. Of course, the specific situation in each of these regions is extremely different, but the security interdependence of all members of the international community is the same. The INF Treaty became the first breakthrough in the area of real disarmament, and it has opened up favorable prospects for reducing other types of armaments.

Today, we view as one of our main tasks the application of new political thinking to the field of practical politics and the prevention of a breach between declarations and concrete realities. Radical economic reform, the growth of glasnost and democracy in Soviet society, perestroika in the process of forming foreign and military policy—these are the most reliable guarantees of a consistent and irreversible realization of new political thinking and the growth in general security.

REFERENCES

Gorbachev, Mikhail S. 1988. *Materialy XIX Vsesoyuznoy konferentsii KPSS.* Moscow: Politizdat.

Kokoshin, Andrey, and Valentin V. Larionov. 1987. "The Kursk Battle in the Light of Modern Defensive Doctrine." *Mirovaya ekonomika i mezhdunarodnyye otnosheniya,* No. 8: 32-40.

McNamara, Robert. 1986. *Blundering into Disaster.* New York: Partheon Books.

Sagdeev, Roald, and Andrey Kokoshin, eds. 1987. *Strategic Stability Under Conditions of Radical Reductions in Nuclear Weapons.* Moscow: Moscow Agency Press News.

Shevardnadze, Eduard. 1988. XIX All-Union Conference of the CPSU: Foreign Policy and Diplomacy. *Mezhdunarodnaya zhizn,* No. 9: 3-35.

Zhurkin, Vitaliy, Sergey A. Karaganov, and Andrey V. Kortunov. 1987. "On Reasonable Sufficiency." *SShA: ekonomika, politika, ideologiya,* No. 12: 22-30.

_____

CHAPTER 14

Prospects for the Development of Soviet-American Economic Relations

GEORGI ARBATOV

SOVIET-AMERICAN ECONOMIC RELATIONS: PAST AND PRESENT

Economic ties between the Soviet Union and the United States have not developed as they should have, and, with the exception of certain periods (the pre-war five-year plans, Lend-Lease deliveries in wartime, and the first half of the 1970s), they have not played a vital role in Soviet-American relations. The primary reasons for this are the dominance of an anti-Soviet course in the policies of American leaders and the lack of historical economic links such as those that exist between the United States and many European states.

As a result, the potential for an increase in economic relations between the Soviet Union and the United States remains essentially unrealized. Of course, this fact cannot help but exert a negative effect on political relations between the two countries. There is no sound material base and no serious mutual economic interest underlying Soviet-American relations.

During détente, both sides took steps to create favorable conditions for the development of Soviet-American economic relations. An overall treaty and legal basis was established for the extensive development of Soviet-American trade, and economic and scientific-technical cooperation (a trade agreement envisaging reciprocal adoption of most-favored nation status, an agreement on reciprocal granting of credits and on financial procedures, and an agreement on furthering economic, industrial and technical cooperation) were promoted. The intergovernmental U.S.-U.S.S.R. Trade and Economic Council (USTEC) was also established.

American business circles displayed an interest in developing economic relations with Soviet organizations, and this resulted in the conclusion of a number of long-term agreements, including, for example, those with Occidental Petroleum, Pepsico, Armco Steel, IBM, and Ingersoll Rand.

That more agreements were not realized is, in our opinion, mainly the fault of anti-Soviet circles in the United States, which blocked the mechanism established to develop trade and economic relations with the Soviet Union and also capitalized on events in Afghanistan and Poland to carry out a policy of broad economic sanctions and an embargo against the Soviet Union.

Under these conditions, there was an increase in the Soviet Union's trade orientation, that is, trade with the developed capitalist countries of West Europe and in part with Japan, which, despite American pressure, pursued a more flexible policy vis-à-vis the Soviet Union. Soviet trade with the United States was reduced to grain purchases, while most other trade was reduced to a minimum.

At the same time, a failure of economic levers to exert pressure on the Soviet Union's foreign and domestic policies forced the Reagan administration to reexamine its attitude toward developing trade with the Soviet Union. The "grain embargo" was lifted under pressure from agricultural interests; then, after unsuccessful attempts to disrupt implementation of the plan to supply Soviet gas to West Europe, the ban against supplying oil and gas equipment to the Soviet Union was revoked. Today, the expediency of the entire American export control system, in particular the ban on deliveries of dual-purpose goods (those that may be used for both civilian and military purposes), is being called into question. The Reagan administration did not support any of many repeated attempts by representatives of the right wing in Congress to harden trade conditions with the Soviet Union, and it promoted the consistent application of antidumping legislation with respect to deliveries of Soviet carbamide. A decision was also made that contracts already in effect would continue to be honored, irrespective of new restrictions or bans. All this was done despite the predominance of conservative elements in determining U.S. foreign policy. The new direction was crowned by the appointment of William Verity, Secretary of Commerce in October 1987 and former co-chairman of USTEC, a man known for his devotion to developing trade relations with the Soviet Union. We may conclude from all of the above that the American administration adopted a more balanced position on the question of developing economic relations with the Soviet Union.

The more constructive approach to this matter by a majority of the industrially developed capitalist countries interested in trade with the Soviet Union has had a certain impact on U.S. policy with the Soviet Union. Thus, Washington's West European allies, including the United Kingdom, did not yield to American pressure in carrying out the gas pipeline project and a number of other important economic projects with the Soviet Union.

The recent effort to strengthen the United States' unstable position in the world economy and global trade is influencing U.S. foreign policy and relations with the Soviet Union. It is considered increasingly important to develop exports, improve the competitiveness of American products, and search for new markets, which makes the potentially enormous market of the Soviet Union attractive, especially when the Soviet economy is being restructured.

Confidence among American business circles that trade conditions are improving is growing, with few exceptions. Business leaders have taken note of the fact that the federal government is not impeding negotiations with Soviet agencies, that trade limits are now rather broad, and that licenses required for exports to the Soviet Union are now generally approved.

At the same time, some Americans feel that the Soviet Union, while proclaiming a devotion to developing trade, contributes little toward its real success and impedes the growth of business partnerships. At the beginning of the 1980s, limited trade was attributed to the Soviet Union's cautiousness, but today many point to the foreign economic problems of the Soviet Union, the lack of hard currency for imports, and the lack of goods meeting world standards for exports.

It must be admitted that part of the blame for the small amount of reciprocal trade also rests with the Soviet side. The Carter administration's actions to limit Soviet-American business ties

confirmed an opinion in the Soviet Union that Soviet organizations should limit contacts with American business until political
conditions were normalized, should not display initiative in trade
and economic relations with the United States, and should embark
upon cooperation only when proposals from Americans were
clearly more attractive than proposals from other countries.

The officially announced primacy of political over economic
relations (a concept first advanced by the U.S. government) resulted
in Soviet economic organizations virtually stopping work on the
American market, turning down inquiries from American
companies, and severely reducing the number and level of business
contacts. The role of the Ministry of Foreign Trade was reduced to
arranging provisions for the trade in grain, while calls for
rescinding the politically motivated Jackson-Vanik and Stevenson
amendments replaced a search for real opportunities to expand
business ties.

We should note that American business circles, while readily
acknowledging the generally negative effect these amendments
have on the atmosphere of cooperation, do not consider these
restrictions to be the main reason for stagnation in trade. They
tend to believe that giving the Soviet Union most-favored nation
status would not change the present structure and volume of Soviet
exports to the United States.

There is no doubt that political considerations will influence
economic relations between the Soviet Union and the United States
into the future. Still, if more attention were paid to economic
cooperation, it would seem that such cooperation could and must
become an important means of working toward the normalization
of Soviet-American relations. For this to happen, however, economic ties must begin to live their "own life." The Soviet Union must
actively pursue all opportunities to penetrate the American market,
revive business contacts with companies, attract them to participate
in rebuilding existing industrial enterprises and constructing new
ones, launch a lobbying campaign in the United States in favor of
trade with the Soviet Union, and reinforce and activate Soviet
economic missions in the United States.

It would seem that a favorable situation for such activity exists at
present in the United States, conditional on a number of external
and domestic factors, including progress on arms reduction, the

activation of a bilateral political dialogue, and the need to reduce the U.S. foreign trade deficit. American business circles' interest in the Soviet market has been stimulated by economic reforms in the Soviet Union and by hopes for positive changes in the economic mechanism, which would make economic cooperation more realistic.

The Washington and Moscow summits in 1987 and 1988 created a more propitious situation for the development of businesslike cooperation between the two countries, and this was reflected in the joint Soviet-American documents signed at the summits. These documents not only express a firm intention to broaden mutually advantageous trade and economic relations, they also provide for the creation of a joint Soviet-American commission on trade questions and the preparation of specific proposals to achieve that goal. This would permit a new approach to the question of developing Soviet-American trade relations and open up new and unique opportunities for progress in this area.

TOWARD A NEW APPROACH

On the eve of the 1990s, conditions are ripe for economic relations to become a dynamic force in Soviet-American relations. This presupposes both an increase in the amount of trade and economic exchange between the two countries and a change in its structure. However, the absence of a long-term concept for the development of Soviet-American trade-economic and scientific-technical ties is a serious problem. Therefore, neither we nor the Americans are certain that the warmer climate in bilateral relations will lead to stable and long-term economic relations. The need for stability is especially important due to the changes in the Soviet economy, specifically a new management system that should improve Soviet economic links throughout the world. The scale and nature of the Soviet Union's influence on the world economy will depend on achieving a consensus with the United States with regard to mutually acceptable actions in developing a world trade and currency system, and the conditions for joint enterprises.

At the same time, we must consider the fact that existing opportunities for a "breakthrough" in trade may be lost for a long time if the Soviet Union and United States do not succeed soon (evidently within the next two or three years) in developing greater economic cooperation. It is important that noneconomic issues be allowed to subvert programs on the economic front. The reasons for this follow.

First, both sides will continue in the foreseeable future to make trade and economic relations dependent on the solution of political, military-strategic, and humanitarian problems. It is also possible that progress in reducing arms may slow down by the 1990s; attempts by conservatives to discredit perestroika in the eyes of Americans and to sabotage Soviet foreign policy initiatives would intensify. When the positive propaganda effect of the Soviet Union's "peace offensive" will fade (if only because "Soviet themes" will no longer be a sensation among the general American public), the federal government will very likely lose some of the stimuli for a radical improvement in trade and economic relations with the Soviet Union.

Second, the absence of visible progress in reforming the Soviet Union's foreign economic practices and the continuing contraction in Soviet foreign trade turnover even now allow representatives of American business circles to conclude that the reform is of a gradual, not revolutionary, nature. A further delay in applying political and economic levers to regulate foreign economic ties with the West, such as setting a real ruble exchange rate, bringing domestic and world prices into line, providing economic, stimulation for foreign trade development, and introducing customs tariffs and new progressive forms of foreign economic cooperation, will make it difficult for the United States and other western countries to embark on wide-ranging cooperation in trade, credit funding, and scientific-technical cooperation. It will be equally difficult to persuade these countries that the Soviet Union is striving to move toward generally accepted methods of cooperation and regulation of foreign economic practices.

Evidently, the time has come to initiate negotiations on setting into motion the treaty-legal mechanism created in the first half of the 1970s, which calls for the renewal of intergovernmental agreements on trade, science and technology, questions of credit and transportation, and the creation of normal conditions for developing economic relations on a stable, guaranteed basis.

Instead of waiting until such a legal system goes into effect, we could take a number of concrete steps to develop Soviet-American trade and economic relations:

1. We could initiate a study of an American (USTEC) proposal for cooperation between American and Soviet trade consortiums with a view to signing a General Agreement on this matter as soon as possible, after having defined the principal spheres of cooperation (agrobusiness and oil and gas, et cetera).
2. We could carry on detailed negotiations with a number of American companies interested in developing cooperation in the Soviet Far East (in mining, oil, metallurgical, and cellulose-paper industries). Aside from production-economic benefits, such cooperation with American companies would spur Japan on to increase economic cooperation with us in this part of the Soviet Union and would help speed up implementation of the program for complex development of the Far East.
3. We could initiate work on setting up joint Soviet-American enterprises in the Soviet Union, the United States, and third countries. For this purpose, it is essential to expand the range of activities of these joint enterprises beyond industry and agriculture to include planning, consulting, research, financial, trade and rental, legal, insurance, transport, and tourist services.

The opportunity to set up joint enterprises as a way of penetrating the Soviet market over the long term is attracting special attention from American business leaders. At the same time, they have justifiable doubts and uncertainties in this matter. Here it is very important to conclude an agreement on reciprocal protection of capital investments and the avoidance of a double tax assessment. Broad consultations should also be held with interested American companies and organizations on all aspects of joint enterprises; this would clarify a great deal for us and would enable us to work out conditions for their operations, which truly would be mutually advantageous and would attract American capital. U.S.-Soviet joint enterprises could become the cornerstone of Soviet-

American foreign economic ties. However, success in this field depends on taking the following circumstances into consideration:

1. Existing American export controls over advanced technology transfer make it difficult in the foreseeable future for the Soviet Union to gain access to certain fields of science and technology, and it should therefore plan to carry on its own research. The more advanced and productive Soviet research is, the sooner the American side will have to begin gradually removing existing restrictions.

2. Experience in scientific-technical ties has shown that the American side is interested in cooperating in areas where Soviet science and technology have achieved notable success (or success equal to that of the United States). Therefore, we should not wait until restrictions on advanced technology transfer to the Soviet Union are lifted; it is essential to link the American side's access to Soviet scientific-technical achievements to reciprocal access to American scientific and technical innovations by interested Soviet organizations. This would be a way of making breaches in the system of American export control, guided in each particular case by the principle of reciprocity.

3. It would be useful if interested Soviet departments, establishments, and organizations (for example, the State Committee for Science and Technology, Soviet Academy of Sciences) had a coordinated plan listing scientific-technical problems that it would be economically tenable to solve within the framework of Soviet-American scientific and technical cooperation. This would enable Soviet organizations to help form the scientific-technical ties that the Soviet Union needs, while at the same time paying due consideration to the interests of American companies.

4. It would be useful to tie small and medium-sized American companies specializing in science-related products to scientific-technical cooperation. If necessary, these companies, which are generally in need of financing, together with American specialized companies, could be granted special credits to carry out work of interest to Soviet organizations. Another form of cooperation with these companies could be the organization of joint incorporated (*vnedrencheskikh*) or "venture" enterprises.

5. As a possible step toward removing U.S. restrictions on the export of advanced machinery and technology to the Soviet Union, we could propose joint scientific research for military purposes, on the condition that there be mutual guarantees against the use of imported machinery or technology. Observance of such guarantees could be secured within the framework of the joint enterprises formed in the Soviet Union or the United States by means of an appropriate verification system analogous to that designed for the INF Treaty. Such an agreement could be viewed in the context of creating a system of trust and economic security in East-West relations.

6. It would be useful to organize a joint Soviet-American consultative-intermediary company attached to the Soviet Academy of Sciences; its mission would be to seek out partners to work in the field of scientific and scientific-production cooperation, as well as to set up joint enterprises to solve particular scientific-technical problems when that would be economically justifiable. It would be appropriate for this company to organize a data bank of technological, engineering, and other services that Soviet and American organizations could offer each other.

The field of advertising and information offers considerable potential for developing bilateral economic and scientific-technical ties. Agreement at the highest level to promote the dissemination of reliable information on the Soviet and U.S. economic systems, their scientific-technical and production capabilities, and the positive effects of foreign economic cooperation could help create a favorable climate for the development of foreign economic relations.

It would be useful to form a specialized joint enterprise that would provide foreign economic advertising and information on a commercial basis. It could be responsible for selecting proposals by American and Soviet enterprises on cooperation, looking for suitable partners, advertising in the Soviet Union and United States by commercial means, and disseminating information on export commodities and services. Such a joint enterprise is needed because Soviet advertising organizations are not ready for independent activity on the American market of advertising and middle-man services.

A relatively narrow group of large and medium-sized companies is currently interested in trade-economic and scientific-technical links with the Soviet Union. Here, we should note that medium-sized and, especially, small businesses embracing 90 percent of all American companies and producing more than 50 percent of GNP are not economically interested in developing ties with the Soviet Union. Meanwhile, Congress and the federal government attribute great importance to medium and small businesses as being the most influential elements of the electorate. The influence exerted by farming associations on the development of Soviet-American trade, and the powerful lobby they have in Congress, are relevant in this connection. That is also why it would be useful to invite representatives from medium-sized and small-business associations, along with senators and congressional representatives, to the Soviet Union to learn of current opportunities for business cooperation.

An important element in Soviet-American relations should be a constructive dialogue on a broad range of complex problems facing the world economy and the search for mutually acceptable approaches to solving them. One form such dialogues might take would be regular bilateral consultations on various levels, including those among scientists, to evaluate the state of the world's economy and its prospects for development.

Needless to say, the development of Soviet-American economic relations could have great economic, political, and international significance. We must, however, keep in mind that implementation of the measures proposed will not yield *rapid* results in the stable growth in Soviet-American trade or in economic and scientific-technical cooperation. The level of American alienation weighs too heavily on both countries, creating barriers that hinder normal, stable, and predictable relations. Nevertheless, simple movement from estrangement to rapprochement in the sphere of economic relations is important, especially at this stage.

In view of the U.S. preeminence and leading role in a number of important branches of the world economy, as well as the enormous potential of its market for selling a wide range of commodities, the development of economic ties with the United

States could give the Soviet Union appreciable economic benefits and could facilitate the Soviet economy's transition to one based on intensive growth.

The very movement of normalizing economic relations between the Soviet Union and the United States will exert a favorable influence on economic relations between the Soviet Union and other western countries. It will also help to weaken and eliminate political and economic barriers in this area, as well as intensifying competition for the Soviet market, because our involuntary one-sided orientation toward West European countries often weakens terms of trade with these states.

Finally, normalization of economic relations with the United States will facilitate greater cooperation with West European countries in international economic organizations (including our participation in the GATT), and will improve chances for promoting the concept of international economic security as proposed by the Soviet Union.

NEW EAST-WEST RELATIONS AND NORTH-SOUTH ISSUES

While many global problems confront humanity today, the main one remains the prevention of war and the demilitarization of U.S.-Soviet relations. This problem remains a basic source of tension, aggravates regional conflicts, and diverts enormous material and spiritual resources from creative goals. Annual expenditures on military purposes worldwide now amount to about $1 trillion, and the number of soldiers and those engaged in military research and production has reached 100 million. In the mid-1980s, one-quarter of all capital investments in the world went into military production, while total expenditures for military purposes exceeded two-thirds of the GNP of the poorer half of mankind. It is especially dangerous that military expenditures are growing rapidly not just in the developed countries, but in the developing countries as well. The poorer countries are burdened by huge foreign debts and urgently need funds to fight hunger, disease, and illiteracy, as well as to carry out measures for environmental preservation.

From the Soviet perspective, the time has come to take practical
steps to realize the concept of "Disarming for Development."
Experts from the Soviet Union and the United States could embark
very soon on joint work to determine the amounts of material and
financial resources to be earmarked for aid to developing countries
from what would be saved as a result of reductions in atomic
weapons, conventional arms, and other possible steps in the cause
of disarmament.

Perhaps negotiations on limiting weapons sales to other
countries should be renewed with the aim of ending the "poor
man's arms race," local wars and conflicts, and terrorism, which
has perhaps now become a global problem, and one that is
growing more acute. Weapons flow freely from local war zones,
and some wind up in the hands of terrorists. The practice of using
terror as a method of political struggle has increased significantly
in recent decades. This cannot but cause alarm, especially because
modern society, with its complex economic infrastructure,
communications network, nuclear power plants, chemical factories,
and fuel depots, presents very "attractive" objects for terrorist acts.

It seems to me that we have as yet done very little to work out
effective international cooperation in the fight against terrorism.
To forge such cooperation, we must first renounce double standards
in questions of international terrorism. There can be no "good"
and "bad" terrorism; the identical actions must not be considered
terrorist acts in some cases and the exploits of selfless "freedom
fighters" in others. Moreover, it is extremely important to
recognize the direct link between terrorism on the one hand and
economic backwardness on the other. It is very unlikely that we
would have run into terrorism on such a scale in Third World
countries if we had managed to break the vicious circle: economic
backwardness = social instability = political extremism = further
worsening of economic problems.

We must not allow ourselves to ignore and dissociate ourselves
from the growing economic problems of the Third World. Such
attempts have been made in the past, both in the East and the
West. We in the Soviet Union have often said the problems of
developing countries are a vestige of colonialism. We are not to
blame. We are ready to answer to anyone concerning our former
colonial regions—the Caucasus, Central Asia, the Far East. Let the

other great powers provide as much help to their former colonies as we have given ours.

While we feel we are not to blame, we also understand that today no single country has the right to retreat from global problems. Feelings of compassion and morality are not the only reasons that we should undertake extraordinary measures; security considerations also play a role.

Of course, our two countries cannot solve global problems by our own efforts alone. The Soviet Union and the United States, after all, make up only 10 percent of the population of the planet. Over the long run, our opportunities to influence the course of events in the world will more likely decrease than increase. The opportunities are nevertheless great. The economic and military might of the Soviet Union and the United States, and the breadth of their political interests, which extend to virtually every part of the globe, predestine the two powers to a special responsibility for preserving peace, strengthening world security, and ensuring favorable conditions for the social and economic development of all mankind.

What should be done first of all? It seems to me that we should begin by recognizing and overcoming old mistakes, delusions, and omissions that our countries were guilty of in the past. If you look at the history of international relations in the Third World over the past few decades, it would be hard to avoid the conclusion that both our countries allowed the Third World to be turned into an arena of confrontation and competition, drawing it into the "Cold War," and this hampered the process of overcoming backwardness in former colonial countries, which bred many acute crises. Smoldering conflicts, inflamed from outside, to this day undermine the weak national economies of dozens of countries and even whole regions of the globe.

We think it essential to bring a principled new approach to the developing world. These new policies must be founded on recognition and respect for the interests of the developing world, on a refusal to regard it as an arena for confrontation, on an understanding that it is not "ours" or "yours," and on an acknowledgement that politically it will travel its own road. The sooner we understand this, the more mistakes we can avoid. And we must inevitably reach the conclusion that our common interests lie, at a minimum, in not interfering, but, wherever possible, in helping these states solve their problems. We would welcome an exploratory search for possible joint efforts in this regard. For us, the Third World should not be an arena for competition, but a sphere for cooperation.

As the Soviet economy shifts to a new system of management, our country will become increasingly interested in actively influencing the development of world economic links on a global scale. Real influence in the global economy, as it presents itself, is impossible without achieving a certain mutual understanding with the United States (and with the West as a whole) with respect to world trade, the currency system, and credit policies. If a consensus in our approaches to development of the world economy were to be reached, it would inevitably have a positive effect on bilateral economic ties.

Thus, in touching on the question of a new international economic system, it is important to stress that the lack of a fruitful East-West dialogue on current economic problems stands in the way of achieving agreement on such a system. In this connection, it would be worth discussing the following proposals for expanding Soviet participation in reorganizing the world economic system:

1. We should examine the possibility of Soviet participation in discussions on international economic matters, primarily East-West relations, at annual meetings of heads of government of leading capitalist countries.

2. During the proposed exploratory talks to be held under the aegis of USTEC, we should develop a concept for increasing Soviet-American trade and economic links and provide for discussion of more general global economic problems, as well as a mechanism for their practical solution (regulation of joint enterprises, systems of technology transfer and scientific-technical cooperation, and governmental renunciation of boycotts and sanctions, for example). All of these developments could serve as a model for a new framework for international economic relations.

3. We should organize bilateral talks between Soviet and American experts to develop a concept of economic interdependence among countries of the East, West, and South in

order to focus attention on global problems in world development. Such a plan would not only permit us to find a common basis for active cooperation among countries, it would clarify specific ways to achieve compromises in the Soviet-American dialogue on bilateral economic relations and global problems, including the problem of reorganizing international economic relations.

A major threat to international stability today arises from economic stagnation in the developing parts of the world. A dangerous trend toward increasing disparities in developmental levels between the industrially advanced North and the relatively undeveloped South has become increasingly evident during the 1980s. This is already a major problem in the world's economy and politics; under conditions of interdependence, it can lead to a serious deterioration in the state of the world's economy, increased pressure toward the disintegration of international trade and currency systems, and an aggravation of regional conflicts.

It is perfectly clear that the process of disarmament and the fashioning of a new system of international stability require that attention be focused constantly on developmental problems, both to strengthen trust on an international scale and to prevent an intolerable rise in propensities toward the forcible redistribution of wealth.

During recent years, the fulfillment of their international obligations by developing countries led to a steady decline in their economic position and prospects for development. On the one hand, this was a consequence of unfavorable trends that arose in the 1970s, trends associated with the growth of inflation and a decline in criteria for the efficient use of capital on an international scale. On the other hand, it is clear that the responsibility for this development is shared by all participants in the international economy, and that to place the principal burden of adjustment on the developing world cannot be justified, as U.N. decisions have emphasized.

The developing countries rightfully expect that their policies, directed toward greater integration into international economic links, will promote a real improvement in living standards, including standards of nutrition, education, health care, and consumption. It is nevertheless apparent that relations between the North and the South, which are based on the criteria and norms of a free market, will not lead to the fulfillment of these expectations, at least not in the short or medium term.

In this connection, it would be useful for industrially developed countries to adopt special measures to protect the developmental process. This would help strengthen confidence in world affairs and improve prospects for a political dialogue on all levels. It is vital to note that the developing countries are making serious efforts to improve the efficiency of their economies in a complex international economic situation, acknowledging the concept of responsibility for international obligations at their main forums. In other words, these countries are prepared to cover their commitments.

A complex approach to the problem of developmental protection should include the following points:

1. Formation of public opinion in the industrially advanced countries favoring development of the Third World, because, in the final analysis, a vital acceleration in the rate of development is hardly possible without taxpayers' money. In this connection, it is instructive that, according to a Gallup poll, only about 40 percent of Americans today think that problems of the Third World directly affect their interests.

2. Governments should undertake serious efforts to improve the international trade and currency systems with the goal of creating a better climate for the trade of developing countries. More than half of world trade now suffers from various restrictions or is affected by the deforming influence of subsidies. Meanwhile, the principal ideas of international trade exchange, reinforced in the GATT, remain viable. Discriminatory barriers against goods from the developing countries must be completely eliminated in regulating a series of markets in the developed countries (which are of great importance to Third World countries).

3. Make wider use of the principle of nonreciprocity in trade with developing countries, especially with the poorest ones.

4. Write off the debts of developing countries to official agencies of western developed countries (the so-called Paris Club credit

line). Write off a certain portion of developing countries' debts to socialist states.

5. Reduce the role of security assistance in national economic aid programs. It is widely recognized that such assistance is economically ineffective and is conducive to increased military tension. It is also vital to expand assistance for projects designed to overcome the most acute manifestations of poverty in the developing world. Specific projects could be developed by the joint efforts of companies from both capitalist and socialist countries.

6. Important and effective steps could be undertaken by international currency-financial organizations. Here, the United States bears a special responsibility because significant achievements can be assured only on the initiative or with the approval of the United States. It is essential to conduct an expert evaluation of alternative proposals to increase the liquidity of developing countries with a view to improving their chances of financing the structural deficit of the current balance.

   As is well known, the developing countries are not pushing the idea of eliminating the conditionality of credits. Effective international control over the use of international funds is an essential characteristic of multilateral official credits. However, it would seem that the developing countries' requests that their conditional nature be made more democratic are justified, considering the inflexibility of this mechanism as demonstrated in recent years.

   International private credits will remain in the foreseeable future an important element in financing in the developing countries (though their role has diminished in recent years). In this connection, it is essential to work out and perfect a mechanism to protect development interests from a change in conditions on the lending-capital market.

7. A particularly acute question today is that of forming an international information order, especially the technological aspects of this problem. This is because of the growth of global telecommunications systems, which are viewed by the developing countries as a threat to their technological advancement, one that could lead in the final analysis to further reinforcing their unequal status in the international division of labor. In

this regard, it would be useful to develop a mechanism for protecting the interests of developing countries in the field of technology when negotiations on questions of technology and information are held in the framework of a new round of the GATT.

8. As far as the activities of transnational corporations in the developing world are concerned, it must be acknowledged that they represent an important channel for development. Such a situation will continue, at least for the immediate future. However, in recent years they have tended to reduce their interest in conducting business in developing countries, at least in those fields that determine the progress of development.

Transnational corporations and banks are not by nature bearers of the idea of protecting growth. If new investment possibilities related to development of the scientific-technical revolution were to arise, a dangerous trend toward foreign companies' disinvestment in the Third World could develop, despite reduced restrictions by developing countries on their activities.

We thus are confronted by the extremely urgent task of creating an effective mechanism of cooperation among governments of the developed countries and international business.

The problem of international indebtedness is of central importance to the global economy of the 1980s and is similar to the importance held by the new world price for oil in the 1970s. By the end of 1987, the debts of developing countries had reached a total of $1.2 trillion. The burden of indebtedness has an oppressive effect on the economies of developing countries and contributes to a potentially explosive situation in the international credit and currency-financial mechanism and, on the whole, to the entire system of international economic and political relations.

In recent years, it has become quite clear that a considerable portion of the debts of developing countries will never be completely repaid. It is equally clear that until now attempts to solve the problem of indebtedness have failed. The main reason for this failure is that solutions to the debt problem are pursued within the framework of the existing unjust credit system, a mechanism that no longer functions in accordance with the realities of today's world.

The growing danger of this situation makes it increasingly urgent to put a stop to a crisis of foreign indebtedness. This will require a political settlement of the debt problem in the context of restructuring the entire system of international economic relations on the basis of justice and equality of all countries, regardless of the paths they have chosen or their level of development. Such an approach presupposes joint actions by the governments of debtor and creditor nations, a purposeful interference into the "free play" of market forces.

The international community could reach agreement on the following immediate steps:

1. lower interest rates for bank credits to a level corresponding to state developmental assistance, with the national budgets of creditor countries absorbing the difference;
2. decide on additional privileges for the least developed countries;
3. limit annual installments of debt payments to a fixed proportion of annual export earnings, in amounts not detrimental to development;
4. accept exports from debtor countries as debt payments along with hard currency; eliminate protectionist import restrictions by creditor countries; and
5. relinquish additional interest when refinancing debts and when deferred payments on loans are presented.

Such measures would comprise a program of quick actions to lighten the debt burden of developing countries. It would be aimed at renewing a stream of financial resources to the developing states and liberating international credit from the abuses of private banks to the maximum extent possible.

Our principal task over the long term is to limit the arms race and to utilize part of the resources released as a result of reduced arms expenditures for developmental purposes. That is how proposals made by the Soviet Union on the idea of developing a concept of international economic security define the issue. We are ready to examine other proposals directed toward a global and fair settlement of the debt problem, particularly those that take into account the socioeconomic needs of developing countries and the interests of the world economy.

The world food problem is today a pressing economic and political reality for all mankind. After the 1972-1974 food crisis, the general situation improved somewhat, though the circumstances in a number of major regions (especially in Africa) remains unstable. If the United States and the Soviet Union pooled their efforts, they could do a great deal to help solve the world food problem. The question now is not the quantity of food produced in the world annually, but its distribution. Here, there arises a whole set of problems that needs a fresh approach.

Indeed, at the beginning of the 1980s, several developing countries (Argentina, Brazil, India, Thailand, and others) made great progress in achieving self-sufficiency in food and even began exporting food. This development not only improved their economies, but it also had a beneficial effect on world trade in foodstuffs, helped to lower prices for food products, and, consequently, made food supplies more available to people in other countries experiencing food shortages. However, it is just this last factor that makes it particularly complicated to take advantage of the opportunities offered: the low standard of living denotes a low level of solvency; the lack of qualified personnel in the agrarian-food complex of food-deficient countries does not permit the effective use of either gratuitous assistance or credits for developing agriculture and the food industry. In short, such measures provide only temporary relief and do not permit these countries to solve the problems of producing and distributing food products; as a result, foreign debt continues to rise.

The world's powers have already come to the realization that today all countries are interdependent, that their economies are bound together, and that the world's food problem is a universal one, despite persistent and substantial discrepancies in the level of food consumption. These discrepancies impose special moral and material obligations on developed countries, which are capable of redirecting a part of the resources made available by the disarmament process to the world food problem. They can also organize bilateral and multilateral programs to speed up progress in agriculture and the agroindustrial complex of the developing countries.

GLOBAL ENERGY AND ECOLOGY

Under modern conditions, it is impossible to assure stable rates of continued economic growth with the present raw material energy base. Growth in the output of traditional power sources is limited by objective economic, political, and ecological factors. An increase in oil and gas production is limited by the inevitable rise in capital and labor costs, while the use of coal is restricted by the high level of expenditures on environmental protection. Further development of nuclear power will result in dramatic cost increases because of additional expenses for safety, overtime work, and the need to dispose of an increasing amount of radioactive waste products.

A change in the structure and nature of energy consumption and production could play a decisive role in solving the world's energy problem. New opportunities are appearing to make radical improvements in the efficient use of minerals and fuels, as well as broader use of new and renewable energy sources. Energy conservation is becoming one of the most important of these sources. The application of modern machinery and technology is leading to a substantial decline in specific power outlays, with costs of conserving one kilowatt hour of power two to five times less than the cost of producing it. Developed capitalist countries possess sufficient scientific and technical potential to restructure their economies toward a resource-conserving type of industrial production.

The growing necessity of choosing an optimal strategy for developing and using the world's raw material energy base places a special responsibility on both the Soviet Union and the United States, and also opens up broad prospects for mutually advantageous cooperation between our countries. As is well known, the Soviet Union consistently supports developing countries in their struggle to establish a new world economic order and to create a firm basis for achieving a system of stable economic and political security.

Soviet-American cooperation in this area could be directed toward a search for new ways to conserve resources in industry, including the development of effective energy-conserving and ecologically clean technologies with closed cycles of nonwaste-producing processing of primary raw materials. Joint work could be of great importance in the following areas: reducing consumption of materials in finished production, introducing completely new construction materials, and conserving power resources in the process of operating machinery and equipment.

Promising directions include high- and low-temperature thermonuclear synthesis, mastering high temperature superconductivity, and industrial exploitation of such renewable sources of primary energy as solar energy, wind currents, surface ocean waves near shore, geothermal waters, and the primary and secondary biomass. Joint work on improving thermal pumps and introducing high-efficiency cogeneration of heat energy in industry could have important practical results.

We must not neglect the ecological situation in the world when discussing cooperation between the United States and the Soviet Union in solving global economic problems. The processes of ecological destabilization are proceeding rapidly on the planet, and this is bound to have an effect on economic development. Seven percent of the world's soil resources are being lost every decade. Almost 80 percent of the agricultural land in dry regions of the globe has been affected to some extent by desertification. Mainly as a result of losses of land resources, agriculture in forty developing countries yielded a lower per capita grain harvest in the 1980s than in the 1950s. Forests covering an area equal in size to Finland disappear every two years. It is hard to imagine, but every day, on the average, one natural species disappears, and the world's genetic fund is correspondingly reduced. Additional technical and material resources are needed to "ecologize" modern production and to prevent or neutralize the dangerous consequences of environmental pollution. As a report by the World Watch Institute notes, these circumstances make it necessary to think of the fact that "if present trends continue, world economic production may reach a level beyond which further growth would bring more losses than gains."[1]

1. Lester Brown, Director, World Watch Institute. *State of the World*. 1987. Annual Report of the World Watch Institute. New York/London: W.W. Norton & Co.

The unity of these problems reflects the ever-expanding scope of security issues in U.S.-Soviet relations. The director of the World Watch Institute, Lester Brown, wrote the following:

> Extensive destruction of natural protective systems and the deteriorating ecological conditions which are apparent in a large part of the 'third world' comprise a threat to national security which now rivals the traditional military threat. A report by the International Commission on Development and the Environment, headed by Norwegian Prime Minister G. Bruntland, states that ". . . it is extremely important that a new concept of national security be adopted, one that would go beyond the traditional definition. This is not only because the nature of the threat has changed, but also because new instruments are needed in the fight against it. Military means are completely useless in the struggle against ecological degradation."[2]

Cooperation on a broad scale is unavoidable in the historical process. This inevitability is related to the objective limited nature of national programs ("global problems require global resolutions"), to their mutual interest in the experience of regulating the interaction of social and natural processes, and to the major powers' responsibility before the rest of the world, in that their entire scientific, technical, and economic potential would be utilized to prevent ecological catastrophe.

The practical realization of disarmament offers new possibilities for large-scale cooperation between the two major powers in the support of global ecological stability, assuring steady economic development along with it. A substantial part of the military-industrial potential of the two countries could be successfully used to guarantee ecological security in the world. And it is not just that disarmament would free up financial resources needed to solve many global problems. The formation of a country's "ecological-industrial complex," in contrast to the existing "military-industrial complex," would win great popular support and help bring closer the interests of business circles and the wider community.

Of course, an approach on this scale to the problem of world ecological security requires new thinking, a new vision of the world. It would also require a long-term change in the "psycho-

2. *Ibid.*

logy" of the state administration, as well as the reorientation of the material-technical base of society. However, the first steps in this direction could be made even now. One example would be to develop and implement joint Soviet-American plans supporting ecological stability in developing countries.

Prospects for East-West
Economic Relations[1]

ED A. HEWETT

I am going to argue for six propositions about East-West relations for the future. Although these propositions are economic in nature, they have political implications, both for the Soviet Union and for the United States. Let us examine these propositions and then return to each to substantiate the argument. First, East-West economic relations are now in the early, most primitive stage. This relatively underdeveloped state of affairs is attributable primarily to eastern economic systems; western policies play a minor role. The key to the difficulties in the East is found in Soviet economic reforms, not so much in the economic reforms of other countries. Additionally, Soviet economic reforms are following a rather sporadic course, though some very exciting things are happening. Over the long term, there may well be genuine progress in Soviet economic reform, but quick results will not occur. Finally, western governments can do very little about this process because they have only a limited role to play, despite what some would argue.

PRIMITIVE ECONOMIC RELATIONS

If you think about the institutions involved with East-West trade and economic relations and how they have developed over time,

1. This paper is the lightly edited transcription of the keynote address delivered at the Geonomics conference held in Middlebury, Vermont, September 22-24, 1988.

then "primitive" is the best word to describe them, and that description becomes more fitting with each passing year. The internationalization of production, of asset ownership, and of financial flows that has occurred in western countries simply has not happened in the eastern countries, neither in their mutual economic relations nor in their relations with other western countries. Eastern countries relate to the world economy through simple trade—one commodity for another.

The internationalization of production processes and asset ownership now commonplace in the West is an exception in the East. This is certainly true within the Council for Mutual Economic Assistance (CMEA), and it is doubly true in economic relations with the West. Efforts within the CMEA to replicate the process of the internationalization of trade and production, efforts that have been going on for the last three decades, have failed. CMEA bureaucrats talk about economic cooperation with little result; western business leaders actually do it without the "help" of bureaucrats.

New efforts in the CMEA, dating back to 1985 with programs for specialization in trade projected to the year 2000, are already showing signs of another disappointment. East-West economic relations are now even less interesting from an institutional point of view than they were before. To be sure, there are possibilities to establish joint ventures, but the costs required to establish and operate such ventures typically far outweigh the likely benefits.

EASTERN ECONOMIC SYSTEMS

Why have eastern countries found it so difficult to foster the specialization and trade they so desperately want? Most of the problems lie in eastern economic systems, not in western economic systems or policy. I am acutely aware of the fact that I am a western economist making these statements, but I will nevertheless make my argument.

Certainly, western policies play some role in suppressing East-West trade and in constraining East-West economic relations. The list is familiar, but it should be recalled nevertheless. The export controls that we impose, while they have in many cases political or strategic motivations, also have some economic motivations behind them. I, for one, have argued against many of the export controls, at least in the United States. In the European Community, import quotas protect domestic enterprises in Europe in its competition with eastern goods, and certainly suppress the level of trade and affect the structure of trade. Special rules for antidumping procedures, applied in the United States and Europe, are a form of protection that should be eliminated.

Also, simply the political fallout of the relationship is unfortunate. I met a woman in Britain who works for the government; she began work on the Soviet Union a quarter-century ago. She has not been able to travel in that country since she began work. This poisonous political atmosphere, the atmosphere of the Cold War even during the current thaw, has an effect on business and a serious effect on East-West economic relations.

Nevertheless, despite these regrettable policies, I do not think they are the primary problem. In fact, I daresay that if economic reform in, first of all, the Soviet Union, and then in East Europe, took off, many of these western impediments to trade would melt like butter, at which point it would become clear that they are not the problem. The primary problems lie in eastern economic systems: the bureaucratic barriers that attend any attempt to set up a trading relationship, and the price system, which makes it very difficult for western businesses to make decisions about profitability. Even planners on the eastern side cannot trust business decisions, because they cannot trust their own price system; thus, they fear, with some justification, that they may sign apparently profitable agreements that in fact give away national income.

Another only too apparent problem lies in the inconvertible currencies, which force businesses to construct elaborate attempts involving complicated barter deals to get around the fact that there is no real money in the Soviet Union or East Europe. The weak infrastructure, a capital stock that tends to be rather old and outmoded, and a labor force that often has undesirable skills from the point of view of western business are further impediments to economic relations. These are interconnected features of eastern economies, which together erect formidable barriers for those wishing to establish a trading relationship not only between East and West, but among the eastern countries.

In addition to the systems themselves, there are policies pursued in these countries that contribute to the difficulties in expanding the economic relationship. For example, the job guarantee in East Europe and especially in the Soviet Union has become a job guarantee particularized for individuals in factory labor. The factory focus of the job guarantee is under attack by some Soviet economists, but not yet successfully. Thus, there is a strong incentive in the Soviet Union to protect those industries from import competition, affecting the structure and level of East-West trade, particularly of machinery and equipment. The policy of excess aggregate demand pursued in these countries has led to an excess demand for imports, necessitating controls on imports and justifying some of the bureaucratic obstacles to trade. It is these economic problems, and not many of the other diplomatic problems, that impede the development of East-West economic relations. Frankly, no amount of goodwill will overcome this problem. The only solution lies in economic reforms in these countries.

THE IMPORTANCE OF THE SOVIET UNION

The third proposition is that the Soviet Union is the key. Impediments to economic reform in East Europe are primarily within East Europe; that is, they are indigenous to these societies. They reflect the fact that the parties in these societies have become entrenched, and they fear the loss of power with the coming of the gradual economic reform. Until now, they have been successfully able to resist the radical reforms that would be necessary to improve dramatically economic relations.

There are two actions that could break this impasse. Radical Soviet economic reform would eliminate one of the major excuses that East European countries have used. It is important to deny that excuse. But even more importantly, true economic reform would dramatically change Soviet policies toward East Europe. If Soviet reforms really succeed, trading with the Soviet Union would become like trading with the West. We can see the beginning of this process, though it is intermingled with the changes in the Soviet-East European relationship that go well back into the 1970s, and stem from the Soviet dissatisfaction with the relationship with

East Europe. The subsidies that were being given to East Europe by the Soviet Union were not bringing the returns that Soviet leaders expected. In fact, the subsidies have gotten out of hand, in part because the price changes in the western world had nothing to do with the Soviet Union. So, from my point of view, the key to reform in East Europe is the Soviet Union.

Secondly, the key to reform in the CMEA is, very clearly, the Soviet Union. The Soviet Union is currently leading a discussion of reform in the CMEA, and Soviet leaders themselves are not quite sure what they are going to do. The lack of clarity in Soviet reforms translates into a lack of clarity in CMEA reforms.

The CMEA is not a separate body; it is not an institution that can be reformed, per se. It is a collection of centrally planned economies that traditionally have protected themselves from each other. Economic reform is beginning to attack this protectionism, and to the extent that each country reforms, the CMEA can reform. To the extent that they do not reform, you can talk within the CMEA forever and nothing will change, except perhaps the number of CMEA bureaucrats who travel and meet with each other. The Soviet Union sets the tone, the pace, and the agenda, and it also determines how far radical reforms can go.

The current foreign trade reforms that have been introduced in the Soviet Union are *very* modest in scope, and they will have very little impact on Soviet foreign economic performance. Reforms in the way the Soviet Union relates to the rest of the world are less important than reforms in the Soviet domestic economy for determining how it relates to the rest of the world. Foreign trade reforms simply affect the external visage of the system, but the system has not changed. If GOSPLAN (the State Planning Committee), GOSSNAB (the State Committee for Material and Technical Supplies), and GOSKOMTSEN (the State Committee on Prices) are still working in that system, then foreign trade reforms are much like CMEA reforms: much talk, but little change in the substance of the system.

There is much discussion in the Soviet Union about convertibility and price reform as preconditions to an improvement in East-West economic relations, and now it is catching on in the West. As far as I am concerned, it is too early to talk about convertibility. Convertibility is a symptom that an economic reform is working, it is not something you do prior to a reform. The Soviet Union can, to be sure, declare external "convertibility." It has sufficient control over its balance of payments, so if it chooses to establish external convertibility, it can make it work. But that is not the real convertibility that we talk about with western economic systems and market economies. It is certainly not the sort of convertibility that would induce someone to hold rubles; rather, it is the sort of convertibility that would allow an exporter to accept rubles in payment, and then get rid of them as quickly as possible. The only reason the Soviet Union might declare that sort of convertibility is because it would be very useful in an attempt to sell their economic package to the world economic community, especially the IMF.

SOVIET ECONOMIC REFORMS

This is a remarkable time in the history of the Soviet Union. If I had known before I was born that I was going to be a Soviet specialist and that these events were going to happen, I would have chosen these years to be about the age I am. I feel very fortunate to read in newspapers and to see on Soviet television events I did not think I would ever see in my lifetime. Much of the excitement is, of course, about politics, but it is also about economics. For me, the most extraordinary aspect is to witness a reopening of the debate about the essence of socialism, whether there is a way to construct what might be called a modern socialist economic system, capable of supporting a world-class superpower. And as far as I can tell, there are very few limits on that debate, either economic or political.

I would also say that the economic reform itself, as it was outlined in the June 1987 Central Committee Plenum, in which Gorbachev gave a speech on economic reform and outlined the principles, is exciting. I have seen only two other philosophical foundations for reform on this level: China and Hungary. Three fundamental principles run through the Gorbachev reforms. First, central authorities will plan less and plan better than they have in the past. To gain control of the system is to stop trying to micro-manage it and to focus instead on the issues that are really important to the Soviet economy. Second, individuals will have much more room to maneuver than they have had in the past, but they will also take much more responsibility for the decisions they make. A weak bankruptcy procedure is now in place, so enterprise failure is now possible. There is, on the other hand, the theoretical possibility that enterprises that do very well can increase their retained earnings. More importantly, there is now a law on cooperatives, which allows individuals to form cooperatives, and, if successful, to retain the income after the taxes. Third, the price and financial systems will now have to take on functions they have never served before. Prices will have to somehow move to reflect supply and demand. There must be a financial system capable of moving funds from where they are generated to where they can best be used.

These three principles run through the intentions of the reform, and, from my point of view, the intentions are right. It is extraordinary that Gorbachev, the man at the pinnacle of the political and economic system, has supported these principles and continues to support them in an impressive way. It makes me a long-term optimist.

On the other hand, the problem I have with the reforms and the reason I say that they are moving sporadically is that there is not a sufficient appreciation of the very important details that follow from the logic of the reform. There is as yet no concept of what I would call workable competition—not perfect competition, not pure competition, but workable competition. Without workable competition—which I define as a free entry and exit within the system and within various industries, a relatively unfettered price system so that prices can move to reflect supply and demand, and an income tax and subsidy system that protects individuals from the worst effects of the fluctuations of prices and of their income—the flexible price system will be a disaster.

Because Soviet industry is highly concentrated and there is an excess demand for goods, simply to free up prices will result in high rates of inflation. Conservatives lying in wait for high rates of inflation will have sufficient ammunition to argue quite successfully against the reform. To create a system with sustained quality improvements, enterprises must be faced with competitors. Enterprises will not improve the quality of their goods and services because they enjoy doing so. They are not going to do it because the government asked them to. They will only improve quality if they have no other options. Competition is also necessary to increase hard-currency exports. Finally, competition is the route to increased factor productivity. New decrees will not increase efficiency. It is the institutionalization of competitive pressures on the system that bring about dramatic improvements in the efficiency with which all resources are used.

The workable competition I am arguing for is not necessarily one that will involve import competition. The Soviet Union could attempt to emulate Japan, which has developed without heavy reliance on import competition. But the Japanese did foster a very tough domestic competitive environment to force enterprises to export to be profitable. Soviet policymakers would have to do the same thing by sticking to a "no subsidies" policy for failing enterprises, allowing wages to fall within enterprises that are unsuccessful in marketing their products, and so on. The Soviet economy is large enough, sufficiently well endowed with resources, and sufficiently developed to pursue just such a strategy.

If competition is going to be workable, obviously the government must introduce true elements of macromanagement and give up on micromanagement of the economy. This will be hardest for General Secretary Gorbachev. He is having a terribly difficult time right now in actually accepting the fact that if he tells ministers that they should not interfere in the affairs of enterprises, then he cannot hold ministers responsible for the affairs of enterprises. He gives almost weekly speeches, castigating ministers for interfering (bureaucrat "bashing" has now replaced chess as the national sport) on the one hand, while on the other singling out ministers by name, telling them that they are responsible for what did not happen in their ministry last week or last month or over the last six months.

There are Soviet economists, now beginning to write in public, who say many of the things I have said, but there is no consensus at present. The opinion of the majority in the Soviet Union is so far removed from this position that it is inconceivable to me that it will soon become true policy. There is still an argument going around in the Soviet Union about what word to use for "competition," because there is the rather impolite word *konkurentsiya*. It is better to use the much more polite words *sorevnovaniye* or *sostyazatel'nost* to talk about competition. In fact, competition is not polite, nor is economic reform.

The other point I want to make about economic reform is that it is easy for someone from the United States to identify the weaknesses of Soviet economic reform. Yet very few economists I know, and certainly I am not one of them, have a good idea about how to accomplish this kind of transition. Economists find it easy to tell you that you are better off at B than A, but they find it very difficult to tell you how to get there and survive the trip.

From a political point of view, I think I understand the problem. Indeed, the way I have come to think about it is something like this: you are in an airplane, a regular, piston airplane. You are losing altitude slowly, and you have decided that you must fix the plane without landing it. You, the pilot, are Gorbachev, and you want a jet. You have told your engineers to fix the plane, and when they get the new jet engines, the new wings, and the new tail on, then you will get rid of the old engine, wings, and tail, but not until then. The economists keep saying, "This plane cannot fly with five wings, six engines, and two tails." And what you say as a politician is, "Sorry, but I am not going to take the chance. I am going to wait." The result is a rather protracted attempt to fly a six-engined, five-winged, two-tailed plane, and it just does not fly very well. That is the situation the Soviet Union is going to be in for some time to come, in part for political reasons, but also in part because the transition is very difficult to accomplish.

REASONS FOR OPTIMISM

Toward the end of the century, it is conceivable that Soviet economic reform will look much better than it does now. There has been a recognition, from Gorbachev on down, that the future cannot replicate the past. The mistakes that were made in the past, the problems with the system, were such that the Soviet Union simply cannot go back. While irreversibility is a strong word to use about this reform, certainly every new month of glasnost makes it more difficult to go back. Indeed, Gorbachev the politician is now quite skillful at portraying the past as a crisis, perhaps more of a crisis than it was.

The social dialogue in the Soviet Union is impressive and important because the only way reform will succeed is with a consensus on some of the principles of the reform. It may not be a complete consensus, and I do not know if one would want to put it up to a vote, but radical reform cannot be accomplished by ambush. It takes time and considerable debate. Soviet intellectuals are now using the Soviet media to talk about economics, not only to each other, but to the population at large. That "conversation" is critical to the long-term prospects for perestroika.

What makes me an optimist is my belief that the political reform will ultimately be a good thing, although in the short run it could be extremely destabilizing and lead to some difficulties for the economic reform. It is going to take time, and there will be reversals in the immediate reform process. There will be retreats and moves forward. We may be in the midst of a retreat right now. However, I am optimistic because the General Secretary is an extraordinary politician with the capacity to learn, qualities he has exhibited frequently in the past three years.

THE WESTERN ROLE

My last proposition is that the role of western governments in this entire process will be, and should be, modest. The economic reforms themselves are really the affair of the Soviet Union and East Europe. It is not our business. It is not our business in the sense that we probably do not know enough to make it our business. Even if we did, it is a social, political, and economic process that these societies need to work out.

Should eastern countries become members of international economic organizations and get into trouble, western officials may end up recommending courses for economic reform. Even here our influence will be marginal. To the extent that we have an effect, it will be because groups within that society are already pushing hard for reform, and international organizations offer marginal support.

The one area in which there is a potential for conscious influence on this process is in East-West economic relations, but here I should advocate only that we follow neutral policies, that is, that we allow economics to drive the relationship. I do not support western governments becoming deeply involved in special subsidies for East-West economic relations or special encouragement for western firms to go into eastern countries to help reforms or to help East-West economic relations in general. What I would like to see western governments do, and what actually our government seems (probably by accident) to be involved in doing now, is pretty much to get out of the way and allow the economics to drive this relationship. In a period of successful economic reforms, the economics could be impressive and could bring about an increase in economic and trade relations.

We just finished a project at Brookings, "Restructuring American Foreign Policy," about the changing assumptions that underlie the foreign policy decisions we will be making for the rest of the century. Early on, there are chapters written by economists on the American economy, the international economy, and the socialist economies. The macroeconomists for the United States projected a large deficit over a long period of time and were looking for a way to close it. They had given up on Europe and were hoping that economic reforms in the Soviet Union and East Europe would take off and provide at least the imports to make up a part of the deficit. My reply to them was that right now, if you combine the trade of China, East Europe, and the Soviet Union, there is East-West trade roughly equal to that of Australia. If the eastern countries take off, the effect will be like Australia taking off, and that is not a launch many people are going to sit around to watch. Maybe by the next century it will be something important, but it is not going to happen soon, even if things go very well in the Soviet Union and East Europe. It is not going to be an extraordinary event that will drive demand for exports anywhere near, say, what happened in the postwar period.

Let me conclude by saying that I know this assessment is maybe not the most optimistic, but it is, nevertheless, realistic. In analyzing East-West economic relations and what keeps them from developing, we must identify what is fundamental. The fundamental issues in East-West economic relations are economic, not political. As I have tried to make clear, the primary problem right now is in eastern economic systems, and if their reforms are successful, the natural consequence will be a rapid expansion in East-West relations. If, on the other hand, the reforms are not successful, there is is nothing we can do to achieve a major secular improvement in existing or wished-for East-West economic relations. East-West economic relations are hostage to reforms, and not the other way around.

INDEX

ABOUT THE CONTRIBUTORS

GEORGI ARBATOV is Director of the Institute for the Study of the USA and Canada, People's Deputy of the USSR, and member of the Central Committee of the Communist Party of the Soviet Union.

BELA BALASSA is Professor of Political Economy at the Johns Hopkins University, and Consultant to the World Bank.

JOZEF M. VAN BRABANT is Staff Member of the Department of International Economic and Social Affairs of the Secretariat of the United Nations.

JOSEF C. BRADA is Professor of Economics at Arizona State University, and Editor of the *Journal of Comparative Economics.*

MICHAEL P. CLAUDON is President and Managing Director of the Geonomics Institute, and Professor of Economics at Middlebury College.

H. STEPHEN GARDNER is Ben H. Williams Professor of Economics at Baylor University.

ED A. HEWETT is Senior Fellow, Foreign Policy Studies Program, at the Brookings Institution.

ALEXEI KVASOV is Scientific Secretary at the Institute for the Study of the USA and Canada.

IGOR MALASHENKO is Scientific Secretary at the Institute for the Study of the USA and Canada.

MICHAEL MARRESE is Associate Professor of Economics at Northwestern University.

PETER MURRELL is Professor of Economics at the University of Maryland, College Park.

VLADIMIR POPOV is Senior Research Fellow at the Institute for the Study of the USA and Canada.

PETER REDDAWAY is Professor of Political Science and International Affairs at George Washington University.

CATHERINE SOKIL is Assistant Professor of Economics at Middlebury College.

ALEXANDER VOLKOV is Research Fellow at the Institute for the Study of the USA and Canada.

ABOUT THE EDITORS

MICHAEL KRAUS is Associate Professor of Political Science and a member of the Soviet Studies Program at Middlebury College. He received his Ph.D. from Princeton University and was a Ford Foundation Fellow at the Kennedy School of Government, Harvard University, and a Post-Doctoral Fellow at the Harriman Institute for Advanced Soviet Studies, Columbia University. Dr. Kraus' research and publications focus on the relationship between the Soviet Union and East Europe in both contemporary and historical contexts.

RONALD D. LIEBOWITZ is Associate Professor of Geography and a member of the Soviet Studies Program at Middlebury College. He received his Ph.D. from Columbia University. Dr. Liebowitz has written on political geography, Soviet investment policy, and Soviet regional economic development, and he is the editor of *Gorbachev's New Thinking: Prospects for Joint Ventures*. His current research focuses on the changing spatial and ethnic dimensions of Soviet investment policy as a result of the Gorbachev reform program.